To Laura and Wade

# Acknowledgments

With the hard work of Anne Simpson, this book became a reality. Her dedication to the project was neverending; she has done an amazing job. I felt very comfortable telling Anne my story. It was at times hard, but her sensitivity made it easier. Thank you Anne . . .

To my family, for being who you are. To the many friends along the way—past and present—who have been sources of inspiration, may I say thanks.

Thanks to Gail Reynolds and Jackie MacNeil for your contributions. To the people in the industry that have worked with me, including all the musicians, and the years of commitment from all those who believed enough to be there, thank you!!

# Contents

# PREFACE

I truly wanted this book to be one of inspiration for those who have a dream; but make no mistake, I sacrificed a lot to finally find mine.

I had reasons that sometimes bordered on selfishness, but if it were not for the parents I was truly blessed with (for all our faults—theirs and mine), I would not have made it.

To the true heroes, the true dreamers, Rene and Neil.

This book can only be one story of the thousand stories in my life. There are many other stories I could tell, but this is the one I chose. This is a part of the story. It is not the whole of it, but it can never be. Some people have been left out, but not because I didn't think of them. I thank all those who are part of my story. So many others live within the pages of my heart.

Like life, this book is a beginning. And there are many pages still to write.

> So we wrote a book between us
> And some of the pages don't fit
> But it's an easy read in a familiar theme
> And sometimes it makes me weep.
> > "Field of Daisies"

# CHAPTER ONE

# BIG POND

In mid-May of 1998, my Aunt Lizzie died. She lived only seventeen years of her life in Big Pond before leaving for good, becoming a nun, and finally dying in France when she was in her nineties. A memorial service was held in New Victoria, just outside Sydney, Cape Breton. I left a little late that day and when I arrived at what I thought was the church, I found the parking lot was jammed. I was certain I was in the wrong place until I saw my Aunt Rita get out of her car. Not only was the parking lot full, the church was packed with people, most of whom had come from Big Pond. I found a seat and ten minutes later there was no room at all. It was standing room only. I was astonished. Here were young and old gathered together to remember a woman of whom they had only dim recollections, or no knowledge at all. Yet she came from Big Pond. She was a MacNeil. And they were there to honor her memory.

The priest, Father Everett, is my cousin, and Lizzie was his aunt too. He spoke about how she had left with her sisters when she was only seventeen, to work as a maid in Boston. Then she joined the Little Sisters of the Poor and moved around the United States before being sent to France, where she'd lived through the war and spent three years in a concentration camp. All her life, she remembered her home, although she came back to see it only once, long after both her parents had died. He mentioned that she wrote a long poem about leaving home revealing how difficult it was for a girl from Cape Breton to adjust to an entirely different way of life. I listened to him, watching the familiar expressions of his face. In the pew ahead of me sat people who were dear to me: Catherine and her brother Duncan, and Agnes, who is nearly ninety. All three were visibly older. And yet it seemed like a moment ago that I was a child dropping in at Agnes's house for a freshly baked cookie. Time passed so slowly when I was a child, and each big event, like Christmas or Easter, was anticipated months in advance. The days crawled along, each hour measured in anticipation. Now the days flash by. And when we gather together it is often for funerals. A generation is passing away, and a part of me is going with it.

Maybe that's why I wanted to capture a little of that place I love so much. It is a place that anchors me when I am away from it and gives me strength when I am there. Even when I am far away on a tour, I can shut my eyes and see the wide blue Bras d'Or, with the headlands and islands in the distance. I used to have a feeling of urgency about showing it to people, but that has lessened over time. Now I simply want to spend time there. It is a place where I have been distressed, confused, joyful, and tranquil. It has been all things to me.

◆　◆　◆

I went to stay at the farmhouse in Big Pond this spring, shortly after the memorial service for my Aunt Lizzie. With the light falling through the trees and across the road, it was a short, pleasant drive from Sydney. I was excited about going: the trees on both sides of the road were feathery with new leaves. The colors were rich and varied, from bright yellow-green to softer greens, and the dark greens of the white and black spruce, standing like sentinels among the birches. Some trees, like the pin cherries and the Indian pear, were white with blossoms, while others were red with new buds. In places the lawns stretch down to Bras d'Or Lake, where the fresh green grass meets the deep blue of the water.

Closer to Big Pond, the landscape changes. From the shores of the lake, along which the road runs parallel, the land slopes upwards into meadows and hills. One hill was dense with trees that always remind me of florets of broccoli. The lake below, really an inland sea, was calm and flat as stretched silk that day. Across the water rose the rolling hills of the headland that juts into the lake, with a scattering of white buildings—Eskasoni—close to the shore. The Mi'kmaq paddling by Big Pond called it "Edoobukuk," meaning "the place where soil erodes from both sides." It may have been that they called the settlement by that name as well, but another name for it was commonly used: "Naookteboojooik," which meant "the place that stands alone."

The hilly landscape must have looked like home to those settlers from Scotland, the MacNeils from Barra when they first arrived. The Clan MacNeil are deeply connected to the island of Barra, the southernmost isle in the Outer Hebrides, which they ruled for eight centuries. They trace their roots back to Ireland, where the O'Neils of Ulster departed for Barra around the turn of the last millennium. In the nineteenth century, as times became harder, many MacNeils from Barra found their way to Canada after long, difficult sea voyages. Hard as it surely was, the beauty of the land must have been a comfort, since it bears a vivid resemblance to that little Scottish island.

My family descends from the Barra MacNeils who came to Canada before the Clearances of 1838. In the early 1800s, Roderick MacNeil settled in the Arisaig area, on the Northumberland Strait, near Antigonish. He was known as Rory Breac, a nickname that helped to distinguish him from other Rory MacNeils. "Breac" is a Gaelic word sometimes meaning "freckled" or "spotted," so I suppose he had a skin condition that suggested the nickname. Rory and his family—including a son from whom I am descended—came to the Big Pond area about 1809. It seems that he was the first settler in this area, but there were many settlers around the lake by that time, notably in the

Christmas Island-Iona area where my mother's ancestors settled. Rory was given a grant of two hundred acres with a brook running through it, which became known as Breac's Brook or Brack's Brook. He was married twice, fathering approximately twenty children in all, several of whom took up land near his grant. Rory, and those of his sons who could do so, took up land fronting the water, for this was desirable for several reasons; for example, the lake was the first "highway." While the MacNeils settled in the Brack's Brook area, where I grew up, others (including the MacLellans, who settled the land where the Tea Room is located) settled the Big Pond area, a few kilometers west. So two communities developed here: "the people of the brook" and "the people of the pond."

While my father, Neil J. MacNeil, descended from Ruairidh Breac MacNeil, my mother, Catherine, or Rene, as she was known, was a descendant of Donald Og MacNeil, who fought in the siege at Louisbourg in 1758 in a highland regiment with Donald MacNeil and Findlay Glas MacKenzie. During that campaign, travels took the three soldiers through the Barra Strait in the Bras d'Or, and the surrounding slopes seemed a perfect place to settle. Donald Og went on to Quebec after the siege to fight under General Wolfe's army, volunteering to hoist the British flag after a conflict, whereupon he was shot by a French sniper hiding behind a tree. Before going to Quebec, though, he sent word to his people in Barra that if ever they should decide to come to Canada, the Bras d'Or would be a good place to settle. Many of his relatives did manage to make their way to Canada. In 1802, over three hundred Barra MacNeils arrived in Pictou, where they wintered. The following year they made their way to the island of Cape Breton, settling in the area Donald had mentioned. Whether Donald's sons, Rory and Murdoch, came with them or made their way to Cape Breton independently is not clear, but they did settle in the Iona area, in settlements on either side of the Barra Strait, with the others. Rory's great-grandson, Michael Duncan (known as Duncan), was my mother's father, who moved his family from Glace Bay to Boston and eventually to Big Pond. Both my mother's and father's families had a bond with the Bras d'Or from the time their ancestors first came here. It's because generations of my family have farmed this land that I have such strong feelings for it. It's like a magnet that keeps pulling me back.

As I crested the hill in the van and came down the slope, I could see the tiny white house where I was born, nestled in the trees. Around the bend, on the same side of the road, is the firehall for the Big Pond Volunteer Fire Department. The old schoolhouse originally stood there, built by my father in the late thirties, but it was later moved close to the church. Across from the firehall is the Glengarry Road, the path we used to take when we went berry-picking. I turned and drove down it. The first house I came to was Agnes's white farmhouse, where she and Stevie John S. MacNeil have lived together for so many years. The elms on either side are high over its roof now. The road winds around a curve; when I was young we thought nothing of walking miles on it to get blueberries. Sometimes we spent hours looking for the cows near here, coming back in the dark. At the fork in the road is Catherine and Duncan MacNeil's place with the old sawmill across the road, high above the brook. I crossed the little bridge that spanned it. There are new houses here: a trailer and a small cottage. The trees on one side of the road have been hacked down, replaced by a gravel pit. Soon I came to the land where Joe Hector Campbell's place once stood, a big white house in the midst of all the trees. Now there was a stock car turned on its roof like an insect trying to right itself. The house is gone and I tried to imagine where the foundation had been. All around, the apple trees were covered in lacy white blossoms. I stopped the van for a while thinking of Catherine Joe Hector's mother greeting us at the door when I went to visit.

"Come on in, girls," she'd call. "You don't want to catch your death of cold."

And we'd go in, stamping the snow off our boots, into the warm kitchen and the smell of a stew bubbling on the stove.

Now nothing is left of that. It was long ago.

I turned the van around and went back along the Glengarry Road, coming out at my cousin Jackie's gray house at the main road. He was a teacher for thirty years and still lives in the same house where he grew up, my Aunt Jessie and Uncle John Duncan's place, built by my uncle's father before him. Not only do I respect him, I treasure his friendship, though he was more my older brother's friend when we were growing up. I wrote the song "Realized Your Dreams" for him:

> So you never left the small town
> With your friends when things got way down
> You stood between the tall trees
> Threw all caution to the cool breeze
> You stayed home on the island
> And you watched the evening sunrise
> And you never thought of leaving
> Even when the winds blew cold…
>
> All you want or ever needed
> You found here without leaving
> It's the drifter and the dreamer
> Who often fail to see
> In the heart that never wanders
> Lies a peace that comes with morning
> It's knowing when the day is done
> You've realized your dreams.

I stopped at Jackie's for a cup of tea, going in by the back door to the same big kitchen I knew so well when I was a child.

"Look," he pointed, as he gave me a mug of tea.

I watched the flickering of a hummingbird's wings, its tiny jewel-bright body.

"It migrates thousands of miles to South America," he told me, setting down a small plate of date squares. "One leg of the journey is a five hundred mile non-stop flight over the Gulf of Mexico."

Jackie was the one who told me the genealogy of my parents' families. His study was lined with books: there were hundreds of books on history, literature, gardening, and birds. One day he might write a book of his own.

At one corner of the front lawn, he showed me the tree that Lizzie planted, together with her sister Josephine, on one of Lizzie's two trips back to visit Big Pond. "They put a medal in the ground when they planted it," he laughed. "Maybe that's what kept it from doing well."

He showed me a red oak that was planted by my father, and a silver maple, planted by my aunt and uncle. And Jackie himself has planted scores of trees, from hemlock to red spruce. A pond is habitat to several wild geese that honked when we approached. We crossed a bridge, ducking under a pinkish veil of apple blossoms, as we came back to the house.

"There's a hairy woodpecker," he showed me. "And some pine siskins. Purple finches too." The woodpecker was hanging nearly upside down on one of the bird feeders, trying to peck at the food. "Just this morning there were waxwings in the apple trees."

I got back into the van and thanked him for the tea. He waved his walking stick as I drove out the lane.

◆　◆　◆

A short distance down the main road were Angus Anthony MacNeil's house and store (A. A.'s store, as we used to call it), with their characteristic red roofs. They were built around the turn of the century, and both are gone now. My father's small white store, which he built, next to Angus's, is now McLeod's Grocery and General Store. Gas is still being pumped outside, just as it was when I was young. A lane divides the two stores, which stand on the same side of the road, and up this lane past my Uncle Joe's white house and my Uncle Duncan's turnip field is the hill where my grandmother's house once stood. That house is gone, too, but it was a typical Cape Breton farmhouse with a pitched roof, facing down the hill to the water below. It may have been an ordinary house, but to me it was lovely. Standing in an idyllic setting, with the hills all around, and Balm-of-Gilead trees and apple trees framing it, the house could have been something out of a storybook, with the valley, or intervale, at its back, and the tree-covered hill rising on the other side. The hillside blazes with yellow and red in the fall. A brook runs through the intervale there, and the spot where I used to go and sit beside it was one of my favorite places for fishing, or just daydreaming. The fields behind the house were hayfields, which were ploughed under some years so grain could be grown, and the soil given a chance to recover. There was a barn where about a dozen cows were kept along with the sheep. Two other sheds were close to the house and in one of these, milk was separated from cream and butter was churned, while in the other meat was salted and fish dried for winter. On warm summer evenings, as relatives sat outside, my cousin would sometimes play the bagpipes, walking along the hill between the house and the barn. The sounds echoed in the air as we played all around the house, often until the stars came out, and I walked home in the dark with the others when it was time to go.

"Full moon tonight," someone would say, looking up.

"Then there'll be ghosts out for sure. They'll reach out and grab you by the heels."

We'd run the rest of the way down the lane, tripping over ourselves to get home.

Back on the main road, I looked across to where granduncle Angus's white house once stood, a place filled with dark memories that were still strong in my mind. All that remains is the depression in the grass where the driveway used to be. Next to it is the impeccably kept property of Hector Morais, an Acadian with a gift for music. Initially a lumberjack, he knew no English when he first arrived in the village with his wife, who had their baby strapped to her back. Further down the road is Peter Frank MacNeil's place, another haunt for all the children, and for Father Stanley MacDonald, who used to go there for a game of cards. Next come the summer bungalows, overlooking the water, where I used to play as a child, and beyond that the new bridge, which recently replaced the wooden one I knew long ago.

Not far away is the Roman Catholic church of St. Mary's, built in 1897 by Father Rory MacInnes, who also built the Sacred Heart church in Johnstown. Its spire reaches high up into the cloudless sky. Like so many churches in Nova Scotia, it is a wooden structure, painted white, with large windows; it sits high on a grassy knoll, facing the lake across the road.

Though it is not a large church, it once seemed more commanding, since it was the place we went at least twice a week, both for Benediction and Sunday mass. To a child, such a country church seems as big as a cathedral; the stations of the cross, depicted in paintings, seemed particularly enormous to me. Each was vividly painted, and the scenes are still etched in my mind.

The church is beautifully built, with a barrel vaulted ceiling arching overhead. There are balconies on either side of the nave, and at the back of the church is the organ and choir loft. The church is painted a soft peach color now, but I remember when it was unpainted. Dark and polished, the wood seemed to glow with richness. A statue of the Virgin Mary stands in the corner of the sanctuary near the door leading into the sacristy, while a large crucifix hangs on the wall behind the altar. Because it is large and life-like, it had the power to frighten me as a child. In the vestibule are a few framed inscriptions on the wall. One of these, by Viola Doncaster, begins: "There is a little Country Church in Big Pond on a hill…"

I thought of Father Stanley, who once presided over that "little country church" with a firm hand. He was gentle most of the time, with a wonderful sense of humor, but in church he kept order like a judge. On one occasion, when he heard no music from the choir loft, he called out, "Don't you know any hymns up there?" And if a child was fidgeting, Father Stanley would call him to task: "Donald Red Dan, it's front you want to be facing. You'll not find the Lord behind you." Once a stool barred his way as he came out of the sacristy and without missing a beat he simply kicked it out of the way. Another time, reflecting on Ingrid Bergman having an illegitimate baby, he declared: "People are just waiting for her to have the little bastard so they can all name their infants after it." There was a gasp from the congregation when he mentioned the word "bastard." He made clear the distinctions between those who were headed for hell and those who weren't. Most of us skated a fine line.

Near the church is MacDonald Consolidated School, no longer in use and moved there for the benefit of senior citizens. It was badly vandalized, the windows taped together in places. Behind it, further up on the slope, is the old one-room schoolhouse my father built, which was also moved here. A small wooden building with a coal shed attached, its door was missing, as well as glass in the windows. Yet there were still touches of craftsmanship about it that showed the quality of my father's work. It might have been restored into a museum of the Big Pond area before it fell into complete disrepair, but now it was too late. It was hard for me to see the schools closed like that; it spells the beginning of the end of small communities.

Across the road was the parish hall, which is now the Tartan Eagle restaurant. It was the scene of many a square dance in its time. Local people would play, like Hector Morais, Martin MacPherson, Joe MacIsaac, and Dan Joe MacInnes. The greatest by far, though, was Winston "Scotty" Fitzgerald, one of the old-time Cape Breton fiddlers. There were milling frolics there too sometimes, originally Gaelic gatherings when people sang songs and beat time with their hands as they shrank or thickened cloth that had been woven on a loom.

Further down the road is a large old house, painted green and hidden among the trees, that was once the Lakeview Inn. Behind the former inn, which long ago was also the first store in the area, is a graveyard that few know about. The victims of a smallpox epidemic lie here, with no stones to mark their graves. Some distance further down the road, on the lake side, is the graveyard where my parents, Rene (Catherine) and Neil MacNeil are buried. Long ago, in 1842, the first church—a chapel—was built here, but it was later torn down and the larger St. Mary's succeeded it. The cemetery is on a green slope, and some of the tombstones are old and slanting, but it was a tranquil place, with the sun making the grass a bright emerald. At the bottom of the slope a new grave had just been dug and a small knot of people had gathered.

At one time, I lived with my two children in a small yellow bungalow close by. Later I moved with them to the building that is now the Tea Room, painted a deep plum with cream trim, which is almost across the road from the cemetery. The Tea Room was originally the one-room schoolhouse that served the village of Big Pond, before the schools were consolidated. It was built about the time my father built the other school-house at the other end of the village, and recently renovated, making it more inviting.

I turned into the parking lot, intending to stay only briefly. It had been very busy in the morning with a few bus tours, but less crowded in the afternoon, my daughter told me. She always had a funny story about something or other that had happened.

"Excuse me, do you think we could have your autograph?"

Several people wanted their menus signed. I wrote notes for each one.

"Who should I write this one for?" I asked. A woman with short, strawberry-blond hair stood by my table.

"Helen." She was a little shy about asking. "Oh," she said, dabbing at her eyes. "I've got tears in my eyes."

I smiled at her as I handed her the signed menu. Her eyes were full.

Needing some time to myself, I went out to the van. My retreat is the old MacLellan farm nearby, when I have time to spend there. When I was looking for land to buy, there was none to be had in the other section of the village, close to Brack's Brook. So I bought this farm in what used to be called Big Pond Centre.

I drove away from the Tea Room to the farmhouse, parked the van and went in, my Yorkshire terriers scampering in front of me.

Little has changed about the MacLellan farmhouse from the time it was built almost a century ago, when a photograph was taken showing construction nearing completion. There was still snow on the ground as two solemn men posed to have their picture taken, revealing a quiet pride in their work. One stood on an old-fashioned wooden scaffold, the water in the background behind him. Now the lake is obscured by the blossoming trees, and is only visible from the second floor.

I treasure my time here. When I sit in the rocker in front of the wood stove and gaze around the comfortable room, I feel that this is my soul space. Small baskets hang from the ceiling and there is a bright quilted hanging on the wall. I put little decorations around: wreaths and wooden tulips; next to the woodstove are two cast-iron owls. The old board walls are painted grey and the trim around the doors pink, which makes it cheery.

My two dogs, Bonnie and Dee Dee, pranced around the hardwood floor, nosing into familiar corners. I've tried to keep the interior much as it was, with the smaller rooms and low lintels of old houses, and in the front room

I kept the MacLellan furniture in the same place as it was originally. I didn't want to change anything. The dining room furniture was moved into the room that now adjoins the kitchen, but it still has pride of place. The chairs, table, and hutch are all a beautiful dark cherry. Upstairs, the bedrooms are small, with slanted ceilings, as they are in many old country houses. On summer mornings I lie awake listening to the birds before getting up.

A lane leads from the house around a grassy field, through the trees and past the lagoon to the edge of the lake. The lagoon was glassy on that still spring day, and in the distance the strand almost completely encircled its shallow waters, where oysters are often gathered. It was that natural lagoon that gave Big Pond—or Loch Mor, in Gaelic—its name. On one side of the lane, in the midst of the woods, is a huge bush, now about six feet tall. It is difficult to believe that it is a rhododendron, planted here fifty years ago. It flowers with a glory of blossoms, an exotic bit of the tropics grown wild in Cape Breton. Further down the lane is the waterfront, where I have a small place by the beach. It was once the trailer, housing the gift shop that used to be at the back of the Tea Room, before we renovated it, with the albums arranged against the wall, and the counter on one side. The kitchen, which was a hub of activity, was where the homemade biscuits, oatcakes, cinnamon rolls, molasses cookies, and apple pies used to be made. It got so hot that several fans had to be kept going at once.

Attached to the trailer is a screened porch, where I can sit and look out at the vista. The water laps against the pebbly shore, a sound that lulls me to sleep at night in the summer.

On that warm spring day the water was silvery blue, stretching out into the western part of the Bras d'Or. In the distance, low blue hills rose out of the water: Red Islands, Militia Point, and Big Harbour Island. I couldn't see Iona, off to one side of the Barra Strait. To the left were green hills through which a truck appeared, coming from Middle Cape on the road above the red cliffs sloping down to the water. Close by there is a man-made pond, where gravel used to be hauled out. Now a sandy stretch traces its outline, dividing it from the lake.

The sunsets here are spectacular, since the trailer faces west. On some summer evenings, the Bras d'Or is true to its name, because the lake shimmers with gold as birds skim the surface. Now and then a bald eagle makes slow circles high up in the air, its white neck visible as it turns. The sky flushes with red, pink, and soft mauve just as the sun sets. Then it fades gradually and evening falls; the stars are tiny points of light in a dome of darkness.

My heart is in this place. I could stay forever.

The lupins are dead now
But they did bloom well now
And the vetch and the wild weeds
That grow in your green fields
And please God if time's kind
And there's still a Big Pond
Oh, I'd love to come back here again.

# CHAPTER TWO

# THE STORE

My eldest sister calls me her "lucky penny." On the day I was born—May 28, 1944—my father took me from the midwife, wrapped me in a blanket, handed me to my sister, and told her she should go upstairs to pray that I wouldn't make it through. It was natural for him to assume I might not, because of my birth defect. He had never seen a cleft lip before and he imagined the worst.

Upstairs, in the bedroom of that tiny house, my sister didn't do as he'd asked.

"Dear Lord," she whispered, eyes closed. "Please let my baby sister live. Please, God. I'll be good if you just let her live."

I yelled lustily.

"Let her live."

To her, I was new and wonderful, like a shiny penny. Pennies were hard to come by in our household, and a bright, new one was rare. I was as much a gift as a shining penny.

"Holy Mother of God," my sister continued. "Please take care of this baby."

I was not about to die. Like the motto on the MacNeil crest, "Vincere Vel Mori," ("Victory or Death") I was determined to live from that moment. By then, my face was a vivid red with crying. My father came to return me to my mother, who took care of me from that moment on. They took me almost immediately to St. Rita's hospital in Sydney, where I had the first of many operations on my cleft lip and partial cleft palate. It was a straightforward job to the doctor, who simply stitched up the gaping hole. Now it would be the job of a skilled surgeon, but it did the trick then, allowing me to drink the milk I needed in order to survive. He told my parents not to worry; I'd be fine. My mother cuddled me in her arms, rocking me to and fro. She decided my name would be Rita, though whether she named me after Saint Rita, after whom the hospital was named, I still don't know. Some time later, I was baptized at St. Mary's in Big Pond, perhaps in a gown borrowed from a relative. My godparents were Cecilia Sampson (the midwife who had assisted at my birth) and her husband, Louis; they were good friends of my parents.

And so I began life in that household, fifth among what would be a total of eight children. I lived in Big Pond until I was about ten years old, included in the rough-and-tumble of life with the rest of the children. There was joy, confusion, and pain in those years, as we moved around from house to house, and finally settled in the store my father built in the late forties. It was a white building with a black shingled roof, and two shiny, white pumps outside, a modern rival to A. A.'s more traditional store next door, with its picturesque roof. Adjacent to the store was the garage, with a grease pit where men could work on cars. We played there from time to time, until my cousin Rose fell into the pit and injured her head. She was taken to the hospital in Sydney, where she was given twelve stitches. Though she was all right afterwards, it put fear into all of us and we never went near the grease pit again.

Along the lane that divided the two stores was a line of boulders that determined the boundary between the land. My father would shift the boulders, but in his absence A. A. would move them back.

My father would move them.

A. A. would move them back.

It was an ongoing battle between them and neither won in the end. In the song, "I Guess I Always Will," I mention "boulders that were boundary lines \ Have faded with the years…"

A. A. also had a mirror fastened to the exterior of his store so he could see the comings and goings. Generally, people were loyal to one store or the other, unless they needed something that one store or the other did not provide. A. A.'s store was darker than my father's, with big old counters, and shelves behind them stocked with staples like bread, flour, sugar, tea, soap, and many other things. Orange soda pop was on sale for a nickel. A nut bar or a package of gum cost the same. And scribblers only cost a few cents. There were dried fruits like apples and apricots in bins. There were different kinds of beans. And there were cookies. It was a true general store and going inside was like stepping back in time. At the back was a glowing woodstove, and on either side of it were two wooden chairs with spindle legs. Here the men of the village gathered, warming their hands and feet on winter days and telling stories for hours. The stories would change over the years until they were tall tales.

When I went into the store, a small child walking across those wide, creaking floorboards, A. A. might look up and grunt at me from where he stood behind the counter by the big white scales. It was said that whenever anyone bought anything, he would keep a finger on the scales, giving the item a little more weight, but that may have just been village lore. I knew from A. A.'s look that he thought of me as a nuisance. Children were meant to be seen and not heard. I hoped he wouldn't say anything, because his voice was louder than thunder and made me jump with fright. He was a big, imposing man with hair so white it almost seemed transparent. Still, I couldn't resist gazing longingly at the candies in the endless glass jars. I was fascinated by the array of toffee, black licorice, strawberry candies, Tootsie Rolls, suckers, and black balls. The hard candies in their colored wrappers were as tempting as red, green, and yellow jewels.

"Father send you over for something he doesn't have in stock?" boomed A. A.

"Ah—" I quavered. "No."

Someone came in then and I slid into a shadowy corner. I could hear the men talking at the back of the store.

"You know that time A. A. got the call from Middle Cape?"

A few of them chuckled. A chair leg scraped on the floor.

"Something about a thief there, and that A. A. should be on the lookout. I remember that."

"Well then, next thing you know there's some old fellow on the road." Someone guffawed.

"Looked like a thief to me," said someone. It sounded like Joe Hector.

"And he starts to run, tearing up the road. So then we call Joe Hector here to run and get his horse and cart and go after the fellow."

"Going like a bat out of hell, he was."

Someone exploded with laughter. "And the thief was flailing his arms and running like a crazy man till he fell down in the field."

"Turned out it was just Joe MacNeil, lying there, doubled up with laughter. Dressed up like a hobo, trying to fool us."

◆ ◆ ◆

There was a delicious sense of terror and wonder mixed together as I listened to some of the stories.

"They're going to fix the bridge," someone said.

"No use trying."

"Ah, you're not going to tell us about the bawkins again."

"Well, someone drowned there way back. That place has been haunted ever since."

"You're as crazy as a bag full of hammers. That's an old wives' tale."

"You put a shovel in the ground there and you can't dig it up. Can't even lift the shovel. There's a ghost there all right."

◆ ◆ ◆

Behind A. A.'s woodstove was another section to the store, where shovels, hoes, rakes, buckets, and other things were sold. The feedbags were piled there, row upon row. I played there with A. A.'s grandchildren, Charlie and Douglas. We'd play cowboys and Indians, never knowing any harm in the game. Once I was asked to dinner at A. A.'s house when his son Alec had taken over the running of the store, since I was a friend of his nephews. Alec's wife served herring and potatoes.

"Now don't go choking on those fish bones," growled Alec, in the same gruff way as his father.

No sooner were the words uttered than I felt a bone stick in my throat, making me cough and spit. I turned blue before the bone dislodged itself, but by then the meal had been entirely disrupted. I recovered enough to apologize and slink out the door, but to this day I worry about fish bones.

Our store was a contrast to A. A.'s. Though the unpainted walls were dark, as were the floorboards, the two front windows were large and light flooded in on sunny days. Bunches of yellow bananas hung from a hook in the ceiling, and ice cream was kept in two tubs in a cooler against the back wall. The counter was against the wall at the front of the store, with shelves behind it: we sold bread, milk, flour, sugar, tea, canned goods, candies, and cigarettes, among other things.

The chocolate bars were lined up alongside the bins of candies, always a delight to us. Once I stole something and my father gave me a tongue-lashing I'll never forget. I never stole anything again. Despite that, I took great delight in "The Funny House," a small, colored cardboard house. For a dime, a customer could punch a hand through the window and win a prize. On Sundays my father allowed one of us to take a turn and I was very excited as I pushed my hand through and pulled out a trinket—cheap and pretty—that captured my imagination. Once I pulled out a pair of turquoise Japanese slippers. To me, they were exquisite because of the richness of the color. Then I quickly ran to hide my treasure from the prying eyes of the others.

I was also very fond of the old piano at the back of the store that belonged to my sister. My father was probably given it by a relative or else he bartered for it, offering to work in return. Pianos were common in many houses then, given the great appreciation for music. I loved to get up on the stool and tinker with the yellowed keys. Even though I never did learn how to play or read music, I was touched by it. I discovered how much music meant to me then, bubbling up from deep inside.

My eldest sister could play the piano beautifully and sang with the voice of an angel. Two songs she sang were especially memorable: "Oh, Susannah" and "Beautiful Dreamer." She was the only one of us who played the piano. My mother tried her hand at the fiddle sometimes, scratching the bow across the strings. She had more of a talent for whistling. My father didn't play an instrument either, but enjoyed music like my mother. He had something of a gift for poetry, as I discovered when he once quoted from Robert Service. Much later in his life he also revealed to me that he'd written some verse.

I took up singing and poured my soul into it. I would have preferred if I could just sing when the whim took me, but both my parents were proud of the fact that I could sing and sometimes they'd get me to sing for the customers. I don't recall precisely when I was first asked to sing for people, but I do remember the sensation of having all eyes on me. It was at once terrifying and exciting. Once a group of wrestlers on their way to Sydney had trouble with their car, so they stopped to see if it could be fixed in the garage. They came inside the store and seemed to fill the space; one of them was called Gorgeous George, a huge man with blond hair and rippling muscles. We'd never seen anyone like them before. Eager to show me off, my father got me to sing for them, setting me up on the piano stool. He always did this if there were lots of customers in the store, but I'd never sung to such an exotic audience. Yet all this attention made me feel even shyer than before. I sang because they wanted me to. I loved to sing, but I didn't always like singing for an audience.

My eldest sister had a Stephen Foster songbook that I coveted, maybe because it was the only book in the house special to me. In it were pictures of large trees and gentle waters, old people rocking in their chairs, young men home from the war, and a couple getting married. In one, a young man serenaded his sweetheart as she listened from her window. A pale woman watched her lover turn his back and depart under a moonlit sky. In "Willie, My Brave," a girl stood on a windswept shore dreaming of her shipwrecked lover. On another page, a young man looked down over a vista of a country village surrounded by rolling hills. I spent hours poring over the illustrations, imagining the stories of all these people. I memorized every scene, until they were all impressed in my memory. They became part of my world, perhaps even more than I knew.

At the back of the store was the small apartment where we all lived. It consisted of a kitchen, a small living room, and two tiny bedrooms. There was running water in the sink, but we had no indoor bathroom. Everyone had an outhouse then, and ours was a typical one, with a window in the door and a catalogue by the seat. It served us until a toilet was installed inside the house some years later. My older brother had a bedroom to himself, while my sisters and I slept in a pair of bunkbeds in the other with only a narrow space between them. My parents slept on a daybed in the living room that could be pulled out at night. Since it was a large family, people came and went. The family soon became grouped in two divisions: the older and younger children. My eldest sister left home at sixteen and my older brother left a few years later to join the army. I remember clearly when my sister left, because she was the first to go. We said goodbye to her at the back of the store and my sister Mary started to cry, which set me off too.

"You'll be all right, dears," she said, stroking our heads. Tears were streaming down her face too. She was young and slim, and her face had a lovely sweetness in it. She had always taken care of us.

The next time I saw her she was wearing a wimple that framed her face and peaked at the top of her head, and she was cloaked in a long, dark habit. She'd become a nun.

◆ ◆ ◆

The kitchen was heated with a coal stove, and I can recall my mother hauling the heavy coal in the scuttle even when she was well along in her pregnancies. Sometimes she and I would take a small piece of coal and chew on it, never knowing how bad it might be for us. I liked the rich taste and the solid crunch of it, as well as the aftertaste that lingered in my mouth.

Once the coal scuttle was the scene of a disaster. Neil was born at Christmas when I was still quite young. My mother allowed the girls to hold him, passing him around our little circle. He was a new Christmas gift to us, and we may have fought over him, tugging and pulling to be the next to hold him. The next thing we knew he had fallen, hitting his head on the coal scuttle. His tiny head gushed with blood. I stood, shocked, looking down at the red blood on the black coal, thinking he might die. He was writhing in pain, and his cries made us flee behind into the store. All we could think of was to hide behind the counter in terror before my mother and father both came running.

"Oh, my God," screamed my mother. "What happened?"

"It's his head. Get some cloths," yelled my father.

We didn't move in our hiding place. Our hearts were banging like hammers.

My mother tended to him, bathing his forehead and pressing a cloth to the wound. The blood kept seeping through. She didn't think of us until afterwards, when we finally came out, an hour or so later.

"Is he all right?" asked my sister Mary, in a quavering voice. "Will he live?"

My mother was angry, but she could see how it had frightened us. "What on earth did you girls do?"

"He fell," she said. "We dropped him by accident."

"I thought I could trust you to be careful with him. Get me another cloth."

"He's going to be okay?" She handed my mother another cloth.

"Yes. I think he'll have a scar, poor thing, but he'll be all right."

Often, during the day, I would sit rocking in the little chair that my father had made for me. I used to rock in it constantly, to the point where it would annoy my father. Through the window in the kitchen, I looked out at the hill rising behind the house, where white spruce and birch thickly covered the slope. It was beautiful any time of the year, whether rain was pelting down, or the trees were brilliant with the fall colors, or the first snow had transformed the world with a dazzle of white. When I sat humming in my chair, I imagined the tops of the trees to be witch's hats.

My mother was often busy cooking. She was a slight woman, with dark eyes and long, dark hair that she wore in ringlets piled on top of her head. Over her blue cotton house dress she wore an apron dotted with sprigs of pink flowers. Her hands lovingly kneaded the dough that might be transformed into the pastry for a delicious pie. Once she put a steaming apple pie outside the back door to cool and my brother and cousin made off with it. Sometimes she was interrupted by customers in the store and if she ran to wait on them, her baking might get burnt in the stove. She called these her burnt offerings, but we would gladly eat them. Even at her worst, her baking was excellent.

She also made cornbread that was golden yellow, light in texture and faintly sweet. Her molasses cookies were richly flavored, too. Each woman in the village had a speciality she baked, and my mother was known throughout the village for her fudge, which was beyond compare. It was so good she used to sell it in the store. The recipe, however, is long lost. Usually recipes were never written down and no one else could duplicate anything exactly the same way.

Just as my mother never bothered to write down recipes, my father rarely worked according to plans, unless he was working for a company. He was a clever, skilled carpenter, able to judge with a keen eye what needed doing and then setting to work. Throughout his life he worked extremely hard, an ethic instilled in him from the time he was young. On days when weather was inclement and he was sent home from a job, he was discontented. He was happiest when he was working. Though not a tall man, he was very strong, and he had handsome features, blue eyes, and thick dark hair. Once I watched him working on the roof of the barn at Nana's (my grandmother's), fairly flying across it. I also saw him put in a new set of stairs in a house and he was worked so fast that the stairs were neatly in place before I knew it. He would give a nail only two sharp, quick blows of the hammer and it would be in place. It seemed to me that he was spitting nails, at the rate he was working. Watching him was like watching an artist at work.

Though they were both good people, my parents were never happy with one another. Theirs was a marriage that had been thrust upon them when my mother became pregnant. They were both young when they married, which didn't help matters. In those days, if an unmarried woman became pregnant, the priest would announce it in church, urging the community to shun her if she did not marry. So my parents really had no choice. My mother's father made her go to the hurried little ceremony in the vestibule of St. Mary's, since such marriages were not performed in the church. My mother wore a green dress, which may have explained her intense dislike for that color later. No photograph exists of the ceremony, such as it was, and no festivities followed. They made a start on married life, though my mother was very unhappy in Big Pond, who lived first in Glace Bay and then moved to Boston at the age of four with her family. The transition of coming from Boston to Big Pond with her family when she was a teenager was especially hard on her. She longed for the city and talked about it often. My father, on the other hand, loved Big Pond.

There was nothing they had in common. When they were together, they exchanged harsh words, each quick to upstage the other. My father had a sharp wit, but my mother harped on him until the quarrel escalated. They'd argue over trivial things.

"Why didn't you put crackers in my lunch can?" he said one evening after work.

"There aren't any," she retorted. "Do you think they're going to drop out of the sky?"

"Well, more likely they'd fall out of the sky than you putting them in for me."

"Put them in yourself, if you want them. You're just lucky you've got something to eat."

"Christ, woman."

Then the silences would follow, and each would sit sullenly waiting for the other to begin again. Or my father would simply turn his back and leave.

I don't know how my parents stayed together. They even attempted to make things work between them. My father went to Boston several times with my mother while they still lived in Big Pond. And he did everything to make ends meet, taking carpentry jobs that came his way, even going to Newfoundland for periods of time. My mother worked very hard in the store, and she tried to make it into a home for us. She planted rosebushes outside one year, but I promptly pulled each one out.

"Rita, what have you done?" she cried.

She gave me my first spanking for it, but that was the end of her gardening.

They had their happy moments, sitting around the kitchen table with relatives, playing a game of bridge or forty-five. My relatives would know when it was a night for a card party, because my father would flick the lights and they would come over. We had no telephone, so the lights were a signal. The card parties were times when the stories would begin, since ours was a world in which people preferred to tell stories rather than read them. Much stock was put in how well someone could unfold a tale, pausing for suspense, or breaking off when people laughed at a comic episode. They would sit laying bets, offering up village gossip, or mentioning fascinating things like forerunners, those ghosts that were said to appear before a death. They were convinced that they existed, as were we.

"They heard the wagon again last night," said my father.

He meant the wagon up at Nana's house. They had once made coffins there and hauled them down to the door where they were taken away on a wagon.

"They could hear the rough box being slid onto the wagon," he went on. "And the horse whinnied."

There was a silence.

"Then off it went down the lane. Duncan looked out the window, but there wasn't anything there."

We crouched on the floor in the bedroom, listening as the games went on well into the night. It is easier to think of my parents like that, in a moment of peace: my father trading a joke and my mother offering around some molasses cookies.

In the morning, it would all change.

# CHAPTER THREE

# FROM SUMMER TO WINTER

Spring comes late to Cape Breton and it is not unusual to have a snowstorm in late May or even June. The wind whips across the Bras d'Or and the storm clouds can be seen in the distance, rolling over the lake. The snow may turn to rain that falls for days, drumming on window panes. Finally, the sun comes out and it feels warm again; while there is always a fear of frost, the weather changes completely and in less than a week or two spring is followed by summer.

When I was young, summer in Big Pond was always a special time because winter was longer and harsher than it is now. I didn't mind playing by myself and often felt great joy wandering in the woods alone. All the time, music was in my head. I heard it everywhere, especially in the wind. Sometimes I would climb the inviting branches of a tree and sit in the crook of one of them, confiding my troubles to it. I gave some of the trees names. It seemed to me that they were sympathetic to my words. Those

26

same trees had been burdened with the heavy snow months before and in my childish way, I almost felt guilty sitting on a branch that had been bent low in winter. Or I would sit with my legs astride a branch, humming a snatch of a tune my older sister had played on the piano. I could hide in these secret places, looking down at the world through a tracery of green leaves. I didn't have to explain myself to anyone.

It was a world I liked to explore with Everett, my cousin, the same one who later became a priest. One of the things we looked forward to in summer was the empty ice cream containers from our store. When the last scoop of ice cream was gone, my father would give us each a container and we'd go off into the woods, among the spruce trees, where we'd lick them clean. Afterwards, we'd go fishing at the brook where it ran through Nana's fields. We walked up the hill along the lane, carrying our homemade fishing rods.

"I'll bet I'll get more fish than you," I told him.

"Maybe."

"Maybe not." I thought of the two trout I'd caught the last time we went. He'd caught five. "You always get a lot."

"You'll get some."

The place we picked at the brook reminded me of a scene out of the Stephen Foster songbook. The trees towered over us and the brook rushed under the rickety old bridge we had to cross. Everett kindly took my hand and helped me over the rotten sections. Then we sat down in a grassy spot patterned with sunlight at the edge of the brook. Every so often he would sing bits of songs he knew, when the mood took him. When he caught more trout than I, as he usually did, he'd flash a radiant smile at me. He loved being outside as much as I did.

I played with all the village children, but I particularly remember Donald Red Dan MacNeil, Catherine Joe Hector Campbell, Jeannie Morrison, Charlotte MacNeil, Josephine MacNeil, and Rose Keane. Rose was a cousin whose mother, Aggie, lived in Boston. She had brought her daughter to Big Pond to live with Nana and my Uncle Duncan on the hill. My older sister must have helped Nana, though she still had time to play with us. Taking turns with the others, she and I occasionally brought the cows in from the pasture.

Nana's cows were out all day and it was evening before we were able to bring them into the barn. The shadows in the dark woods made us jump with fear. Sometimes we were out for hours, wandering through the woods, imagining we heard them lowing. Whenever we heard the sound of the lead cow's bell, we ran and threw our arms around Bossy's neck. It might be dark by then, but we'd still have to round up the others and bring them in to the pen at Nana's. It seemed that the cows were more important than we were, because if they weren't brought in there was hell to pay. One evening we came back without the cows, perhaps because we'd been play-ing, and Uncle Duncan got terribly angry with both of us.

"Where are the cows?" he asked. His voice was deep and threatening at the best of times, but he was much worse when he was in a bad temper.

"We—we—" My sister looked at me. "We couldn't find them."

"Couldn't find them?" He yelled. "What do you mean you couldn't find them?"

We stood looking at our shoes.

"They need to be milked and you two are just skipping around think-ing of God knows what. I suppose they're in Sydney by now."

I went home because it was late, but he must have said more to her because she ran away. They had to call the RCMP to come and search for her. Finally, after a day and a night had passed, they found her. She had been hiding in a tree all that time, probably without food or even a blan-ket, and still had to be persuaded to come home.

◆ ◆ ◆

Summer was when my father taught me how to swim. I'd put my arms around his neck and he'd swim out into the cold water of the Bras d'Or. He was a good swimmer and would go out even when there was ice on the lake. With him, I learned to float and then to swim. My friends and I used to play close to shore, putting starfishes on each other's backs. Soon all of us got used to the unpredictable nature of the lake. Within hours, it could change from being flat as a platter to a roiling mass of grey waves, capped with white, that would tumble onto the shore. Even when it was calm, I was afraid of going out too far. I had, and still have, a real fear of deep water.

We usually swam at the wharf, and sometimes we would see Father Stanley MacDonald decorously crossing the road in his long black cassock, heading for a swim on the other side of it. He would always disappear to a hidden place where he could swim in solitude. And on one occasion I saw a family drive up and stop at the wharf. The father tied an old brown rope to each of his two small sons. Then he picked them up and tossed them into the water, where they yelped in terror, trying to stay afloat while he barked at them from the wharf, pulling at the rope whenever they went under. This went on for about an hour, before he allowed them to come out, thinking that he had taught them to swim when all he had taught them was fear of the water. I couldn't imagine how I would feel if my father had done that to me. Once I felt something of that fear when my older sister pushed me off the wharf, though I screamed at her. It was terrifying to fall over the edge and feel the dark water close over my head. I surfaced, panicking and thrashing my arms until someone dove in and fished me out. Still dripping, I ran after her, beating at her with my fists and yelling at her never to do it again.

Yet that same fear didn't stop me from daring the others, and being dared myself, to walk the railing of the old bridge over Brack's Brook. The narrow wooden railing of the bridge must have been at least two or three feet higher than the bridge itself, and the drop to the brook below was about twelve feet or more. Each of us teetered precariously as we walked across to the other side, almost falling, but always catching our balance in time. We spent endless hours playing around that bridge. We'd swim in the brook, and hide, shivering, under the big wooden pylons, listening as cars or trucks rumbled overhead. Sometimes we fished there too, or we'd go down to the shore and fish for cod.

When we grew tired of playing by the bridge we'd go home and play hopscotch for a while. Then we might play on the swing set my father had made for us, which was a magnet for all the children in the neighborhood. Even at night, the adults could be seen swinging in the moonlight. If swinging began to pall, we'd play hide and seek for hours. Once I ran down a hill to hide and slid into an ant hill. I came up screaming, bitten all over, and huge red welts formed on my skin. My cousin, Brother, carried me home and there my mother sat up for most of the night watching over me. When her warm, gentle hand stroked my forehead, I felt safe and loved.

Some days we'd take empty milk bottles and walk down the Glengarry Road past Agnes and Stevie John S.'s house as far as Joe Hector's farm, where we'd go into the sun-baked meadows, swatting away flies as we dropped blueberries into our bottles or our mouths. As fast as we filled the bottles and took them home, the blueberries would be put into pies, and we'd go back for more. Sometimes we'd make a detour to the sawmill where Catherine, Duncan, and Benny lived on the same road. We liked jumping into the hills of sawdust left from the cutting of lumber. Our eyes stung for days afterwards because of the tiny wood chips, but at the time it always seemed worth the pain.

One summer day I was playing outside in a makeshift tent behind the store with my cousins. It was one of those perfect days, with clouds heaped up in the blue sky. My cousin, Raymond, said he wasn't feeling well. He was a slight boy with curly brown hair who wasn't often sick. But his head hurt terribly and he wanted to lie down. We walked him over to Aunt Jessie and Uncle John Duncan's house, just on the other side of A. A.'s store. It was the last we ever saw of him. He died a few days later of spinal meningitis.

I went over to the house for the wake, like the rest of my family. Some people were gathered in the kitchen, but the immediate family were gathered around Raymond's coffin in the good room. It would have been an open coffin, and the family must have sat up that night and two more nights for the vigil by Raymond's thin body, looking at his unnaturally calm face. I don't recall going into that room, but I remember that I was stunned by the sight of my uncle in the hallway between the kitchen and the parlor. He was a tall man with the same curly hair as his son, and he was sobbing as if his heart would break, holding on to the wall.

"Oh, God," he cried. "Oh, God."

I had never seen a man cry like that before. I slipped out of the house and ran through the dark field back to the store, crying and stumbling as I went.

The days that followed seemed empty. We were used to old people dying, but it didn't seem possible that one of us would die. It seemed strange to cross the road that year and walk to school, knowing Raymond wouldn't be there. I scuffed my shoes against the pavement as I went. The breeze was soft and warm; it was still summer in September. Yet the teacher was standing on the step ringing the great handbell to bring us all inside. It clanged again and again, as if the bell was reminding us, over and over, that something precious had ended.

The schoolhouse was across the road at a short distance from the store. It was set back from the road, close to the woods, but we couldn't see the lake from the classroom. Still, we were always distracted by what lay outside the six large windows, three on each side of the building. On the left side were the hills, with the peaks of spruce trees at the top, and on the right side were the woods. We might catch a glimpse of eagles. Or we'd see shiny black crows pecking at the ground. Even on the days it rained, I'd rest my head against my hand, gazing at the grey curtain of water. In winter, many of the birds would disappear, but the snow would begin to drift past the windows. Sometimes it whirled in a frenzy of white, or ice pellets would hit the glass like bullets. When spring finally came, along with the rain and mud, the first robins were always cause for celebration.

The schoolhouse had a tiny cloakroom, which opened into a small room with a blackboard that covered one wall and a potbellied stove close to the teacher's desk. The younger children sat closer to the front, while the older children were at the back. We would begin with the Lord's Prayer, but no anthem was sung. Then we would start our lessons. We had such standard fare as reading, writing, and arithmetic, as well as history, geography, religion, health, and social studies. Most of us shared desks and textbooks with one another. Though I didn't enjoy it, I tried to concentrate on my work, because each year we had to pass examinations to get into the next grade.

The teacher taught all the grades. Teachers changed almost every year, but each had a routine of writing notes on the blackboard which we would then copy in our workbooks. If we whispered, she would turn and scold us, rapping her ruler to get our attention. One teacher reprimanded me for something I hadn't done.

"You've been smoking."

"No, I haven't."

"Don't you talk back to me. I can smell it on you."

"It's my mother's sweater," I said. "She smokes."

"And you don't? I don't think you're telling the truth, young lady. Sit down."

I sat down, furious with her. I could have shown her my mother's tobacco still in the pocket of the sweater, but she wouldn't have believed me. That incident hurt me, but soon the teacher was gone, replaced by another one.

Recess was my favorite time of the school day, and since we didn't have long outside, we'd rush to the door. Then we'd often make a dash for the woods, where we'd pick the sap off the bark and chew it. The skin of the sap was hard, but it was softer underneath, and we'd chew it like gum. When it got colder, we might grab an icicle from a rock, or a bit of ice clinging to a tree branch. At lunch hour, after going across to the store for a bite to eat, we might get a chance to run up the road, where ice hung in a glossy white array on the rocks.

"What's the matter with your mouth?" one of the others would start.

"Dad kick your teeth out?"

Everyone would laugh.

Then I'd walk back to school by myself. Not only was I teased, I had to suffer through the attempts of the public health nurses, sent from Sydney to ensure the health of school children. They gave us all immunizations, but they also singled me out, putting a tongue depressor against my upper gums and teeth as they tried to pull them into alignment. It was very painful and did no good at all. All it did was make me feel worse.

"Hey, Rita, did you get that lip in a fight?"

Sometimes I fought them. I scratched at their faces and hit them, but they hit me too. We'd roll over in the frosted grass until the teacher had to run outside and shout at us to behave ourselves, and who did we think we were acting like a bunch of hooligans.

◆ ◆ ◆

We all looked forward to Hallowe'en for weeks ahead. It marked a break in the tedium of school. On that night my father would give us sparklers which he'd light, watching as we ran with the bright, flickering sticks, trying to make pictures or write our names before they burned out. Then we'd go from house to house with our cousins, trick-or-treating. We'd turn over people's outhouses or soap their windows, but the adults got up to more tricks than we did. A cow or a horse might be taken from one barn and put in another. Cars might be missing. Tools from a barn might be hanging from the trees.

At school when it grew very cold, we'd move our desks to be closer to the coal stove, similar to the one we had in our kitchen. The older boys had the job of keeping it going. We didn't want to move our desks too close, or we'd get too hot. If we were at the back of the schoolroom we'd get too cold. No matter what the weather, school was always in session, except for the brief holidays, and the long, wonderful summers. Sometimes there were blizzards, and the children who lived far away trudged through the drifts to get to school. Nowadays they would never be allowed out in such weather. By the time these children got to school, it was nearly time to go home. The snow and ice clung to their clothes as they stood by the stove, half-frozen, while beads of melting snow dripped onto the hot stove. There were little hissing sounds as the droplets hit the stove, and the younger children giggled in their seats, listening.

The smell of woolen clothes dripping by the stove, the odor of burning coal, the slightly bitter fragrance of the sap gum that we chewed at recess, the acrid scent of tobacco in the sweater I wore, and the soft pine smell of the dustbane we sprinkled on the floor at the end of each day all remain in my memory. At Christmas, one of my strongest impressions is the smell of spruce, from the tree that was brought in from outside, filling the small schoolroom and making us fidgety for the holiday that was coming.

By this time, the water in the gully behind the store would be frozen. It froze in tiny waves, making a natural slide. After school, we would grab an old piece of cardboard from the store and slide along the gully until our faces were rosy with running and sliding. We would do it until we were too cold to do it anymore. Other days we would skate on Brac's Brook near the bridge. The bulrushes that fringed the edges of the brook would be rigidly frozen in place, their velvety brown tops turned woolly and covered with a film of ice. We'd rush down to the edge of the brook and sit only long enough to tie our skates. It didn't matter whether the skates were for boys or girls, we would wear whatever was available. They ranged from a size four to a size nine, and if the pair I got were too big, I simply wore lots of extra pairs of socks. With a burning tire for warmth, we would skate away under the shadowy pylons of the bridge where we used to hide in summer, and then circle back to the tire and warm our hands.

If there had been a fresh snowfall, we would rush to make snow forts behind the store. The best snow for this was always the kind that was slightly wet. Then, from our snow forts, we'd make snowballs and lob them at one another. Once my cousin appeared with some cigarette butts that he'd scavenged from home. We took them to an old outhouse no one used anymore, and took turns lighting them, gasping in some smoke, coughing and choking. Then we collapsed in the snow feeling sick.

More than anything, we loved to take our toboggans up to the hill. Then we'd come careening down, screaming all the way. We'd go up and down until the short day began to fade into twilight and when it got too dark it would finally be time to go home. Inside we'd dry our socks at the stove in the kitchen, and if we were very cold we'd put our feet in the oven. Later my mother would make supper with some help from my sisters and while they were working I'd trace my fingers over the designs of the frosted back door window. When it was very cold, the frost didn't melt from that window. It contained wonders, like silvery faces, or caves, or delicate land-scapes. I would blow on it and the magical shapes would disappear, but later they would form into new patterns, each more beautiful than the last.

Soon the supper would be ready and we might sit down to steaming potatoes, turnips, and canned corn beef with my mother's gravy. After the dishes were done, we often had to say the rosary and when it was time to go to bed, I would lie awake thinking of Christmas, only weeks away. I imagined the jingle of bells on the roof or the stamping of a reindeer's hoof, and then, exhausted and excited, I'd fall asleep.

# CHAPTER FOUR

# CHRISTMAS

The Catholic Church ruled our world. It ruled over our days, our school, our family life, our tragedies, and our celebrations. I couldn't imagine what life might be like outside its tight circle. Each day at school began with a prayer and many evenings after supper, particularly during October devotions, we went down on bended knees as my father said the rosary, moving the beads as he said the fifteen decades of Hail Marys. We never dared to move during this ritual, because if we did my father would be provoked. He spoke rapidly, but it always seemed endless. Each decade, or ten beads of the rosary, would begin with the Our Father, and then he would launch into the rest of it.

"Hail Mary, full of grace, the Lord is with thee," he began. Then the words began to run together. "BlessedartthouamongwomenandblessedisthefruitofthywombJesus."

Then he would begin again, slightly louder: "Holy Mary, mother of

God," but this too, would trail off into "atthehourofourdeathAmen."

After each Hail Mary he would move his fingers to the next bead, finishing with the Glory be to the Father, but then it would begin all over again for the next decade. Even when he was finished the decades, the ordeal wasn't over, because the litany followed after this. Only then could we get up, but if it happened that I went over to my Aunt Jessie and Uncle John Duncan's later, I might find myself in the middle of the same thing. There too, I would have to join in the rosary, again without moving an inch.

I loved the Bible stories, and could listen to them over and over, particularly when my father sat with me on the daybed and told them to me. I could imagine Noah and the ark as the dove flew back with the olive branch. I could visualize the story of the wise men and shepherds following the long-tailed star to a stable in Bethlehem, where a child, haloed in golden light, had just been born. And I loved the tales of Jesus curing the sick and the blind. But then my father began telling me about the Devil and I wanted him to stop. The terrifying world of Satan and the fiery pit of Hell, which was such a part of our upbringing, began to haunt me.

Before each church service, the bell would ring loudly, its sound echoing throughout the village. It was wise not to be late, because the heavy front door squeaked when it opened and the priest might be there at the door to show his displeasure. There was no escaping either benediction or Sunday mass and on both occasions we were all expected to be attentive, even the youngest ones. On one occasion we fidgeted with our shoelaces during mass and Nana mentioned it to my father. We were sent to bed early that night. The masses were all spoken in Latin then, and seemed interminable to me, even though I learned to be perfectly quiet. The pews were hard as rock and the kneeling benches were designed to torture the knees. If we were lucky, the choir up in the choir loft would sing loudly and it would alleviate some of the pain.

When Hilly MacPherson sang, those who had begun to nod off lifted their heads to listen. It was better to be jolted awake by Hilly than by Father Stanley's stern glance. Her low, rich voice, resonating like an instrument, shook the rafters of that little church. When she sang Dies Irae, I was carried away by the sheer power of her voice.

There was abuse and alcoholism in our village, but no one discussed it. Men who were abusive to their wives still went regularly to church and came back from receiving the host with their heads bowed. There might be a whisper or two, when such a man was kissing the altar rail at the front of the church: "Did you see him eating the altar rail?" Yet women were cowed by their husband's authority over them. More often, the whispers at church were about what other women were wearing. There would be endless discussion if one of them wore something new: "Now, where'd she get that fur coat?" Or there would be talk about the poor woman who had been wearing the same hat for years: "She's been wearing that since the cows came home." The aging Sunday suits of the men, worn shiny in places, never came under the same scrutiny.

My older brother and our cousin Jackie were both altar boys, and had to wear white surplices over soutanes or cassocks. One day my brother didn't make it to mass. He and Jackie had gotten hold of some tobacco and a pipe, which they smoked in the outhouse. It made them both sick, but while Jackie staggered over to the church for mass, my brother was nowhere to be seen, still recovering at home.

Father Stanley always wore a black suit and the traditional white collar when he visited our house, as he did at least once a week. He was a tall, handsome man with a good sense of humor, and he looked a little like Winston Churchill. Certainly he carried himself with a presence that couldn't be ignored. When the Canso Causeway was opened in 1955, he was asked to give a short speech of three minutes. Then the allotted time for the speech was shortened to only one minute. He used that one minute to berate the politicians, including C. D. Howe, in Gaelic. Everyone clapped, even the dignitaries from the mainland, who didn't understand a word of what he was saying. All the Cape Bretoners understood though, and loved him all the more.

When he came over to our house, he let me groom his white hair with a black comb and then he'd laugh when I'd pull the hair off and put it in the garbage.

"What happened to your nose, little Rita?" he'd ask.

"Joe Louis punched me." This was the answer my father prompted me to say.

When he heard my answer he shook with laughter, uttering only a bubble of sound.

"Joe Louis the boxer?"

"Yes, Father."

Then he took me up and blessed my lip. I expected a miracle to take place immediately, but when I looked in the mirror, everything was just the same as before. If a miracle could happen at Lourdes or Fatima, it could happen in Big Pond. And so I waited and hoped, imagining a transformation that didn't come. Still, Father Stanley made me believe in a miracle, and that hope kept me going.

Because he was suspected of taking a few drinks, the village men felt it was their duty to report it to the bishop. My father was one of them, and from that day on, Father Stanley never came to visit us. He had found out very quickly who had reported him. I couldn't understand why he never came to bless my lip again, and I was sad to see him walk by the store without coming in.

"Why doesn't Father Stanley come in to see us?" I asked my parents once, as I watched him walk past.

They glanced at each other. They were keeping something from me.

Years later, in Sydney, I saw Father Stanley when he was living in a nursing home. We exchanged greetings and his tired old eyes revealed that he was grateful for the visit. He waved goodbye feebly, making the sign of the cross, but I never saw him again.

When I was old enough for first communion, I took catechism classes for a few weeks at school. We were given grey paperback books, filled with beautiful pictures. We had to know everything: the Ten Commandments in big, bold print, the seven virtues, seven sacraments, and seven deadly sins. We were not to forget that the seven virtues were divided into divine and moral, that sins were either venial and mortal, while the seven deadly sins, all potentially mortal, paved the way to the burning pit of hell. We had to know everything else besides, like the Hail Mary, as well as the Litany of the Blessed Virgin Mary. Then there was the Confiteor, the Apostles' Creed, and the Act of Contrition. Anyone unfamiliar with the Our Father had to memorize that too, but it seemed that was engraved on the heart at birth.

Like the other girls, I wore a white dress, white socks, and white patent leather shoes. We looked like little dolls, our mothers told us. My friend had a cigarette butt in her white sock and I wondered if it would fall out when we went up for our first communion.

If church was a trial for me as a child, I still looked forward to Christmas every year. Though people didn't put lights outside their houses as they do now, they would put their Christmas trees at the window so that the colored lights could be seen by those passing by. My father would cut a tree for us as he did for the school. The trees were usually missing a few branches, but my father would nail the base of the trunk to a stand of two pieces of wood, and we would turn the bad side to the wall, tying it firmly with string. Then we would trim it with a string of lights, a silver garland, and lots of colored paper decorations. There were also a few delicate red and silver bells that my parents must have bought once in Sydney. Of all the things on the tree, I loved them best.

Even the tree at the school would be garlanded with our handmade contributions. Each year, there was a Christmas party. Our cards and decorations made the room a festive place, not the bare schoolroom it was ordinarily. Some of the parents came, we exchanged small gifts, and even a poorly disguised Santa Claus appeared. I vividly remember walking home from one of those parties with a glass Scottie dog, a gift, clutched tight in my mittens.

Just before Christmas one year, Catherine Joe Hector invited me to her house to stay overnight. I was a little apprehensive, because I'd heard that her father was gruff. We started out after school, and what was an easy walk in summer was much more difficult in winter. Each day Catherine must have walked two miles each way to school. Yet that afternoon, it was a great adventure walking along the snow-covered Glengarry Road to her house.

Joe Hector's farmhouse was set back from the road and to me it seemed like the biggest house I'd ever seen. It was a huge white house, and its whiteness was exaggerated by the snow all around it. Inside, it seemed forbidding, with all the heavy dark furniture. The kitchen was the cheerful room I expected, but the dining room was like a cavern, with a large, dark table and heavy chairs. This was where we ate our supper. Catherine's mother, who looked so much younger than her husband, was kind and friendly, but Joe Hector, a big, imposing man, only grunted a word or two.

Catherine had told me that I was not to go up the stairs that led up from the kitchen. And under no circumstances was I to go in the good room. When I saw Joe Hector going up the stairs after dinner, his huge black boots disappearing into that gloom, I wondered what sort of monster lived up there. Or maybe there were ghosts up there. Maybe it was the ghost of Catherine's brother.

I knew Catherine's brother had died when he was still a baby. Joe Hector had gone out to the road the morning after he'd died when he saw my father pass by.

"Mister," he called. "The baby died in the night and we need a coffin for him."

So my father made the coffin, a tiny little box for Catherine's brother. I wondered if she ever worried about his ghost.

In her bedroom, which was just off the kitchen, we jumped into bed. It was large and cold. Even the sheets were icy, though her mother put a hot water bottle under the covers for us. When I glanced up at the bed post, I saw the usual rosary beads hanging from it. No house was without them. Catherine and I tried to get warm, talking until we fell asleep.

"What do you think you'll get for Christmas?" she whispered.

"I'd like a little rocking horse with a red saddle."

"I'd like a sleigh."

"No, I think I'd like a doll instead of a rocking horse."

"Or one of those talking dolls."

"With blue eyes that open and shut."

"Yes, blue," she said sleepily.

When my father was away in Newfoundland working, I was allowed to sleep with my mother on the daybed. She would turn on the radio as she often did in the evening. We could get a station in Wheeling, West Virginia, that she used to listen to a lot. Sometimes we heard shows like "The Inner Sanctum," "Charlie Chan," or "Amos 'n' Andy." But on those evenings in December we listened to Christmas carols sung by a choir. Outside, it was storming and cold, but in the warm kitchen the music was beautiful as it lulled me to sleep. It is one of my most treasured memories, lying in bed with my mother as the choir sang "O Holy Night."

Christmas was always white, and the snow transformed the village into a fairyland. Snow would be piled up on either side of the road by then, and sometimes we were simply snowed in and no one could travel. One year when the roads were blocked all the way to Sydney, about twenty-five miles away, my father walked the distance to get our supplies and then walked home. It was no ordinary walk. The wind was bitter and it would blow the snowbanks into drifts on the road. Sometimes the snowbanks were as high as the eaves of the houses.

No doubt it was easier walking in the morning, but when my father had warmed his hands and filled his knapsack at the store, the biting wind was likely in his face as he began the return trip. The daylight begins to diminish around four o'clock in the afternoon on December days, and becomes darker even earlier when it storms, so he would have had to hurry to make it back before night fell. There were probably moments when he questioned the wisdom of making the journey. If he had fallen and injured himself, there would have been no one to help, since the farmhouses were few and far between. As well, when it was very cold, there was always the risk of becoming drowsy and being tempted to rest. If he had stopped, he would have frozen to death. So he kept walking, imagining the lights of the store and the faces of his children as he came in the door. Finally he made it, completely worn out with the effort.

◆ ◆ ◆

By Christmas Eve we were wound up with excitement. The few presents under the tree were pretty in their red, green, or white tissue-paper wrappings. We hung up our socks in the kitchen and put out cookies and a glass of rum for Santa. Then we went to mass at midnight. The wind might be blowing hard that night, or it might be calm and tranquil with the stars spangling the darkness. Without city lights to diminish them, the stars seemed very close in Big Pond.

The church was a different place in the middle of the night, full of hope and beauty. It may have been my imagination, but people seemed more willing to smile at Christmas and enter into the spirit of the season. Candles lit the altar and made the entire church a mystical place, and shadows fell on the huge pictures showing the stations of the cross. Then Hilly would begin to sing a carol, like "Silent Night," and we were enthralled listening to her. The service seemed to pass in a kind of golden, incense-clouded haze. Then we would walk home, hoping that by some stroke of luck we might catch a glimpse of Santa's sleigh, flashing across the sky like a falling star.

> I looked through the night
> Thinking and praying and hoping I might
> See one little reindeer fly through the snow
> Thank goodness this season will never grow old.

On Christmas morning, we would get up and look in our socks for whatever Santa had left for us. We never believed he would leave a lump of coal. Usually we found an apple, an orange, and a few candy kisses. My parents didn't exchange gifts with one another, though. Christmas was a time for children. There was also a mass on Christmas day, but when we arrived home we ate our big meal of the day. My mother would have cooked a turkey, stuffed with dressing, and gravy, which we would pour over the mashed potatoes and thick slices of turkey. We also had turnips from our uncle's field, and my mother would have made a pie for dessert. It was always a delicious meal and afterwards we'd sit around the table drinking tea. Nana would drop by in the afternoon and we'd show her our presents. I was too young to make presents for the others, but they gave me ones they had made. One year my father made me a wooden doll cradle which he had shoved under the bunkbed in our room. I discovered it, but I was told that it wasn't for me, even though I wondered about it. Another year he made a rocking horse, and once he made a wagon for my brother. My sister Mary made me a doll out of the head of a mop, with two button eyes. All of these were precious treasures.

In the afternoon, we'd go over to our cousins to see what they'd received, but we'd usually end up playing outside. There we'd stay almost until the stars came out and then traipse home across the snowy fields. Christmas was over for another year.

# $\mathcal{R}$ELATIVES

I f the Catholic Church ruled most aspects of our lives, my relatives ruled the rest. They lived all around us. They were our neighbors, our friends, and occasionally even our enemies. We were like spokes in a wheel that radiated from Nana's house, since she was the matriarch of our family. Her house on the hill was at the centre of things, with its commanding view of everything below.

Born Mary Elizabeth Campbell, Nana was a gentle person, who must have had steel in her soul to endure the difficulties of her life. Altogether, she had given birth to fifteen children, but two boys died in infancy. When I was young, my grandfather had already died, and while eleven of her children had moved out of the house, my Uncle Duncan still lived with her. She worked the fields as hard as he did. Three of her daughters—Elizabeth (Lizzie), Mary Catherine, and Josephine—became nuns and she never saw them again. Another daughter, Agnes, moved to Boston and married there. There were still four daughters who lived close by, as well as three sons, besides Duncan. But that didn't mean that she could take life easier in her declining years.

She continued as she always had, but during those infrequent moments when she rested, she might sit in her wooden rocker, looking out the window for company that failed to come by. She was a small woman with an enormous hump on her back, which may have been caused by osteoporosis, and because she was stooped, she appeared smaller over time. Her hands were worn and wrinkled as shoe leather. Her grey hair was gathered up into a bun, and her blue eyes were clear and wise. Over her dress she usually wore a sweater she'd knitted and adorned with pretty buttons, the sleeves rolled up above her cuffs. She always wore stockings and old-fashioned black shoes. That's how I saw her when I wrote "Grandmother."

> Grandmother sat by the window
> And stared out at December
> Falling flakes reminded her
> Of good times she once had.
>
> We all know when the mind grows old
> Dreams are closer to the soul
> And memories mean so much more
> Than they ever did before.
>
> Grandmother sat in her rocker
> That spoke to her of comfort
> The window served as a looking glass
> And took her back through time...

When I came by, she was always pleased, but like all my relatives she wasn't demonstrative in her love. Yet I knew she was very fond of me, as she was of all her grandchildren. She often talked about her husband, John, known to everyone in Big Pond as John the Widow, because his mother had been widowed young and named "the Widow." Her offspring were known as "the Widow's children." My father was known as Neily John the Widow, while I was known as Rita Neily. People generally included our fathers' names with our own in order to place us in the family.

Nana explained our family history to us, never letting us forget that we were the fifth generation out of the isle of Barra in Scotland. She herself spoke Gaelic, as did her children. But Gaelic was not passed on to us through my father. She and my father spoke of the old country with a longing in their eyes, as if they knew exactly what it looked like. It was their spiritual home. "The Crossing," a song I wrote after visiting Barra, tells of their nostalgia:

Our generations came from here
My father told me stories
Of how he would return one day
And in a time of glory
We were distant by our many miles
Made distant by the sailing
I've come to stand in father's place
I heard the night winds wailing.

He was haunted by a melody
He heard so long ago
It came from in his mother's heart
And touched his very soul
Oh, I've often heard him speak your name
Although we've never met
I've come to see for father now
To put his mind at rest

And when the night lies over you
And I lay gently dreaming
Although the candle burns no more
The journey's now completed...

Nana was a staunch Catholic, and it was probably because of her firmly held beliefs that she was such a strong character. She went to church every day of her life. Before Vatican II, she had to fast until the early morning mass was over, though she got up very early and did chores before going. Even when things changed after Vatican II, I don't think she ever followed the new way of eating an hour before taking communion at mass. Her rigid adherence to the old ways of Catholicism never faltered.

Whenever we went to Nana's, we would use the back door where some black belting, perhaps a scrap piece from a mill, was spread across the step. This door led into a small room that had a shelf, basin of water, and mirror, where people tidied up before going into the kitchen, which was the biggest room in her house and the hub of activity. She stored food and prepared for baking in the pantry, just off the kitchen. At the other end of the room were two windows where she could sit in the rocking chair and look down at our store.

The kitchen was heated with a woodstove at the back where a bucket of wood stood ready. Coal could also be burned in it. The oilcloth on the floor, worn through in places to the wide floorboards beneath it, was printed with red or blue flowers on a cream-colored background. Because it lay in front of the stove, it was burnt in places from the cinders that escaped the fire. Sometimes when I turned up a corner of it, I'd find the few dollars that she'd put aside for a rainy day.

Her days were filled with work. Every morning she got up early and did the chores in the barn. She was always the one to milk the cows, since it was considered women's work. She did all the inside work as well. Like the other women of her generation, Nana used the sheared wool from her sheep, which she then combed, carded, and spun on her spinning wheel. When she was growing up some people probably wore home-spun clothes, but by the time I was a child no one did. Laundry was another time-consuming task, taking up most of a day. On Saturday she scrubbed her floors and then covered them over with brown paper or newspaper until after church on Sunday, when she was ready for company. She always had baking ready for anyone who dropped in. Her bannock and biscuits were mouth-watering, but what I remember the best was spreading her homemade butter and sour cream on a slice of her bread. For a treat, she would spread the cream on a slice and then sprinkle it with sugar. Then we'd sit at her kitchen table and enjoy it.

The hall that led from the kitchen to the front door had a few dips in it. There were often no basements in those old farmhouses and the foundations were always shifting a little. Doorways were often slightly crooked, and a door might not be properly hung, so a draft would come in underneath it. At the end of the hall was the front door, which would have opened at the top of the hill, facing the Bras d'Or, had anyone ever used it. Also opening off this hallway was the front room, which we never entered unless someone died. This forbidden room was filled with pictures of relatives, mostly dead by that time, a few photographs of children who had taken first communion, and one or two wedding pictures. On the floor were a few scattered, handwoven rugs, and above the doorway hung a wooden cross. There was a sofa and matching chair, with beautifully stitched doilies on its arms. The wallpaper was flowered, but in the corners it was coming loose since the room was closed for such long periods of time. I was always curious about that room, but I didn't dare go inside it.

I saw it only on the day Nana died. Over the years, she became frail and finally quite sick. She was taken to the hospital in Sydney, where she stayed for a while and was brought home to live her last days. She died in winter, and her house was crowded with family at the wake, all shivering with cold. My father glanced at the picture of the Pope, hands pressed together in prayer, at the top of the stairs.

"It's so cold that the Pope has his hands over his ears," he remarked.

It was strange to go into the frigid front room and sit around Nana's coffin. She looked just as she always had, except now her hands were folded on her chest and a rosary hung down from them. Her face was pale and composed. We would never again see her waiting for us in the rocking chair by the window. We wouldn't see the gentle expression on her face as her smile creased her wrinkled face. Nor would we ever look into her clear blue eyes.

◆ ◆ ◆

Besides my grandmother's house, I was always welcome at my Aunt Jessie and Uncle John Duncan's. My cousins Mary, Sharon, Genevieve, Jackie, Brother, and Raymond lived there and we spent a lot of time with them. While our store had some fascination for them, we were happy to have the open space of the farm to play. We especially liked playing in the hayloft, riding in the hay wagon, or hiding in Uncle Duncan's turnip field nearby, hoping we wouldn't get caught. We often did, but that was half the fun.

Whenever we went inside Aunt Jessie's house, she would offer us a biscuit and tea. I don't remember ever seeing her without an apron. Her nylons were always rolled down to her ankles and her hair was tied back in a bun. She had a slightly quizzical expression, as if she were anxious about something. When she spoke to us, it was in a thick brogue that made us feel welcome. If we picked rhubarb from her field, she was quick to reward us with a dish of the steaming, cooked fruit with a hint of brown sugar. She was a kind and gentle woman, who gave all to her family. I spoke of her in "Lupins":

> And Jessie at noontime
> Oh, she'd have the tea on
> And I'd sit in her kitchen
> And I'd quietly listen
> To the talk of the coming
> And going of people...

Jessie's husband, my Uncle John Duncan, often seemed stern, but when he laughed it softened his hard edges. They are both gone now, as is their daughter Mary, two years older than me, who died a few years ago of Lou Gehrig's disease (or amyotrophic lateral sclerosis). When I drive by the old farmhouse now, I recall seeing her in the window of the house where her brother Jackie lives now. I wrote about her in the song "I Guess I Always Will," in which I recalled a few special people of the village:

> There's a light in the window
> Of a house upon the hill

And I see Mary looking out
And I guess I always will.

On my mother's side, my grandfather, Duncan MacNeil, was still living when I was a child. He had remarried when my grandmother died, and whenever I went to visit him, he seemed a big, jolly man. He lived "over the road" on the lake side, about a mile away.

I tried to imagine what my maternal grandmother, Mary Elizabeth, must have been like, a woman I was told I resembled: her daguerreotype shows a lovely, gentle woman with brown hair, soft dark eyes, and wire-rimmed spectacles. According to my aunts, he abused her, probably because he was a heavy drinker at one time. No one interfered, because what a man did in his home was his own business. One day, when my grandmother decided she would cut off her long brown hair, she hid in the barn for a few days, afraid to come out for fear of what her husband would do. Yet when I knew my grandfather he had stopped drinking and was a kindly person. I loved him.

My mother's sisters, Mary and Christie, often came by. Her brother, Uncle John, lived there too, and my mother was very close to him. Yet I have stronger memories of the times my aunts would visit, my mother would put the kettle on, and they'd sit down to a game of cards, sometimes chatting nostalgically about Boston. Aunt Mary was a large woman, with the same long dark hair as my mother, and she also wore it in ringlets piled on top of her head. Aunt Christie was a gentle, pretty woman, who'd had polio when she was young. It had affected one arm and hand. One of them mentioned to my mother that I should be kept out of sight when company visited.

If drinking had been a problem for my grandfather, it was becoming one for my mother. She had mood swings, and would go from being very vocal to being extremely tired, when she would disappear for a nap. Often, she'd send me over to A. A.'s store for vanilla or lemon extract, telling me it was for her baking. I used to think she did an extraordinary amount of baking. Later, behind the old outhouse, I discovered a heap of hundreds of these small brown bottles. She'd been drinking the extract, probably in the safety of the outhouse. Because she felt trapped and frustrated in that small village, she must have seen it as an escape.

My father drank too, and was apt to quarrel with my mother, but for long periods of time he'd stop altogether. On occasion, though, my Uncle Joe and my father would fight over some obscure disagreement. My eldest brother would come between them to break it up, but it never seemed to be resolved. If these two drank together, it often seemed to end up this way.

"You're crazy to fight with him," my mother told my father afterwards.

"It's no business of yours."

"It's business of mine if everyone who comes into the store asks me what was going on here last night."

"Goddamn it, you stay out of it."

◆　◆　◆

There were other shadows in my life. We often ran across the road to my great-uncle's house when we were playing. Uncle Angus could be cross as an old bear, but he sometimes invited us into the kitchen, giving us cookies or candies before sending us out again. It seemed to us that he warmed to our company, laughing with us over a joke. He had a wiry build and grey hair, and was known for his ability to step-dance even when he was very old.

Occasionally, he'd coax me back inside, but after a while I'd run off with the others. Dusk would fall and the bats would swoop low over the grass. We had a terror of getting them in our hair so we'd scream and run for cover. Once, when the other children ran home I was slower than the rest and my uncle called me inside. In the gloom, he reached out and grabbed me.

"I'm going to do some things that'll be good for you," he said. "But you can't tell anyone, ever, or you'll get into trouble. Do you understand?"

I nodded, but my heart was racing. I felt his gnarled hands on my skin under my dress, stroking and squeezing me. When he finished, he reminded me never to tell anyone about it and then he let me out by the back door. The front door opened almost directly across the road from the store.

I never did tell. It terrified me, but the consequences of telling someone seemed worse. I felt something was very wrong, and that I'd better not tell anyone or I'd get into more trouble. It may have been the worst thing I could have done, because from then on, my uncle found any excuse to get me over to his house. Usually he would ask my parents to send me over to get money so I could go for cigarettes for him. Whenever I was over there, he'd lock the doors, close all the blinds and in the dark room he would sit on the kitchen chair. He'd pull me onto his lap. I tried to leave, but he was always very persuasive in getting me to stay.

"This will make things better," he'd tell me.

Then he'd begin to take my clothes off. He'd take off each article one at a time, though I clung to them. He was very quiet and slow, calculating his movements. All the time I felt paralyzed, as if I was caught in a trap. I couldn't bear to look at him because of his strange little smile. It sickened me. So I looked anywhere else but straight at him. I studied his black rubber boots. If I had a piece of string, or a candy wrapper, I'd fiddle with it between my fingers. But I remember everything.

I remember the porch and the back door that led straight into his kitchen, the coal stove and scuttle, the old oilcloth on the floor, the table and three chairs by the window, and the bedroom that led directly off the kitchen. The smell of that house was curiously musty, and it surrounded me, like something unclean or dead. It was always very dark, with only thin strips of light coming from the blinds. He'd take me in his arms from the chair over to the old brown couch in the corner. I'd feel his hard hands on my childish body and want to scream as they moved over my skin, up and down. I didn't make a sound, trying to concentrate on the mildewed smell of the couch, but I was entirely rigid as I lay there. Other times, he'd take me into the bedroom and put me on the iron bedstead. Then he'd lie beside me, holding me close. He didn't smell clean. His hair scratched me. I was very frightened of him. He'd push himself against me, never penetrating me, though he did just about everything else he could without raping me. There was a window outside that bedroom and I used to yearn to be outside in the light, away from his fumbling embrace. It all took no more than an hour at most, though it seemed like years. When he was done, I'd dress quickly. Each time he gave me a cookie or put a penny in my pocket, before sending me home by the back door.

"Just remember it'll help you grow up to be a good person," he said. "And don't you ever tell anyone."

I ran away from him, anywhere, as long as no one else would be there and I could be in the sunlight. Sometimes I went into the woods or down to the gully, places that I loved. I'd sit and rock, trying not to think about it, as if the experience were a dirty old dress I had to take off before I could be myself again. I had the feeling that I was the only one he victimized, probably because I was so young and vulnerable. I know that it went on for years, but then it stopped. I have no idea what put an end to it, unless someone suspected and warned him. It may have ended when we moved away. It is all still unclear to me. I only know it disturbed me deeply, as a child living in a village where there was no escape from it. I didn't have dreams about it then, but when we moved to Toronto, I had nightmares about it almost every night. It has only been in the last two or three years that I have mentioned it to several people. It was difficult: I cried each time I talked about it.

It profoundly affected me. Certainly it marked the point at which everything changed, because it was a traumatic passage out of innocence. And it changed the way I dealt with my sexuality later on. I'm still haunted by it. I have dreams in which I am creeping across the road, coming back from his house in the darkness.

Even now, I see his calloused hands, yellow from smoking, and the two twisted fingers of his right hand.

# CHAPTER SIX

# ℳOVING

The break from Big Pond didn't happen overnight. In the mid-fifties, we sold the store and went to live in Sydney before going to Toronto. My father went on to Ontario ahead of us and stayed with relatives, while my mother, well into her last pregnancy, stayed with us. This meant enormous upheaval for everyone, although the two eldest children had moved out. There were still five of us, besides my mother, crammed into a tiny, ugly apartment above a store. It had no bathroom and we all had to go down the hall to use the toilet. The first time I ever saw rats was in that place. It must have been hard on my mother, who was often sick during that pregnancy, so my sister Mary took care of us as best she could, but she was working at Crowell's Department Store and there was only so much she could do. Then my mother gave birth to my youngest brother, so she had to attend to him. I was at elementary school, where I knew no one, but occasionally Sister Saint Agnes would stand me on a desk out in the hall and get me to sing. That was a bright moment, but I didn't like going back to the apartment. While the landlords downstairs were kind to me, giving me candies now and then, I longed for life to go back to the way it had been before.

Yet my life was to change even more radically. My father came back and one morning in 1955 we all piled into the black Ford, with whatever belongings we could take. My father drove, though he was sick at the time, next to a squalling infant in the front seat with my mother, and the rest of us in the back seat, excited about the journey across the country. We'd never been to the mainland before, let alone seen anything else of Canada. None of us knew what to expect, least of all my parents.

Mary—who can't have been more than twelve or thirteen—helped my father with the driving. It seems unbelievable to think of her at the wheel of that big car, but she managed well enough. We went through Big Pond on our way and it was an odd sensation to leave the village behind, but I wasn't aware how much I would miss it. At Port Hawkesbury we crossed the newly built Canso Causeway and then continued through northern Nova Scotia and up through New Brunswick where it seemed to me that the trees were the tallest I'd ever seen. It was evening before we stopped somewhere in Quebec at the cheapest motel we could find. There were only two beds for all of us, and the five of us were crowded into one bed where we had trouble sleeping, excited as we were, while my parents were in the other bed, probably with the baby between them. For us it was a great adventure, but it couldn't have been for my parents.

It took us all day to drive from eastern Quebec to Toronto, and when we got there it was dark. The city was jewelled with lights everywhere we looked, spread out in profusion just to welcome us. We had our noses pressed against the windows as we drove through it, amazed by everything from skyscrapers to streetcars. It was a long way from a village in Cape Breton to this panorama of lights.

I don't know how far ahead my parents had planned, if at all, but after staying briefly with our relatives, we found a place to live on Close Avenue, between King and Queen streets, not far from Lakeshore Boulevard. For the next three years, I lived in this neighborhood with my family, never venturing as far as High Park to the west, or even to the downtown further east. We lived in a duplex, and our apartment was on the first floor, while another family lived above us. My parents had a bedroom with a window that faced the street, and further down the hall was a living room, where we had a black and white television and a piano. A small kitchen adjoined it, only large enough to hold a stove, refrigerator, table, and chairs. At the end of the hallway, which must have run the length of the house, were two bedrooms for the rest of us. There was an enclosed porch attached to the back of the house, where my mother's adopted brother lived for a period of time. He had already been living in Toronto before we came. Other visitors from home would stay in that room when they came.

And so it all began. It seemed to be a good place at the beginning, when we were all still hopeful. My father got work as a carpenter, and my mother seemed to enjoy the novelty of being in the city. I started school at Holy Family Catholic Elementary School and immediately liked my teacher, Miss Adam, who was kind. She had brown eyes and honey-colored hair, and walked with a bit of a swing to her gait. Still, it was hard to be with so many children I didn't know. They made fun of my cleft lip and I was hurt by it, more than I had been in Big Pond. Maybe as a result of that my parents took me to the Hospital for Sick Children to be assessed. Different doctors were involved in this, but one stands out. Dr. Ord took one look at me and regarded my parents.

"Did a butcher sew this up?" he asked.

His comment made me feel terrible, but he was the one to do several operations on my lip and nose while I lived in Toronto.

There were some bright moments at school. The teacher often asked us if there was anyone who wanted to sing, dance, or recite a poem for the rest of the class. How I ever managed to get up in front of the others escapes me now, but I did. I was shy, but I also wanted people to notice me. I stood up in front of the class and in a high, clear voice sang the Irish folk song "Molly Malone":

> In Dublin's fair city, where the girls are so pretty,
> I first set my eyes on sweet Molly Malone,

She wheeled a wheelbarrow through streets broad and narrow,
Crying, "cockles and mussels, alive, alive, oh."

Everyone clapped when I finished. The teacher congratulated me and the children who had kept their distance before now came up to talk to me. I basked in the praise. In the afternoon I went home happier than I'd ever been and told my mother, tears running down my face. And it was because of singing that song that I was asked to participate in the Irish concert at school, which was another highlight.

There may have been some routine to the days when my mother was still at home, but she had grown restless. Eventually, she went out looking for work and found a job at Eaton's, where I later worked myself, once I was on my own. She was very excited about this job since it changed her long, unhappy days into much more stimulating ones. Now not only my parents were working, but Mary too, who had gotten a full-time job at Power's Grocery on King Street not far away. She didn't go to school during the time she lived there. That left me at school and the younger ones at home with babysitters.

With two jobs, my parents could afford to drink as soon as they came home from work. They'd have a few drinks of rum and then begin to argue with each other, bickering into the small hours until they fell into bed exhausted. Sometimes they quarreled about going back to Cape Breton, their voices rising as an argument became a battle.

"I'm not going back there to live in some dump," my mother cried. "I've got a job now."

"Well, for Chrissakes, get a job there."

"We're staying here."

"What, so you can put on make-up every morning and parade around Eaton's looking like a whore?" yelled my father.

"And what are you?" A bottle crashed against something. "Jesus, Mary, and Joseph, what are you? You're a bastard."

"And you're a whore."

Their bedroom would be in complete disorder in the morning, with fragments of rum bottles scattered on the floor. They always managed to get up for work the next morning, but then it would all begin again when they came home. And despite the craziness of our family life, my father still insisted that we go to church each Sunday at Holy Family Church on King Street. If we didn't go to mass, he would rage at us. I remember going with my mother, but I must have been self-conscious because I wouldn't take my hand away from my face. Only once did I lie to my father when he asked if I'd been to church, but he was quick to discover the truth. He yelled at me, his face contorted with anger. He never once hit me or the other children, but his words were brutal.

We found ways to avoid the pain in our lives. My other sister, just a little older than I was, took to roaming the streets. On weekends I would do the same, and grew quite used to walking on King Street at eleven o'clock at night. The lights comforted me, reminding me of the spectacle we'd seen when we first arrived in the city. I also started to skip school, going around the corner and down a flight of steps that led to a basement apartment, and hiding in the shadows of the doorway until I knew all the others would be in school. Then I went my own way for the rest of the day. Perhaps the only thing that kept me going was the idea that I was going to make a record of my own music. I went across Lakeshore Boulevard where I had a confused notion there were booths where I could make a record. I had no idea what was involved, I just knew I had to do it.

I wandered around there. The lake glittered in the light and if it was warm there were people out sunbathing. There were kiosks selling hot dogs and French fries. Once I came across a group of bikers. They had "Hells Angels" emblazoned on the backs of their studded leather jackets, but I didn't know what that meant. They were big men with long hair and beards, and their huge, shiny motorcycles fascinated me.

"Hey, kid," said one. He had a tattoo of a heart and a cupid on his arm. "Aren't you supposed to be in school?"

I didn't answer. I stood there.

"Poor kid," said a woman. She had white-blond hair that was black at the roots.

"Come over here," said one of the men. "Ever seen one of these?"

I went a little closer. I looked at his motorcycle. I stared at his heavy boots.

"Come on, I'll take you for a ride."

"Don't go with him," laughed another one. "He's nuts."

I climbed on the back of his motorcycle. I put my arms around the burly man and he revved his engine. Then he took off down Lakeshore Boulevard, his hair blowing out behind him. I felt the wind rushing by as he wove in and out of cars. Then he circled around and brought me back to the others.

"Hey, he brought her back alive," said one of the men.

"Did you like that, kid?"

"Yes," I said, thinking he might do it again. "I did. Thanks."

"We'll get you an ice cream. Every kid likes ice cream."

Somebody got me an ice cream. I ate it all, even the last bit of the cone.

"What's your name?" asked the woman with the blond hair.

"Rita."

"So why aren't you in school, Rita?"

"I'm going to be a singer," I informed them, wiping my sticky mouth with the back of my hand. "I'm going to make a record."

They laughed. "Well, that's good." They were getting ready to leave, straddling their motorcycles. "You'll be a star."

Then they all pulled out with their engines thundering, sunlight glinting on the chrome. A couple of them turned and waved at me as they went.

◆ ◆ ◆

The idea of becoming a singer filled my mind. I told the other children at school that I was making a record of my songs, or that I was auditioning as a singer. Word got back to the teacher and she called my father in to tell him; he got angry with me. Whether it changed anything or not, I don't know. I wasn't doing well in school and I don't think I was even passing from one grade to the next during the three years we lived there.

Everything was in turmoil. There was nothing Mary could do to stop it, though she kept on working. A child herself at thirteen, she was responsible in the midst of the ups and downs of our life there. Having met some very kind people, such as the manager of the grocery where she worked, she relied on them and they helped take care of her. Once my father went to the store as she was counting the cash with the manager at the end of the day. He was drunk, but he had the idea that groceries were needed, so he went up and down the aisles tossing things into the cart. Mary, scarlet with shame, had to talk him into leaving the store. It distressed her that the manager would see her father in such a state. Yet he was concerned for her and made sure she got home safely from work each evening. She had other friends with whom she spent a lot of her time and sometimes I would go with them, just to get away from the house.

At some point during those years, she decided to leave and go back to Cape Breton. She could only have been in her mid-teens, but she was approaching life as an adult. She took the train to Sydney, where she arrived without a dime in her pocket and went immediately to Crowell's to see if she could get her old job back. They took her on, but all the time she worked there she had terrible headaches. She'd had a bad time in Toronto and it continued to haunt her.

Meanwhile, I was virtually on my own. I knew a few children I got along with, but it wasn't the same as it had been at home in Big Pond, where we had so much fun with our cousins and friends. There were none of the wonderful times swimming at the wharf in summer, or skating on the brook when it got cold. Playing wasn't something I did much of anymore. Instead, I'd sit inside the dark apartment and listen to the radio. Such stations as CHUM were new then and I listened to it constantly, singing along to an Elvis Presley song, like "Love Me Tender" or "Blue Suede Shoes," rocking back and forth on my parents' bed when they were at work. I rocked until the mattress was worn threadbare in one place.

We watched television quite a lot during that time and on one station from Buffalo we often saw "Uncle Bob's," a talent show, which called for auditions from children. My parents asked my cousins to drive me there for an audition. It was a two-to-three-hour drive to Buffalo and I was excited about it the whole way there. I auditioned in the studio, singing "A Tear Fell," a song by Teresa Brewer. I was picked to be one of the contestants on the show a few months later. Unfortunately, they called when I was in the hospital recovering from a nose operation. To console me, an article ran in the *Toronto Star* about a sick little girl called Rita who should be comforted by the fact that her American debut had not been cancelled, just postponed. When I did finally play in the United States years later, I recalled those words.

My father thought he would comfort me by bringing the newspaper to the hospital. He arrived drunk, with my mother, his white T-shirt brown with dirt as he waved the newspaper in his hand. He was thrilled about it and while I knew it was nice that someone had written it, I cringed with embarrassment at the sight of him. Eventually, my mother was able to get him to go home with her.

It took me time to recover from those operations at home, and perhaps because I was there anyway, my parents kept me out of school longer to take care of the younger children. My impression is that I spent months at a time babysitting. I tried to do my best with them because they needed me, but I was too young to be looking after them. Sometimes my father would volunteer my services to someone else, so there would be extra children to look after. I'd buy clothes for my brothers and sister at the store up the street where we had an account and I'd also get food at the grocery store next door. I don't remember my parents ever sitting down for a meal together, so I made sure the younger ones were fed. And if there was a holiday, like Easter, I bought them small things like colored baskets with a few treats. Each day, before my mother came home from work, I'd line the three of them up and wash their hands and faces with a washcloth, comb their hair, and send them to get a caramel out of the drawer. Then they'd go down the street to wait for my mother when she got off the bus.

Once my mother brought home a gift for my younger sister, Ann. It was a large pink plastic case with a snap. Inside was a doll on one side, separated by a compartment where her clothes were kept. Ann was overcome with joy, and she carefully laid out each article of clothing on the bed, trying first this one and then that one on the doll. She had never owned anything quite so wonderful before. In the night, however, my parents destroyed it during one of their arguments. My sister was distraught as she tried to tell them they had done it, but they laid the blame on her, not remembering what they had done. Other things were ruined during the course of those fights, and one morning we woke up to find that the fish bowl in the kitchen had been upended and the two goldfish were lying dead in a pool of water. The brightly colored fish were still intriguing to the little ones and they played with them all morning on the kitchen floor.

We got visitors from Sydney now and then, but they didn't stay long. My parents were hardly aware of their guests. Once, in the evening, I was sitting with one guest in the living room watching television. It was about seven o'clock, but my parents had been drinking before that.

"I found that tube of lipstick in the car," my mother screamed. "And it wasn't mine."

"What are you trying to say?"

"I'm saying that if I find lipstick in the car I'm going to put two and two together."

I turned up the television and then sat down again, but their voices seemed to get louder and louder.

"You're a bitch."

"No, you're a son of a bitch."

I turned up the television again and we all sat there in the growing dark gazing at the black and white screen, listening to them. It was impossible to block it out.

It went on and on relentlessly, even when the neighbors complained. At one point, I decided I would call the police, but then I didn't have the courage to carry it out. Perhaps I should have. Even on the rare days when my parents weren't drinking, their conflicts would often lead to my father hitting my mother. They never beat us, but their violence hammered at us constantly. It seemed to me there was sadness everywhere I turned, because the man who owned the neighboring grocery store married and soon began abusing his wife. I would hear her cries mingling with the sounds of my parents slamming doors, smashing bottles, and trading curses each evening: it was all part of the same vicious cycle. And each night when I went to bed I had terrible dreams, nightmares about Uncle Angus's house in Big Pond, sneaking across the road, or being in a dark and frightening place.

One night I was wakened by piercing screams, different than anything I'd ever heard before. My mother was crying out for help, a sound that seared my heart. I hovered in the corner and then crept down the hall. The door to their bedroom was open and I was frightened to death of what I might find when I looked inside. There was my mother with her head wedged in between the bedsprings, while my father pushed down on it from above. I don't know if he saw me, but he stopped and my mother somehow or other managed to pull her head out. I crept back down the hall and knelt down in the darkness, but it didn't end there. The quarreling and crying went on all through the night, as it always did. It was a wonder they could get up for work the next day, living as they did. I went into the bedroom the next morning and it was as though a tornado had swept through it. My mother was getting ready for work, trying to daub her bruised face with make-up. She was literally black and blue. At that moment I hated my father fiercely.

I had no idea if all families lived this way. My relatives, the only family we had ever visited there, didn't seem to live like this. Theirs was an ordinary household. Yet something was terribly wrong with ours. I began to think of my parents' bedroom as a sort of torture chamber. With all the violence that went on within those four walls, it was a wonder that anyone came out alive. I used to feel shivers up my spine whenever I passed that room on my way out the front door.

Word got back to our relatives at home that something was wrong, and my mother's brother, Uncle John, came to see what was happening. He could be counted on to take her side. Perhaps he challenged my father when he came home from work. However it started, I recall the two of them locked together in a fight like a pair of bulls in the living room. They were crashing around, banging things off tables, smashing into the piano, and pounding at one another with their fists.

"You good-for-nothing bastard," yelled my uncle, as he punched my father's face.

"You Christly—ooff—you Christly excuse for a man," cried my father. "Goddamn crazy idiot."

This wasn't going to change anything between my mother and father. Like us, my uncle was powerless to stop their problems.

Only my older brother was able to change things. He had come before with my sister Mary to try and reason with my parents. The last time he came he'd had enough. He told them they had to stop. They had to come home. They listened to him, realizing he was right. I don't know what would have become of us if it had gone on like that, because we were all at the breaking point. He suggested to my parents that the family could live with him in Sydney. My father was homesick all the years he lived in Toronto, and the idea of moving home was something he'd been longing to do. My mother didn't want to leave her job, but she must have wanted to change the circumstances of her life there. Neither of my parents had known how to break the pattern of the life they'd been living, but now there was a solution, however temporary.

So one morning we all loaded into the Ford again, belongings pitched in the trunk. We headed out of the city with none of the wonder we'd felt when we first arrived. It had defeated my parents. They had less money than when they'd started, so we returned to Cape Breton with nothing to show for our time away. We stayed in cheap motels, just as we had when we left. Yet I realized how much I'd missed Cape Breton when we crossed the causeway and drove northeast towards Sydney. The blue islands out on the Bras d'Or, the mist hanging over the water, the tree-covered hillsides were all so familiar. We were finally coming home.

# CHAPTER SEVEN

# SETTLING DOWN

We stayed with my brother and his wife Ruth for about a year. It was generous of him to give us a refuge for that time, a place in which we could heal after the explosion out of Toronto. In that year, my parents stopped drinking almost completely, and my father was happier. It seemed that a light had gone out in my mother, though, because she hated to leave her job in Toronto. However, life had a semblance of normality. There was always tension between them, but we weren't living the nightmare that we'd been living before. And the presence of my brother, and Mary who was working and living on her own, and the occasional visit to my older sister at the convent, helped to make things better. My brother lived in the Meadows, just outside Sydney, and I started going to school in East Bay. I was thirteen now and finishing grade eight. I walked back and forth to school, though the distance was quite a few miles. I didn't mind the walk; what I minded was being teased by the others about my lip. Remarks that I'd shrugged off as a child in Big Pond now hurt me deeply. If anyone made fun of me it made me angry. I was shy and sensitive, and I was afraid to be around strangers because I sensed they were making comments behind my back.

Soon we moved out of my brother's house, into a small apartment on Prince Street in Sydney, which was all we could afford. It was cramped, even though there were fewer children living at home. The living room was tiny, as were the kitchen and the two bedrooms. There was a woodstove in the hall and a washer in the bathroom. Every Saturday night, I'd wash out my beige jacket and put it over the radiator for church the next day. I had started a new school—Sheriff Junior High School—which was very demanding for me. I had to work twice as hard to get good marks because I didn't have much of a background in any of the subjects. By the end of that year, though, I had a high mark in history and I'd won the science prize for the top mark. The science teacher made the remark that he never thought I'd be the one to win it. Despite that disparaging comment, I was very proud of that prize. No one else in the class had worked as hard as I had.

Sometimes I visited Mary at Crowell's. She was on the nylon counter at the front of the store, and in winter, whenever someone came in, she'd get a blast of frigid air. Yet it was a good place to work and my sister didn't complain. She lived in a plain little room at Philpott's boarding house, with just enough money to pay for room and board, and a little left over that she saved. She had to wash out her blouse for work since she couldn't afford to buy another.

At least Mary managed to be on her own. My parents' relationship hadn't really improved, nor had either of them given up drinking entirely. Since we had all moved out of my brother's house, there was nothing to stop them from reverting to their old ways. One Christmas Eve, the tree was trimmed with lights and the small gifts were under it. These were pre-sents that Mary had bought for us out of her meager savings. We couldn't afford any gifts that year. It must have been difficult for my mother to watch my sister offer us things that she and my father couldn't provide. Mary came by early in the evening, saying she would come back, but when she did, my parents had been drinking. My mother began yelling at her.

"I don't want you giving them anything," she screamed. "Take your presents and go." A toy teapot caught my little sister Ann on the side of the head as it flew through the air. "Go." She ripped the wrappings off the presents and tossed each of them down the hall. Then she went into the bedroom, slamming the door.

"Don't go," I pleaded with Mary as she went out the door. "Please."

"I have to," she said, tears sliding down her cheeks.

I followed her out. There were stairs on the outside of the building and she was already halfway down.

"Please don't go," I called, shivering in the cold.

"No, I have to."

We picked up the presents, mangled and broken, with the wrapping paper torn, but it didn't do any good. No one had any heart for Christmas. My parents slept late the next day and Malkie had to come and kick at their bedroom door to get any response.

"What's going on here?" he cried. All he had to do was to take one look at the darkened, disordered room to realize they were in no shape to listen.

He went into the tiny kitchen and began putting together a Christmas dinner for us, but he was still angry. He slammed the turkey into the oven. And he stayed with us until my parents sobered up late in the afternoon, telling them that they would have to apologize to my sister. It was as if he were dealing with children. They both cried, promising that it wouldn't happen again. Afterwards they called Mary who came over to hear them ask for forgiveness. Of course she forgave them—we all did—and they cried, hugged, and kissed. Yet the whole thing was another one of those traumatic episodes in a long line of such things. There was nothing to ensure that it wouldn't happen again.

Because my parents were unhappy, it was a life of extremes. Sometimes they were in their own world, carping at each other, and other times they were loving towards us. Once I was very sick with flu, and my mother stayed up all night stroking my head. She had gentleness in her character, but she was embittered about her marriage. Yet she still had a strong will. While we lived there, she decided not to continue going to church.

"I'm never going to darken that door again," she told my father firmly.

"You can't do that. You'll rot in hell."

"There are worse places to rot."

Maybe she didn't see the point in it any more. It caused havoc in our household, but there was nothing my father could do about it. Once she made up her mind, she never went back to church again. The rest of us still went though, regularly as clockwork. And I was deeply religious then, imagining that I might go into the convent one day. Like most Catholic girls, I had a vision of myself as a nun. I thought I'd go one step further and join the cloistered order of the Sisters of the Good Shepherd. I was gently dissuaded from this path; I was still young. I had lots of time to decide if that's what I really wanted to do.

We moved out of that small apartment into a house on Mechanic Street in 1959, which was just around the corner on a fairly nice street. We lived there for a number of years. I was happier there, and I know my mother liked it better. All her life she wanted a house that they owned, but there was never enough money for that. This house was much more spacious than the apartment, with a living room facing the street, a den where we watched television off the large kitchen downstairs, and three bedrooms upstairs. My parents had their own room and Ann shared a room, while I had a room to myself for a while for the first time.

My parents bought some furniture for that house. When the three-room grouping arrived in the van, Ann watched from an upstairs bedroom window. I was hoping for a rocking chair, but I was afraid to look in case there wasn't one.

"What are they bringing in now?" I asked her.

"A kitchen table," she reported. "And now some chairs."

"A rocking chair?"

"No."

"Now there's a green chesterfield."

I waited.

"And a matching green chair."

"What now?"

"They're talking. Now they're having a smoke."

It seemed interminable.

"Oh, now more stuff is coming out. Oh!—"

"What?"

"You won't believe it when you see it!"

"Is it a rocking chair?"

"Yes, and it's got a chrome frame and white padding on the seat and the back, and some kind of pattern on it. It's the most beautiful thing."

I shot to the window to see for myself.

"Oh," I breathed. "My rocking chair."

It was the most wonderful rocking chair I had ever seen in my life. The chrome frame was dazzling. The padding was covered with tiny gold stars. When they put it in the den I sat down in it and began to rock back and forth, blissfully happy.

My parents had never tried so hard to make things better for us. It was good for me that things were quieter at home because it was difficult dealing with the world at large. At fifteen, I was now at Holy Angels High School, but I didn't like it any better than the other schools I'd been to. I had a white blouse and a navy blue uniform like the others. I even had a new green coat. At least I dressed like everyone else, but they still made nasty remarks about me, nudging each other as they whispered.

"What's wrong with her mouth?"

"And look at the way she just stands there, rocking."

Each whispered comment was like a little blade going deep into my skin.

On weekends I usually stayed in, listening to the radio in my parents' room, rocking so much that I wore a hole in their mattress, just as I had done before. I even rocked while waiting at the bus stop. All I ever did was dream of performing music. I tried taking music lessons at the high school, but I was shy and the teacher did most of the singing. I suppose I was able to take the lessons because my sister was a nun, which helped my situation a bit. I also sang at some of the local Kiwanis festivals, but I'd break down halfway through a song, run off the stage, and then cry all the way home.

In school I had to pretend that I had a solid background like the rest of the girls. In order to make things sink in, I'd come home after school and immediately do my homework. I'd write all the lessons and homework in chalk on the wall of my bedroom and pretend I was teaching. And it seemed to be a good way of learning things, because I improved. One of my favorite subjects was religion; I was interested not only in Christianity, but other religions as well. I was captivated by the stories, just as I'd been by the Bible stories my father used to tell me when I was young. I also did well in history, receiving marks in the eighties. I was very proud of my high marks, and even the average grades I usually got in math and science seemed miraculous to me.

Both my parents loved it when I sang for them. My father would come home from a long day at work and lie down in the den, inviting me to sing. My mother would sit in the kitchen. Sometimes she'd hand me the broom to use as a microphone. For a while, "Danny Boy" was the song they wanted to hear over and over. Sometimes they liked to hear "Sinner Man," "Old Man River," or "Peace in the Valley." My mother especially loved "O Holy Night." They never lost their faith that I would have a career as a singer, and my mother and I talked about it constantly, perhaps because it gave her a reason to dream. Occasionally, my aunts came by to visit my mother. She'd get me to sing for them and once my Aunt Mary remarked, "That girl has a million dollars in her mouth." I couldn't understand exactly what she meant. A million dollars in my mouth?

◆ ◆ ◆

If she was resigned to things, my mother still helped to establish a routine, which was what we needed. She was there when we left for school and when we returned. She still smoked a lot, like my father, and when they woke in the morning their hacking coughs sounded horrible. When my father tried to start the car in the yard, he'd cough, hawk, then cough again. It sounded like an alarm through the neighborhood. On Thursdays they went together to buy groceries, which rarely varied. They bought meat, fish, potatoes, turnips, carrots, a few cans of beans, bread, butter, sugar, tea, and a bag of assorted cookies. Many times the food didn't last until the next pay day, so we'd be low for a few days before we had some cash. My father's pay had to cover the rent, fuel, car payments, and clothing, as well as groceries. We couldn't afford any extras, and if something had to be bought or repaired we went to Household Finance for the money. Whatever our financial situation, my mother always prepared a feast on Sundays. My brother-in-law, Johnny, still contends that she was the best cook he's ever come across. She had her own special ways of making food taste delicious. Her gravy was rich and smooth, with a savory taste, her mashed potatoes were buttery and light, and her turnips were spiced with nutmeg. She herself ate very little, but it made her feel satisfied to know that we enjoyed her meals so much.

When I went to bed I could hear the radio from my parents' room. My father would leave it on until the small hours and usually all he would get was static. Some nights I would listen to Don Ho's "Aloha," from Hawaii, which I loved. It seems amazing that we were able to get a station that far away. I was soothed by the sound of waves lapping against the shore and the soft Hawaiian music.

Sometimes my mother went to card parties, since she was involved in a group in which each member took a turn. She always got excited when it was her turn, tidying the house and making sandwiches. Then she would put on her blue house dress that she reserved for such occasions. She fussed over the plates, cups, and saucers, laying out napkins, and arranging the teaspoons just as if she were getting ready for the queen. If anyone asked, she told them the spoons were from the United States, when they really came in the Red Rose tea packages. At the time I remember thinking, "Well, God love her. They're going to find out."

One of the women who came to those card parties was heavy-set. She claimed her chair as soon as she came in the house: it was always my rocking chair. One day she broke it, but my mother politely said nothing about it. When I discovered that it had been broken, I was crushed. I cried inconsolably. My brother welded it together again, but it wasn't the same as it had been. And when the woman came back for the next card party, she sat in it again. It broke, and again no comment was made. It happened again. Each time my brother fixed it. If I could have pulled that rocking chair out of the den, I would have, but it wouldn't have been allowed.

It was around that time that my father taught me how to drive in the red Ford Falcon. He was always very patient with me, never raising his voice. Only when we got home did he point out what I'd done wrong.

Once when I was out by myself I crashed into the back of a bus when it stopped unexpectedly. I went to the shopping mall, and still shaking from the shock of it, got the hammer from the trunk, and tried to pound out the dent. It was no use. The dent remained, big as life. I went home and hid upstairs, afraid to tell my father.

The next morning he said calmly, "Well, I hear the lamp posts were walking around the parking lot and one ran right into you."

◆ ◆ ◆

I made a few friends in that time. Carolyn Tobin lived across the street. She was fair-skinned with red hair, and she was very bright, as well as having a bubbly, outgoing personality. She was like her father, who had a good sense of humor. I was often over at her house. Shirley was another friend who lived next door to her. We often went to school together, either walking or taking the bus, and we might join up with Betty, who lived on the same street. Lorraine was another of our friends, though she lived further away. Together, we made plans for dances at the parish hall.

I'd get money for pop bottles I'd collected to pay my way into the dance and then go over to Carolyn's to plan our strategy. We had to get together to put on our hot pink lipstick and blue eye shadow. We spent hours curling our hair. Then we'd finally set out for the dance, though I was always gloomy about going. I'd watch the others, but I was destined to be a wallflower. Carolyn always danced, Shirley had a boyfriend, and Lorraine managed some dances too. I stayed hidden in the shadows, self-conscious about my lip. I didn't think I'd ever be asked to dance. If the boys noticed me, they might make a cruel comment, which made me bitter for a while. Still, I loved the music, and it was because of it that I kept going back. When I came home the kitchen light would be on. My mother would be waiting up for me, worrying, and when I came in the door she'd comfort me.

"Did you have a good time?" she asked each time. "Did you dance?"

"No," I said, bursting into tears. "No one ever asks me to dance."

"They will, dear. One of these times it'll all change."

It helped that they took me to the orthodontist. He had to rework my jaw bones in order to bring my upper lip out to meet my bottom lip. It was very painful for me, but afterwards he made a partial plate, with three front teeth attached. Now I could smile without feeling so conspicuous. The day I got it I went first to show my sister at Crowell's. Then I went immediately to St. Theresa's, got down on my knees, and thanked God. Everyone in my family was delighted, my mother most of all. Yet she didn't know if I would still be able to sing the way I had, so she got me to take out the plate when I sang. Soon she realized I could sing with it just as well as without.

If school and dances were difficult for me, my solace was in my siblings. I was always close to the three younger children and we often had fun together. I'd sometimes take them to the midnight horror shows. Other times I'd babysit them and occasionally I'd cover myself with white powder and a sheet. We'd play ghosts or we'd play spotlight out on the street at night. On Sundays, Carolyn would come over and we'd listen to the hit parade, dancing all around the kitchen in our socks.

And I always looked forward to visits with my sister at the convent. I also liked the times Mary or my brother came over for a meal during the week. We adored them both. One day, Mary informed us all that she was going to get married to Johnny, her boyfriend of many years.

"Marriage isn't what it's cut out to be," said my mother.

"I love him," my sister answered simply. "And he loves me."

Mary looked lovely on the day of her wedding, in a full length white gown which set off her figure. She had a coronet around her dark hair and a veil that hung down to her shoulders. She had never looked more angelic to us as my father walked her down the aisle and she stood at the front of the church. She had made a good choice too, because Johnny was a good-natured, steady man. He looked handsome that day in his dark suit, standing beside his young bride. When they went outside and the bells rang, we covered them with a flurry of rice.

Yet the saddest part of it was that my mother didn't get out of bed all day. She couldn't bear to see her daughter marry, because there had been so much pain in it for her. In her darkened bedroom my mother must have heard all of us across the street at Johnny's parents' house where the reception was held. Before they drove off, Mary kissed us goodbye. She was dressed in a pretty blue stroller suit, all set for her honeymoon, but Ann was determined to go with them.

"Don't go," she screamed, clinging to Mary. "I want to come with you."

"It's all right," said Mary, bending down to hug her. "I'll be back. I'm just going for a little while."

"No," she cried. "Let me come."

Ann was heartbroken. It reminded me of the time that Mary had tried to make Christmas special for us: she was our salvation. So we all cried when she left. Yet we knew that she had chosen a good life for herself, and that of all of us, she deserved it.

CHAPTER EIGHT

# On my own

In 1960, my best friend Carolyn Tobin and I had a dream of going to Toronto where we would live like queens with her sister. We used to sit on her front porch talking about it on late spring evenings. There were big trees near the house and the wind blew lightly through the leaves, an occasional soft rustling. The air was warm, lulling me as Carolyn talked about her sister. I imagined her living in the lap of luxury in a white mansion where she wore white satin gowns as she gracefully descended a white staircase.

We decided to go and look for work there after grade eleven, if our parents would let us go for the summer. They did, so long as we were under Carolyn's sister's care. We found a driver who was willing to take us there for fifty dollars each, but first he had to be interrogated by my parents. He was to take us straight to Carolyn's sister's door and no funny business or he'd have the police on his tail.

So off we went. It took three days to reach Toronto. The white mansion was just an ordinary house in the east end of the city, and Carolyn's sister Jean wasn't the sort to keep long white gowns in her closet, though if she'd descended a spiral staircase everyone would have turned to look. She was one of the loveliest women I'd ever seen: she was tall and had Carolyn's long red hair, but her skin was smooth as cream. She was cheerful and kind, helping us start the search for work. I was so shy when we went out job hunting that I used to hide behind Carolyn and let her do the talking. I liked being in the city, but I also felt frightened and alone now and then. We found work fairly quickly at the CNR, sorting checks in the office, and working one day a week in the cafeteria. I was proud that I had a job. The summer flew by and suddenly we were back in Sydney, thinking about school again.

I couldn't settle down when I got back home. I kept thinking of Toronto and the people I'd met. It made me restless. I was seventeen and I'd already been out working on my own. I went back to Holy Angels High School for grade twelve, carrying an extra subject—French—that I'd failed the year before. I didn't see the purpose in continuing school, especially since I'd worked for a while and known what it was like to be able to earn a living. So I quit. For a while I worked as a housekeeper for a woman who had five children and was pregnant with the sixth. I worked each day of the week and found the hours long and the work tiring. On Friday I was paid: I made twelve dollars.

I talked to my parents about going back to the city. They understood; one of them must have gone to Household Finance for money and my father bought me a train ticket. So back I went to Toronto, the first time I'd ever taken the train. It was the late fall of 1961, the air was crisp and cold, and there were still some bright leaves clinging to the trees. I was a little apprehensive, but also excited. This time I was going to make a career for myself in singing.

I stayed with Jean for a while and decided to see if I could get some work at Eaton's. My mother had gotten work there and maybe I could too. I arrived at the personnel office, filled out an application form, and sat frozen in a chair while I waited.

"Rita MacNeil," a voice called.

I didn't move.

"Rita MacNeil."

"Is there a Rita MacNeil here?"

Finally I got up and followed a woman into a small office where I was interviewed. I must have done all right because I was given a job. I would be making forty-eight dollars a week. I was thrilled.

The next day I went to Eaton's and went in through the main doors where there was a big statue of Timothy Eaton. On the main floor were the cosmetics and perfume counters, the leather goods counter where soft kid gloves and leather purses were sold, and another counter where nylons were sold. There was a counter for jewelry, another for watches, and another for colorfully arrayed silk scarves. I could smell the fragrances of good leather and French perfume as I went down the aisle on my way to the escalator.

That first day I was put to work answering the telephone. There were six black telephones on a counter and I was responsible for handling calls on one of them. I sat down in my chair and waited, terrified. What would I do if I couldn't speak? What would I do if someone asked me a question I couldn't answer? Would I be fired? The telephone rang. I picked it up, gingerly.

"Good morning, Eaton's Customer Accounts Services," I said.

A voice was yelling into my ear. I dropped the telephone and ran into the washroom, crying. I couldn't do this job. If only they'd given me something else to do instead of the telephones. Now I'd be fired, just as I thought. The supervisor came into the washroom, though, and gently assured me I could do the job. She'd come and help me with it, telling me exactly what to say. And no, I shouldn't worry about being fired.

I wiped my tears and followed her out, back to the telephones. "Now," she said, sitting down beside me. "Just take your time and listen to what the caller is saying."

It rang again.

"Good morning, Eaton's Customer Accounts Services," I said. This time the voice wasn't angry. It was a crisp, pleasant voice. I was able to talk to this customer. When I didn't know the answer, I put my hand over the receiver and asked the supervisor. She stayed with me the whole day, giving moral support. I never would have made it without her. By the end of the day I was exhausted, but I'd learned to deal with all kinds of requests.

I treated myself to a few things that first week. I bought an outfit for work and a pair of black slingback shoes with spike heels. The skirt had to be long enough; one girl had been sent home because her skirt was too short. My purchases seemed extravagant, but they were worth every penny. I gazed at the scarves, looked at the cosmetics, and tried the perfume testers. It was still hard to believe that I could buy a few things for myself.

Soon, to my relief, I was moved into the accounting department. I was in charge of keeping accounts for hundreds of ledgers, with each ledger representing an account. I had to sort thousands of bills into the proper ledgers. I also answered the telephone for customer services. And I was responsible for authorizations if a clerk phoned up from the floor. Once or twice we discovered that credit cards had been stolen and I had to keep the clerk on the line until the house detective could catch the so-called customer.

It took some time for me to feel comfortable with my job, but everyone was very helpful. Those with experience made sure that we knew what we were doing. Two supervisors were especially kind: Stella and Mrs. Conklin. There was an air of goodwill about the office, a sense of loyalty to Eaton's, and a true professionalism in the way people worked. People came from all over, particularly from Europe. There were Poles, Ukrainians, Germans, and Italians. I got to know Anna Kaminski, a Polish woman who lived in the west end. She had a room to rent for sixty-five dollars a month. With my wages, I thought I could manage it and still be able to save some money.

She took me home one day after work to see the place. They lived on Wright Avenue in a brick house with trees lining the street. At the end of it was High Park, with the trees looking wintry at that time of year, though it was magnificently green in the spring and summer. Anna, her husband, and two daughters lived on the first floor of the house, while other tenants lived on the second. On the third floor was another apartment. The windows at the front looked onto the street and at the back they overlooked the yard, which was full of flowers in spring. There was a tiny sitting room and a kitchenette with a stove and a small fridge, and a bedroom with two single beds as well. It was cozy and clean. I loved it immediately and as soon as I could I gave her the first month's rent.

I began to feel settled about my life in Toronto, proudly phoning home that I'd gotten a job at Eaton's. Each day I took the streetcar from Roncesvalles Avenue along Queen Street and got off at the Eaton's store at Yonge Street. And each day I went in through the heavy glass doors of the main entrance, past the statue of Timothy Eaton, and up the escalator to the sixth floor. I worked hard. At noon I went to the cafeteria with the others from my department and that was a treat. I even enjoyed working overtime. I soon made friends with a blond Polish girl called Sophie Paris, who lived around the corner from me. There were others too, but she was my closest friend.

For the first time, I watched the Santa Claus parade. The others took me upstairs so that we could have a good view. I'd never seen anything like those floats going past on Yonge Street. People lined both sides of the street, but we had the best view by far. The parade was just the beginning. The staff were busy decorating the store, putting up wreaths, garlands, and lights. Every department was festively decorated. On the first floor was a big Christmas tree, trimmed with beautiful baubles and colored lights. Best of all were the windows decorated in ways I'll never forget. People came from all over to see those windows. One year there were fairy tale characters, like Little Red Riding Hood, Goldilocks and the Three Bears, and Snow White and the Seven Dwarfs. The little figures moved, lifting a waving hand, or bowing low. They delighted me. Another window showed a winter scene of people dressed in old-fashioned clothes, skating on a pond with trees covered in powdery snow. The figures glided, a little jerkily, in circles or figure eights. In another window an electric train ran around a group of animated toys—a nutcracker, toy soldiers, and dolls. Each of the windows was designed with great imagination and I gazed at them entranced, just like the children who pressed close to see.

Once we were allowed to leave work to see the Christmas carollers on the first floor. There was a Christmas party for the staff as well. We went up by elevator to the ninth floor where we went into the Georgian Room. Here we were seated at tables with linen cloths and served sandwiches, squares, and tea in china cups and saucers. I'd never felt so special before.

While Christmas was an extraordinary time at Eaton's, there were other events throughout the year that I loved. Often musicians played on the first floor, and I particularly recall Tommy Hunter, whose songs I knew well, and Peter Appleyard. There were others too, and I always made a point of seeing them. It gave me some hope that I would make it in that world too.

Once I was settled, one of the things that I had determined I would do was have another operation on my nose. I looked up Dr. Ord, now at the Medical Arts Centre, the same doctor who had done the two operations when I was younger. I had to pay for it now, since I no longer had medical coverage, but he allowed me to pay him on a monthly basis. He scheduled the surgery and I got some time off work. During the operation he took some cartilage from my ears and tried to build up my nose. After a day, he brought in a mirror and I watched as he took off the bandages. It looked slightly straighter, though it was hard to tell because of the swelling and bruises. When the swelling had gone down and I was back at work, Sophie and I had our photographs taken in a little booth on our lunch hour. Afterwards I cried, because the nose I'd hoped for was not the one I'd have to settle for.

◆ ◆ ◆

In the credit department, which was on the same floor as the accounting department, I met a young man by the name of Allan. He was handsome, with wavy brown hair and white teeth. All the girls in my department were determined to meet him. I got to know him because he loved music and was a member of a small singing group. Once he invited me to go and listen to them rehearse. Soon the girls were flocking to my table at lunch hour, interested in what Sophie and I were talking about.

"So how did you get to meet Allan?" one asked, patting hair that was teased into a beehive.

"You're not dating him, are you?" asked another, with loaded sarcasm. She already knew the answer.

"No," I said. "We just talk about music."

"What kind of music?"

"All kinds. He's in a singing group."

"You've heard him?"

"Sure."

"You have?"

One of them got out a compact and patted her nose.

"God, he's cute, don't you think?"

"I guess," I said, nonchalantly.

Allan kept me informed about what was going on, telling me about local music festivals and other places to play. I was impressed that he took it so seriously. It was time I was doing the same. I longed to be singing more, but I was working and there wasn't a lot of time left over to concentrate on music.

If I wasn't singing, at least my life was secure and comfortable. The Kaminskis had become like a family to me. Sometimes they invited me to have supper with them and I loved the food they ate, which was different than anything I'd ever eaten before. They offered me a ruby-colored soup with a rich flavor, which they called borscht.

"Borsh," I tried.

"Borscht," they gently corrected.

"Burscht," I said, and they nodded, smiling.

Anna and her daughters could sew very well and they tried to teach me. After supper we sat in their living room, decorated with Polish embroidery and some pieces of furniture made of teak.

"You take the material like so," said Anna, showing me. "Then you are going to cut out the dress like this."

I tried.

"No," said her daughter Christina, "flatten out the material before you cut it."

I smoothed the material and began cutting.

"Yes, that is good," Anna approved when I finished. "It is maybe a little up and down here, and here, but you will have a nice dress."

I went up to bed tired with my efforts, looking out the window at the bare trees. I opened it a little, but there was a nip in the air. It would soon be spring and the flowers would be out in the garden. In May I'd be turning eighteen. Life was working out for me: I had a job and an apartment. I got along with everyone at work. I had friends. Yet there were times I still felt lonely. I undressed, put on my nightgown, and got into bed.

I'd been to a few dances at the Maritime Club with people from work. I had danced at those, but a friend wanted me to go to another one there and I wasn't sure I wanted to go.

"You can't just sit at home." She looked at me directly.

"Why not?"

"Because you can't."

"I just don't really feel like going."

On Saturday night I found myself sitting at a table in a smoky half-lit room listening to a Roy Orbison song on the record player as everyone else danced. My friend was dancing. I was not. I was not going to have a good time.

"Like to dance?"

Someone was smiling at me, his teeth very white. He had jet-black hair and brown eyes. And he spoke with an accent.

I followed him out to the dance floor. We danced one dance. Then we danced another. We danced to "Little Bitty Pretty One," and "Bony Maroney," and "You Are My Special Angel." He put his arms around me when we slow-danced. There was a clean minty scent of aftershave.

"Who is that?" Sophie whispered as we paused for a rest.

"I don't know."

"Well, find out."

He asked me out for a date when he drove me home. I floated up to the Kaminski's veranda, waved as I went inside, and floated up the stairs to my apartment. I floated to sleep.

He was wonderful.

# CHAPTER NINE

# LOVE

He took me out on a Sunday evening, the night after the dance. I was still on cloud nine from the night before. He had an old two-tone car, partly ivory and partly green, and he opened the door for me to get in. We drove down to Lakeshore Boulevard and got out to walk around. It was a warm evening and there were lots of people out walking.

"Where do you come from?" I asked, wondering about his accent.

"My family they come from Sicilia."

"Where?"

"You call it Sicily."

"Sicily," I said. I thought of men serenading women under windows, as I'd seen in the Stephen Foster songbook. I thought of rose trellises, wine, and sunlight.

"In the south of Italia."

We walked on in silence.

"And now they live here?"

"On Pape Avenue," he pointed east. "You are living with your family?"

"No. They're in Sydney. In Cape Breton."

He looked puzzled.

"In another part of Canada."

"Here, you live by yourself? No family?"

"I manage all right. I have a job at Eaton's," I told him proudly.

"A job is good. I work in a factory."

"What do you do?"

"Make the shoes."

I gazed out at the lights that seemed to float in the ink-colored lake. He took my hand.

"You like to go dancing?"

"Yes." I'd liked dancing the night before. I hadn't enjoyed dances much before that. "I like the music."

We drove around for a while in his car until it got late and he took me home. He turned to me, his eyes a deep brown, as he leaned over and kissed me. It was the first time anyone had ever kissed me. It was a sweet, long kiss. I felt as if the world had turned upside down. We said goodnight and he told me he would call again. I went upstairs to my apartment, scarcely able to believe what had happened to me. Without warning, my entire world had changed.

I'd fallen in love.

◆ ◆ ◆

Not only had I fallen in love, I'd fallen head over heels in love. Mine was a serious case. I sorted bills all day, but I was daydreaming of my new love. He was handsome, he was a hard worker, he was sincere, he was gentle, he was a good dancer, he wanted to keep on dating me, and he knew how to kiss. What more could I ask for?

"Rita?"

"Mmm."

"Rita, it's time for break. Aren't you coming?

He took me out each weekend. Sometimes we would just drive around in his car, or stroll by the lake, or go to the drive-in. I liked watching movies at the drive-in, leaning against him as we watched Vincent Price in *The House of Usher*. Horror movies were our favourites.

Still, I didn't know that much about him. I wanted to meet his family.

"No, that is not possible," he told me.

"Why?"

"You are Canadian. I am Italian. It is not possible."

"What do you mean?"

"They will pick for me an Italian girl."

"What about a Canadian girl?"

"No," he said. "Not a Canadian girl."

I didn't meet his family.

I wanted to go out to dances sometimes, but he'd take me all the way to Oshawa to a dance. Or I'd invite him to the staff party at Eaton's. He didn't want to go. If I asked enough times, though, he would relent. Once I pleaded with him to go to a New Year's dance. Christina Kaminski was going with her boyfriend and I wanted to go too. Finally he agreed to go. I bought some gold material and Anna and Christina promised to help me make a long gown. They invited me down for supper one evening and we cut out the material. The next few nights I went downstairs and we worked together until our dresses were finished.

"You must put it on and we will see how the fitting goes," said Anna.

I went and put it on.

"Ah," said Anna, when I came back into the room. "We have here a princess."

"It's perfect," said Christina.

"And so tiny a waist!" exclaimed Anna.

We went to the party. Everyone else was enjoying themselves, but not once had my boyfriend offered me a compliment. He complained the whole evening. It was a wasted night.

Nothing dimmed my love for him, though.

"My parents have found a bride for me," he announced one night as we were driving.

My heart sank.

"She is not so bad."

I didn't say anything. I watched him park the car.

"I have the picture of her." He took it out of his wallet and looked at it. "She is pretty. Nice eyes. You want to see?"

"No."

"You don't want to see?"

I turned away. There were tears in my eyes.

"Anyway, that is long from now. Now it is you."

I turned back to look at him. He put the picture back in his wallet and pulled me close to him for a kiss.

◆　◆　◆

I had been in Toronto for almost two years now, working at Eaton's. It was 1963 and soon it would be 1964. I was nineteen. The years were passing quickly. I hadn't seen my family in a while, though I called home every week. When I walked home from the streetcar, I shuffled through brown leaves, and there was a bite to the wind.

One day the supervisor made an announcement. She was crying. John F. Kennedy had been killed in Dallas. He had been assassinated. We were stunned; someone began to cry immediately. How could such a thing be possible? What would happen to his wife and those two little children? The rest of the day was dismal. All of us were so shocked it was difficult to do any work.

Still, there were preparations to be made for Christmas. The store was decorated and people were talking about gifts they were buying. I wanted to buy something nice for my boyfriend. I was secretly hoping he would buy me something that would show he cared. He did care about me. He just hadn't said he loved me.

It would happen if I waited. All I had to do was hang on, however difficult that was. Sometimes I phoned him and he would threaten to break up with me. I had to run to the washroom and throw up, shivering with fear. How would I ever live if he broke up with me? Then we would go out on another date and everything would be fine, but it was an emotional roller coaster.

One night we were parked at a place where we could look out at the water. It glittered in the moonlight.

"I love you, Rita," he said.

He loved me. Of course he loved me. I knew if I waited long enough I would hear those words.

"I love you, too," I breathed.

He kissed me.

"Sometime you will come to my house. You will meet my parents."

"Really?"

"Yes. You will have to give time for this."

"How much time?"

"Maybe some years. Maybe five years or so."

I could wait five years. He had told me he loved me. We would get married and he would work at the shoe factory while I worked at Eaton's. We would have children. His parents would love our children.

◆ ◆ ◆

Sometimes I sang at a few functions, like weddings, but I wasn't doing much of it. I still talked to Allan at work, and he mentioned that I should think about taking voice lessons from a music teacher. He went to her and so did a few of his friends. He could set up an audition with her, and on the basis of that she would decide whether to take me. I was interested so he set it up for me and I went one evening to the St. Clair Avenue area where she lived. Farnham Street was a tree-lined street with large old homes in the centre of the city. Allan and a few friends were there waiting for me and stayed outside while I went in. I was very nervous. I sang "Old Man River," unaccompanied. The teacher saw that I had potential, but I was going to have to loosen up and allow my voice to really come out. She took me on, and though it was a little expensive, I was very encouraged. I worked with her for a couple of years, learning to let the songs to pour out of me. She got me to sing gospel and blues, songs I really loved, and by the end of my time with her she was talking about how I could make it as a singer in clubs. She would try signing me with an agent.

While I was taking lessons from her, I went with a group from work to the Colonial Tavern. They urged me to get up and sing, so I did, belting out "The Wild Colonial Boy" and "Ramblin' Rose." Not only did they give me a standing ovation, the whole crowd went wild, shouting and banging on tables. Someone even passed a hat. It was a tremendous feeling to get that kind of reaction from an audience. I wanted more of it. Whenever we went back they'd urge me to get up and sing.

I couldn't explain it to my boyfriend. It was a bone of contention between us. Though he played the accordion and had even taught me an Italian song, "Marina, Marina," he didn't want me performing. I didn't want to lose him, but I still felt very strongly about my singing. The more I tried to make him understand, the less he listened. Many times he was on the verge of breaking up with me over it.

If music was one problem, sex was another. He couldn't understand why I wouldn't make love to him. I wasn't ready. Why wasn't I ready? It was a good thing, it was nice. Why shouldn't we make love? If I loved him, I should prove it to him. And if I didn't, then how could I love him? The truth was that the whole thing scared me. No one had ever talked to me about sex, let alone given me any advice. I knew nothing about it, because it had never come up in our household. Besides, it had always been drilled into me that it was a sin. Yet he threatened to break up with me if I didn't. I didn't know what to do. At work I kept disappearing into the bathroom where I'd cry, wondering what to do.

One night we drove to a park in the east end of Toronto. He pleaded with me until after midnight. I was very tired because I had to get up for work the next day. We had been over and over the same ground, and I kept resisting him. Finally, he threatened he would leave me for good and find someone else. Someone who was easy. That was enough to make me change my mind.

I was frightened. It seemed rough and painful, and it seemed wrong. It felt dirty to me. In fact, it reminded me of those terrible encounters with my Uncle Angus. It certainly wasn't what I'd imagined. We might have

Rita's paternal grandmother, Mary Elizabeth MacNeil—"Nana"—was the inspiration for the song "Grandmother."

Tea Room

Rita's maternal grandfather, Michael Duncan MacNeil, and her maternal grandmother, who was also named Mary Elizabeth MacNeil (nee Campbell).

Print File Archive Preserver. Tea Room

Ann Rickedstaff

Father Stanley MacDonald, parish priest of St. Mary's Church in Big Pond when Rita was a child, was "an imposing man with a brilliant mind."

St. Mary's in Big Pond, where "the doors of the church open to a breathtaking view of the Bras d'Or Lake." It was here that Rita recorded vocals for her second Christmas album.

Tea Room

Ten-year-old Rita stands in the center row, fifth from left, with her Grade 5 class (1954-55).

Rita's parents, Neil MacNeil and Catherine (Rene) MacNeil, at a family wedding in the late 1960s.

A passport photograph of Rita's mother, Catherine (Rene) MacNeil, taken when she was a teenager.

Sixteen-year-old Rita in the living room of the house on Mechanic Street in Sydney.

Rita and her infant daughter
Laura in 1966, at George Street
in Sydney.

Rita's mother holding Laura.

Behind the apartment at Crawford's in Toronto,
Rita poses with Laura (c. 1968).

Rita with her husband, David, in Toronto
(Christmas 1968).

Rita and her newborn son, Wade, at the farm in Dundalk in 1970.

Before it became the Tea Room, the school house in Big Pond became Rita's home in the early 1980s.

Laura just before the graduation dance in Big Pond, 1984.

Wade at the Tea Room in Big Pond, 1990.

Duncan MacNeil (brother to Catherine and Benny) on the Glengarry Road in Big Pond, "where we picked blueberries."

Rita with her two dogs, Bonnie and Dee Dee, in 1997.

Warren Gordon

Rita's Tea Room was newly renovated in 1994.  The school house still forms the central core of the building.

George Wotton

George Wotton

Noreen Basker having tea at Rita's Tea Room in 1990.

Laura is now manager of the Tea Room.

become a little closer, but there was no real pleasure in it for me. As he drove me home, I noticed that my skirt was wet.

"My God," I said, horrified. "I'm bleeding."

"It is all right," he smiled. "Just as long as I am the first one."

At home, I made my way quietly up the stairs to the apartment. I discovered my red skirt was soaked with blood. I quickly took it off and hid it away in a bottom drawer of the dresser. Then I washed and crawled into bed, feeling very strange. It seemed to me that everything had changed that night and I wasn't sure it was for the best.

We continued to date, but I was becoming more dependent as time went on. I kept waiting for things to get better. One of the Italian women I worked with, also named Rita, tried to talk to me after a bad telephone call, when she found me in the washroom crying.

"He will break your heart and marry an Italian girl," she warned. "It will never work."

"No," I wept. "He told me he would take me to meet his parents."

"He is telling you stories."

She invited the two of us over to her house one evening. Her husband and brother were both there, and her brother played the piano while I sang; afterwards they poured us little glasses of red wine. Most of the evening they talked in Italian. Rita wanted to know my boyfriend's intentions and while he was not entirely direct with her, she realized that he did not take the relationship as seriously as I did.

"You are heading for disaster," she told me later. "If you break up with him it will be the best thing."

One of my sisters was living with me by that time. There was enough room for both of us since there were two beds in the apartment. She wasn't convinced about my boyfriend either.

Yet I couldn't break up with him. I loved him.

Surely he loved me.

I continued to see him, not just on the weekends, but also one night during the week. Once we even went to Wasaga Beach. He usually wanted to make love and because I wanted to please him I'd give in. One summer morning, though, I woke up feeling strange. I threw up over and over.

Maybe it was just the flu, I told myself. It wasn't the flu. I went to see a doctor on Roncesvalles Avenue and he confirmed what I already suspected.

I was pregnant. What would I do now?

# $\mathscr{L}$AURA

As I expected, my boyfriend didn't take it well. "Are you sure?" he asked. We were in his car, driving aimlessly around the city. "Yes." "*Madonna mia*. I know a doctor who can look at you."

"Why?"

"To make sure." He slapped the steering wheel. "Ah, *Dio mio. Che cosa successo?*"

He was more frightened than I was.

"There's no need to check. I'm pregnant and that's all there is to it."

"You can try things. Make a bath with the mustard."

"And what will that do?"

"That will stop the baby from coming."

"A mustard bath?"

"Or you try the Ex-Lax."

"I don't think so."

I was angry with him now.

"*E allora*. We go to someone who stops the baby from coming."

"No," I said. "No."

On we talked, going around in circles. He suggested kicking me in the abdomen. At one point he started yelling at me to get out of the car, reaching across and pushing the passenger door open. He had the confused idea that if he scared me I would lose the baby.

I was exhausted.

"This baby will come whether you want it or not," I declared. I patted my stomach and softly crooned a song to the child I was carrying. I had to think of what lay ahead for both of us.

◆ ◆ ◆

I tried to act rationally, but at the same time I was frightened. I even took the dry Keene's mustard my boyfriend had bought, filled a bath, and sprinkled it in, just as he'd told me. It didn't stop my vomiting: I was clearly still pregnant. And what had he meant exactly by someone who could stop the baby from coming? In my confusion, I went to Anna Kaminski and talked to her. She was very gentle. She wanted me to make up my own my mind about this child, but she also wanted me to know what my boyfriend had been talking about. She showed me an article in *Life* magazine, which explained, with photographs of fetuses, all about abortion. Anna was not endorsing the article, but she wanted to allay my fears. Now I understood. I talked to a few people about what I'd read, though I wasn't intending to go through with any such drastic step. And I went with my boyfriend to see another doctor. Before I knew it, someone alerted the police and one day, when my boyfriend brought me home, there were two policemen waiting outside the Kaminskis'. They informed us they were there because they'd been told I was expecting a baby and was considering an abortion. I was aghast.

"If you take any such steps," the taller policeman told me, "you'll be arrested."

I was terrified.

"Sir," he turned to my boyfriend. "We'll need your full name and address."

◆ ◆ ◆

I had to resign my job. My supervisor was understanding and helpful, and I managed to finish out the day. I would work for the rest of the week before leaving Eaton's for good. That evening after work I was slated to go to my music teacher's. I told her as well. She pitied me, but she was kind. Yet I could see by the look in her eyes that she felt it was over for me.

Then I began making plans with a Catholic Church organization that took in unwed mothers. With their help, I could be placed with a family who would provide room and board in exchange for babysitting and house-work. One of my friends suggested that I wait before deciding to agree to this, and I didn't know that my parents had already been notified. My mother and sister were making plans to take me home. My friend ulti-mately revealed this to me, and I felt terrible. It was enough to be dealing with it myself, but I didn't want my family to know.

And I was losing my boyfriend. I knew now that marriage was not an option. My Italian friend at work had been all too accurate in saying that he would not marry me. He still came to see me, but everything had changed. We were both panicking. He couldn't accept what had hap-pened and neither could I.

There was a little going-away party for me at Eaton's, which the others in the accounting department had arranged. One of them gave me a set of washcloths, and another gave me a little white sweater. They wished me well and gave me hugs, but when I went out of the store I was devastated. I loved that place. I passed the watches and the jewelry, the scarves and ties, the gloves and purses. It was 1965; I'd spent more than four years working there. I went out by the side door where my boyfriend was wait-ing. It was raining hard and the little gifts I was carrying got wet.

I looked at him as he drove, his fine profile, his tanned arms, his dark eyes. The windshield wipers slapped across the glass. He had told me he loved me. I thought of the night he said that and how I'd been so touched by the words. We drove in silence, rain sliding down the windows.

"What?" he asked.

The wipers slapped back and forth.

"Nothing."

"You are crying?"

"No."

I said goodbye to him. Then I went upstairs to the apartment, changed, and got into bed, my face to the wall as I wept.

◆ ◆ ◆

My mother and Mary arrived from Cape Breton. I don't know how they came up with the airfare, but I suspect that they'd had a family conference and someone had gone to Household Finance again. I was never so glad to see them in all my life, and we hugged and cried together.

"I can stay with a family and work for them until the baby's born," I said. "It's all set up."

"Dear, we'll take care of you," said my mother gently. She looked sad, but she wasn't going to let me go through it on my own.

"It'll be better if you come home," said Mary.

They were right. There were no words of reproach, and I was grateful, but it was still hard to turn my back on everything I had established for myself in Toronto. That evening, my boyfriend called. I went down the steps to the alcove outside the Kaminskis' to answer it, and Mary followed me. When I answered, she grabbed the phone from me.

"What did you do to my sister?" she cried. "You wouldn't want that to happen to your sister, would you? You bastard."

I took the phone from her and listened to him crying. We talked a little, but there really wasn't much to say.

"I don't know what to do," he said, still crying.

Neither did I. There was nothing either of us could do to change things. My face was wet with tears as I climbed the stairs back to the apartment.

The next morning we were on a plane bound for Sydney. My mother kept fidgeting with an apple. Then it dropped from her hand and rolled down the aisle, which made her laugh until she cried. We all laughed and I realized at that moment that it was going to be all right.

My father met us at the airport, and for the first time since I was a child, I gave him a big hug. He hugged me back.

"I'm so sorry," I said, "for the state I'm in and everything."

"It's all right. Let's get your suitcase."

Both my parents accepted me and whatever was to come. It was a great relief.

They took me to an apartment on George Street where they'd moved. They had the second-floor apartment in a big old green house. We went into the dark hall and up the stairs. The bathroom was on the landing outside the apartment. When my father opened the apartment door, it almost hit the table and chairs in the kitchen. They showed me the bedroom they had prepared for me. My sister Ann and two brothers shared another bedroom while my parents had the third one. My parents and I sat in the kitchen and shared a pot of tea.

"It's a nice place," I said, looking around.

"It'll do," said my mother. "It's got hardwood floors."

There was an awkward pause.

I started to cry. "I'm so sorry," I said.

"It's all right," said my mother. "You'll be all right."

"I never meant for it to happen."

"Don't you worry," said my father. "You're better off here." He drank his tea quickly and put the cup in the sink.

I went into the living room. It was painted a light green and there were red and white floral patterned curtains at the window. I looked out the blinds at the tree-lined street, similar to the one I'd lived on in Toronto. My eyes filled with tears again. I turned and looked at the familiar ornaments from Woolworth's: the two imitation houses and the little boy tending his geese. Against the wall was the green chesterfield I remembered from Mechanic Street, except that now it looked worn. A stack of books propped it up where one leg had fallen off at the back. I didn't see my rocking chair, which had been broken so many times.

My parents were right. I was better off here, however hard it was going to be. And they'd welcomed me home with open arms, perhaps remembering how hard it had been for them when they were young and my mother had gotten unexpectedly pregnant. They'd made it much easier for me than it ever would have been in Toronto.

This was where I stayed until the baby was born. Neither my mother nor my father ever mentioned my boyfriend in Toronto. I'd sent them a framed photograph of the two of us at a New Year's dance; I was wearing the gold dress that the Kaminskis had helped me sew. I found out later that my mother had ripped up the photograph, but she didn't tell me. It was my only link with him and now it was gone too. Some nights I cried myself to sleep with loneliness, remembering him.

Yet I felt comforted with my parents. They were both very good to me during those nine months. I often stayed up late watching "Peyton Place" or "The Big Valley" with her. And they seemed to be enjoying themselves a little more. They even went bowling together on Friday nights, which they'd never done before. My brother-in-law Johnny, who worked as a mechanic, would often take me out for fried chicken on Fridays after work. Then I'd come home and make lemon pie for the younger ones on those nights. It was hard to believe that two of them were already teenagers. It didn't seem very long ago that I'd been looking after them in Toronto.

Once Ann was delegated to take me out for a walk. It was winter, and slippery with ice, but my parents wanted me to go out for some fresh air. I was always accompanied anywhere I went; they wanted to protect me. Ann took me down the street and we crossed at the intersection. I fell flat on my back in the middle of the street. She was terrified when I couldn't seem to get up.

"You'll be hit by a car," she said. "Take my hand." She could see everyone beginning to come out of the church after a mission mass.

"Quick," she said.

Finally I managed to hoist myself to my feet and Ann helped me to get to the opposite side of the street.

◆ ◆ ◆

I could see that my parents were hard pressed financially. I was reminded of when I'd been living at home and they'd sent me to Household Finance to pay a portion of the bills. Ann had taken over that job. Now their situation seemed worse. One day I was in the bedroom and I heard the landlord talking to them.

"You can't miss it again this month," he was saying.

"Just give us a bit more time," my father said. "I'll get you the money."

"Well, you'd better. Or I'll have to evict you."

They desperately needed money. And, like manna from heaven, it came to us a few weeks later. Before I'd left Toronto, I'd bought a sweepstakes ticket, and now I discovered that I'd won over a thousand dollars. I paid off my bills, saved a little for Christmas presents, and gave the rest to my parents. We had fun that holiday, because I felt I was able to give a little back to them. They'd been so good to me. I bought my mother a pair of brown lace-up boots, and I also got a pair of coverings for the chesterfield and chair. My father indulged himself with a few drinks, but it was nothing like the times in Toronto. My mother may have taken drinks now and then, too, but like him, she seemed to have mellowed.

I was very sick with that pregnancy, especially with nausea and vomiting. I was often in the hospital where I had to be put on intravenous because I was dehydrated. So I would spend a few days in the hospital and then come home again. My parents were unfailingly kind to me. When I felt well enough, my father would take me to visit relatives. Once I even sang at a priests' gathering. It was clear that he wasn't ashamed of me.

I sang for my mother whenever she asked.

"It's not over," she told me, gently. "You can still have a career."

"Well," I said. "It'll be difficult."

"You're young."

I looked down at my distorted body. I'd gained a lot of weight.

"And you have such a gift."

I was touched that she'd never given up believing in me, even now.

"If I ever get a break in music, we'll buy Moxham's castle and fix it up so you can live there," I told her. Moxham's castle was the thirty-room home that Arthur J. Moxham, a steel magnate in Sydney, had built for his wife. Moxham was originally from Wales. He and his wife had settled in Ohio, where he'd built an extravagant home, and when they came to Cape Breton in 1899, he had the castle dismantled and shipped to Sydney piece by piece, down to the mahogany panels, fireplace mantels, and stained-glass windows. There was also a greenhouse, carriage house, stables, and gatehouse on the property. Unfortunately, their son Thomas died in an accident in 1901 while helping supervise construction of the steel plant, and the Moxhams returned home. By the 1960s, the mansion had become a ruin defaced by vandals.

My mother laughed. "That place," she said. "You'd need a pot of gold."

◆ ◆ ◆

The night my water broke, my parents rushed me to the hospital. While waiting hours to go into the delivery room, I thought I'd go wild with pain. I kept screaming as wave after wave of pain slammed into me. My mother was by my side, and when she realized she couldn't offer any comfort she ran from the room in tears, tightly clutching her rosary beads. After what seemed like days, they wheeled me into the delivery room in a mad rush.

"We have to take this baby," cried someone. There were two nurses and a doctor with me. They talked about me as if I wasn't there.

"We'll need forceps."

Then they clapped a mask over my face and I went into a hazy netherworld of drugged sleep. When I came to, I was mumbling about some Italian bastard I knew.

I'd been in labor eighteen hours, but now I had a beautiful daughter. It was April 15, 1966.

"Is there anything wrong with her lip?" I asked. "Is she all right?"

She was a fine, healthy baby. I cradled her in my arms, gazing down at her big, dark eyes. I adored her with a fierceness I hadn't expected. She was mine. I touched her tiny fingers, her delicate ears, her baby-fine skin. I gently passed my fingers over her fontanelle, worrying that the nurses hadn't bathed her properly because she had dried blood on her scalp. The nurses bathed her head again when I asked about it. She was only brought to me for feedings and spent the rest of the time in the nursery. I wanted to keep her close beside me.

Another woman was on that ward with me, and each evening her husband came to visit. They talked about their plans for their baby and it made me feel sad. What could I provide for my daughter? How would the world treat her? It was a time when I felt the sting of my situation and hers most keenly.

My family came to see me, but my parents were more concerned for me than for the baby. Or so it seemed to me.

"Don't come to see me," I cried one evening. "Go and see her first."

My parents looked bewildered and hurt. They had only wanted to comfort me, and assure me of their presence. Yet I felt she was being overlooked. From then on, they went to see her and then they talked about her when they saw me.

"I think I've got a name picked out for her," I told them. She was a lovely baby and I wanted a name to match. "Laura."

When my parents took us home, my father proudly showed me the rocking cradle he had bought the day before. The minute we got her home both of them fussed over her continually. It couldn't have been easy for them to have another one in the house, because it meant another mouth to feed, but if my parents were worried about money, they didn't let on. But on days when my father couldn't work because of the weather, he would pace the kitchen smoking.

I was trying to adjust to motherhood. I was tired all the time. And I'd gained a lot of weight, going from 119 pounds to 183, because I'd been eating my mother's good cooking for months. I determined that I'd lose weight and I managed to get most of the extra pounds off, but it was to become an ongoing battle. My weight was never constant.

With my mother's help, I looked after Laura, enjoying the times when I bathed her or fed her a bottle. She was a good baby and quickly fell into a routine.

"Is she sleeping now?" my mother asked.

"It took a while, but she's down now."

"Dear little thing."

I struggled about whether I was going to be able to raise Laura by myself. I cried each day, still feeling shaky about it. Everything had happened so quickly. With my mother, I talked about going back to Toronto to try to launch my singing career once more.

"Laura's no trouble for us," said my mother, taking her from me and kissing her cheek. "She's so sweet-tempered."

"I don't know if I should leave her here and just go."

"You need to get started with your music."

"I'd like to give it a try."

"Once you're managing on your own again, you can come back for her."

It was true that I needed to get started again and try to earn an income, but I never would have considered it if I hadn't thought Laura would thrive. They looked after her every need, with no financial help from me. And they idolized her. Had she had her bottle? Had she been changed? Where was that sunbonnet to cover her sweet little head?

"Are you sure?" I asked my mother.

"Of course I'm sure."

She talked to my father that night: it was all right with him. They would just borrow for the train fare. The next morning my mother and I went to Household Finance, where she borrowed $250 for me. I felt that I was a burden, but she didn't complain. She had faith that I was going to land on my feet this time.

I took the morning train from Sydney. My mother was on the platform to see me off, her eyes filled with tears. She was holding my daughter in her arms. It was hard to leave them, but I had to tear myself away. I knew Laura was better off with my parents for the time being. I boarded the train and waved at them from the window, tears streaming down my face.

"All aboard. This train is westbound for Montreal," called the conductor.

The train began pulling out of the station, and I waved until I couldn't see them anymore. I was on my way once again.

# CHAPTER ELEVEN

# DAVID

How did I think I could make a career for myself, when I didn't know where to begin? When I came out of Union Station, I stood for a moment trying to get used to the light. I felt empty. It was a warm day at the end of summer in 1966. Some people were in their shirtsleeves, and a group of businessmen passed me, walking quickly. The man at the hot dog stand was doing a brisk trade; I could smell mustard and relish. Taxis swarmed in front of the station and the Royal York Hotel across the street. Everyone was on the move.

I had a place to go—I would be staying at the Kaminskis' until I got back on my feet—so I took a cab there. I wasn't sure where I would go to look for work, but it seemed natural to try Eaton's again. I was very lucky to get a job there the next day. I wouldn't have to be dependent on people.

Heads turned when I went to work on the sixth floor. I remembered Allan and a few others, but there were a lot of new people. I knew they'd never expected to see me again. There were some cold looks; there was a real stigma attached to my situation. I hadn't felt it until now, because my parents had sheltered me from it. So it made me feel strange and very lonely. On top of that, everything had changed. There were no more ledgers now, only tables, each with its own telephone. They had begun computerizing our department.

"It's Rita," cried Sophie. "You're back!" She gave me a big hug.

I showed her the pictures of my daughter and she agreed Laura was adorable. We talked about what had happened since I'd been away. During the lunch hour I met Katie and Eileen, sisters from Scotland, whose accents intrigued me. Eileen had glasses and a kind manner, while Katie had big expressive eyes and great enthusiasm. They both had brown hair and soft skin; they dressed in pretty clothes. Above all, I liked being around them because they had such a good time. Like Sophie, they were a tonic for me.

I soon got adjusted to the routine of work. After a while I moved from the Kaminskis' to share an apartment with Katie and Eileen. They always included me in their plans: I went to several parties with them, where I met lots of people from the United Kingdom. Yet it was still a difficult time for me. I was between worlds, and I didn't seem to fit in either one. Once I even went down to my old boyfriend's neighborhood around Pape Avenue. I saw him drive by, but he didn't see me. He was driving the same two-tone car that I knew so well. It felt odd to think he was living the same life, while mine had changed so radically. I think I still loved him a little, even then.

Summer passed into autumn. I sang for a few private functions: a couple of weddings, the odd outdoor concert, a few pubs. It wasn't much, but it got me excited about music again. And it was important for me to be doing it, because it gave me more confidence each time. I didn't go back to the music teacher I had gone to before, though.

Every day I thought of Laura and wondered how she was doing. And when I called home once a week and my mother reported all the new things she was able to do, I felt a little left out. Now she was into everything in the kitchen, crawling all over. She loved having a bath in the sink.

And she had special little games my father played with her. I wasn't to worry, because she was fine.

I thought about her all the time.

"Rita, come out with us," Katie said to me. "There's another party and you've got to come."

They introduced me to people when we got there. I'd met some of them, but there were others I didn't know.

"David, this is Rita," said Katie, turning to me. "Rita, David."

"Hello."

"Hello."

"May I get you something to drink?" he offered.

"Yes, thanks."

David Langham had brown hair, a boyish smile, and a fine-featured, handsome face. I liked him at once. We danced, but I also had a chance to talk to him. He was from England, from Newcastle upon Tyne, and he was living in an apartment with his buddy, Harry. He had two brothers—Ronnie and Bob—and a sister, Brenda. His father had died when he was young, and his mother had raised them. He was in Canada working as a draftsman. He liked tinkering with motorcycles and machines; he wanted to figure out how things worked. Now could he ask a question about me?

I told him I was from Cape Breton. I said I was working at Eaton's where I'd met Katie and Eileen, but I was hesitant about telling him too much.

"Would you like to dance again?" he asked politely.

"Sure."

At the end of the evening he asked if he could call me. I was a little shy, but he meant it. He seemed to like me. And I knew I was attracted to him. We went to another party the following weekend and I met some other friends of his from England.

"Do you like English beer?" someone asked me.

"I've never had any."

The beer was stronger and darker than Canadian beer.

"Do you like it?" David asked.

"Yes." I smiled. "It's different."

We watched the others dance. I told him about my passion for music.

"What kind of music?" he asked.

"All kinds. Let's see, blues, gospel, some hymns, ahh—Elvis Presley, folk songs, Chuck Berry, the Beatles—"

"That's quite a range," he said, his eyes crinkling at the corners when he smiled. "Hymns and Elvis Presley."

"Oh, that's just the beginning."

◆ ◆ ◆

I was moved to the Eaton's store on College Street, where the accounting department was also being computerized. The work was very different, but I began to adjust to it. We had printouts of all the accounts, for instance, which made it easier. All phone authorizations had been computerized too, which was quicker than having to search through accounts before giving an authorization.

Sophie worked with me there and we used to have lunch together.

"Sophie," I said. "I've met someone."

"Who?"

"His name is David," I told her. "He's from England."

"Well, that's great," she said, warmly.

"He's not like—well, he's different than—"

"If he treats you well," she said, "that's the main thing."

◆ ◆ ◆

I was seeing David regularly. We went to movies, to dances, and to Irish halls to hear music. We danced at one of the Irish halls when the Carleton Show Band was there. A few times we drove into the country. On each date, he wore a suit and tie, looking neat and handsome as he opened the door of his old brown Dodge for me. He was proud to be in my company, which was an entirely new sensation. My first boyfriend hadn't wanted to be seen with me. David was altogether different. He was sincere and kind, yet he was also open-minded and outgoing, which I liked. And he had a dry sense of humor. He could tell stories with the same flair as people at home, careful to build suspense. Once at a friend's place, he told us a ghost story that sent shivers up and down my spine.

"I was at home one night reading in bed," he said. "Ronnie was doing something in another room upstairs and Bob was already asleep. I heard footsteps coming up the stairs. We'd heard them before. The house was haunted, but we'd never been bothered by the ghost." He drank some beer. "Anyway, I heard the footsteps come to the top of the stairs."

"And?" I asked.

"They didn't stop there. I could hear them coming down the hall. Clomp, clomp, clomp. They were still coming down the hall. Slowly. They were coming towards the bedroom door."

I waited, breathlessly.

"They came," he went on, "right to the door. I was terrified, wondering what would happen, but I couldn't do anything. I couldn't call out to Bob to wake him. I just sat and waited."

Everyone was spellbound, listening to him.

"And then something came through the door. I could see it, but all I could make out was a gas mask and some tattered sleeves. That was all. I couldn't really make out a body, or even a face."

"So what did you do?" I asked.

"I couldn't do anything. It came over to the foot of the bed. It was all I could do to sit there, watching it. I was paralyzed. Then I heard a few noises—tiny anguished sounds."

"Like groans?" someone asked.

"No, not like that. More like little squeaks of fear."

"Then what?" I asked.

"It vanished."

He drank some more beer.

"We did some research on the house after that," he said. "We discovered that a young man had lived there, but he'd died when part of the house had been blown up during the war."

"Did he ever come back?" I asked.

"I never saw him again."

◆ ◆ ◆

We visited one of David's good friends after he was recovering from a nervous breakdown in the hospital.

"He's in pretty bad shape," David confided in me.

"But he's a lot better than he was," I told him. "He'll get better."

It upset him, but it helped when we talked about it.

We also went to see another friend from Scotland who had wall-to-wall fish tanks in his home. I was entranced by them. There were striped fish, red fish, golden fish with floating fins, darting fish, shimmering silvery fish, blue fish, canary yellow fish. I was told their names, which I immediately forgot. I simply wanted to look at them. It was a wonderful visit, but shortly afterwards we learned that our genial, knowledgeable host had committed suicide.

It was very hard for David. Much as I tried, there was nothing I could do to lessen his sadness.

Difficult as these things were, they were drawing us closer together. I was guarded about my feelings, but I realized that I was falling in love with him. And he seemed to reciprocate it. It wasn't the same as it had been before, because now I was more cautious. I hadn't been swept away by the passion of first love this time. Yet when I looked in his eyes, I knew he had my heart. And if I really loved him, I would have to tell him about Laura. One night, when we were having dinner at a restaurant, I thought the time had come.

"I want to tell you something," I said.

"What?"

"Well, I—"

"It's all right, if you'd rather not tell me."

"Things aren't what they seem. I mean—"

"What is it?"

"I have a daughter." I looked down at the tablecloth. "She's just nine months old now. She's—she's with my parents in Sydney." I waited for him to say something.

"Don't worry, pet," he said. "This doesn't change a thing."

"What?"

"It doesn't change anything." He took my hand. "Tell me about her."

◆ ◆ ◆

It was clear David and I were getting more serious after we'd been seeing each other for about five months. Over that time I'd felt a change in myself. From having very little self-esteem, I had gradually gained more and more. David treated me with sensitivity and respect and I wanted this relationship to continue. One day when we were alone on an elevator in a store, marriage came up in the conversation. Later we discussed it more, and he suggested we could bring Laura to live with us.

"Are you sure?"

"Of course I am."

He sent my father a letter asking for my hand in marriage. He'd explained all about himself and his work, how he wanted to marry me, and that he'd be honored to take care of Laura, too. My parents were deeply impressed when they received it. They wanted to meet him.

We went to Holy Family Catholic Church on King Street. It was the same church I'd gone to as a girl when we lived in Toronto. And while David was a Protestant and I was a Catholic, Father Segman was very good about marrying us.

"Do the best you can do and you'll be all right," he told us.

We were married on a Friday in the early spring of 1967 when there was still snow on the ground. It was a small wedding. There was just David, myself, and two witnesses: David's brother and my sister. I was wearing a royal blue suit and a pink pillbox hat. David was impeccably dressed in a suit. We were sitting in the pews when a man rushed in, calling, "Is there a wedding going on here today? I've got a telegram for the wedding party."

"This is the wedding party," I said, laughing as I took the telegram my parents had sent. "But the wedding *party* comes later." We all started to laugh.

We tried to contain ourselves as we waited for the ceremony to begin, but the man mopping the floor wouldn't leave. It took him a while to realize that a wedding was about to take place, but after a while he departed with his clanking bucket and mop. It set all of us off again, just as Father Segman came out of the sacristy.

We were still laughing during the ceremony.

"Do you, Rita, take this man to be your lawfully wedded husband?"

I couldn't speak. "I do," I gasped, finally.

"If you don't stop laughing I'm not going to marry you," threatened Father Segman, but he was laughing too. It only took about fifteen minutes to get through the whole ceremony and then we went into the back to sign the registry.

We were still chuckling as we signed our names. Father Segman scooped up some snow outside and plopped it into my hand. It convulsed me.

After the wedding we were off on our honeymoon. We went to the basement apartment we'd rented in the Minto Suites on Lakeshore Boulevard, changed our clothes, ate toasted buns with cheese, and went to Honest Ed's, a huge store full of bargains. We had a wonderful time there, buying plastic flowers, tablecloths, and all sorts of things we didn't need. Finally we went home on the streetcar, carrying shopping bags full of things. We couldn't stop laughing about the things we'd bought.

Thus began our married life. We were in love and believed we could conquer the world. David was very gentle with me, though he had difficulty expressing some of his feelings. As for me, I couldn't really explain how I felt about sex. It's true that I wasn't very interested in it, but then I'd never liked it. I imagined it was like that for everyone. We had a few months together before going to Sydney in the summer to get my daughter. During that time David had a job interview in New York, and though he didn't get the job he brought a present back for me: a silver charm bracelet. I put it on and threw my arms around him.

In August, we went to Sydney and my parents had prepared for the occasion. When we went into the apartment at George Street the table was laden with platters of Southern-fried chicken, coleslaw, and my mother's delicious apple pie. They were determined they would welcome us with a party, even if it meant going to Household Finance again. Everyone was excited to meet David. My sister and brothers were all dressed up, my mother was wearing her best, and my father was wearing a clean shirt and pressed trousers. Yet my daughter stole the show. She ran back and forth to my mother, wondering who the strangers were. I had left a six-month old baby and now I found a fourteen-month-old toddler.

My parents had taken very good care of her. They adored her. And yet it was strange not to be a part of her life. I wanted to embrace her, but she ran away. I hadn't given much thought about how it was going to affect her to be whisked away. And I hadn't realized just how hard it would be for my parents, who had given so much to her. I had been caught up in my own world, and now I was simply marching in and taking her away.

My parents proudly displayed all the pictures they had taken. Here she was taking her first steps and this was the time my mother had bought her a new outfit. Here she was sleeping in her rocking cradle, but that was when she still fit in it. And here she was with my father on the old green chesterfield, when he was tossing her in the air. And in this one, my mother was just taking her out for a walk. Here she was with my mother, my father, my brother, my aunt, my uncle, my sister, another aunt, and my mother again. Wasn't she just the sweetest thing?

We had only ten days of holidays, too short a time for me to re-establish much of a bond with my daughter. We took her out with us when we went shopping or when we went to visit people, in an attempt to get her used to us. Then the time came to take her with us at the airport. My mother couldn't stop crying. I was crying. My father was keeping a brave front.

I loved them dearly. I didn't have the words to thank them for what they'd done for me. So I simply hugged them goodbye. Even though they knew it was time for me to look after Laura, it was very hard for them to part with her after so long.

Laura started screaming. She screamed as we boarded the airplane. She screamed all the way over the Maritimes, Quebec, and Ontario. She screamed on the way to the apartment. And she screamed herself to sleep in the crib we'd set up in the apartment. The sobs were loud and heartfelt; they were the saddest cries I'd ever heard. I couldn't leave a screaming child to go back to work, so I quit my job and stayed home with her. Now the three of us would be living on David's salary.

While he was patient and loving with Laura, learning quickly how to father her, I had a harder time of it. It wasn't easy learning to mother her, particularly since she still didn't see me as a parent. I was often impatient. I was frightened I'd do the wrong thing. And I assumed that babies should cry themselves to sleep: if they cried, it meant that they were spoiled. It was the old "spare the rod and spoil the child" school of thought. On the other hand, I loved her dearly and gave her lots of attention. She was a child who loved to laugh and we snapped hundreds of pictures of her.

In time, she began to trust us. The bouts of crying eventually passed, but this only happened after she'd been with us for months. She began to think of us as her mother and father. And one day we realized that we'd become a family.

# $\mathcal{D}$UNDALK

We lived for a while in that small bachelor apartment in the Minto Suites and for a time David and I took on the job of superintendents. He had a full-time job as well, and he'd also decided to upgrade his skills by taking courses. He'd have to fit in his studies whenever he could and sometimes he'd sit on garbage bags in the furnace room of the apartment building as he studied calculus. Sometimes he'd fall asleep over that textbook.

I took pride in keeping our apartment spotless. Once I decided to launder the cushions of our basket chairs, on Sunday, when we reserved a time to do our own washing. My sister Ann had come to live with us for a while and she came upon me in the laundry room.

"What happened?" she cried.

Little bits of foam littered the floor, the walls, the washing machine.

She started to laugh. "It looks like it snowed in here."

I looked down at the little bits clinging to my clothes and started to laugh too.

It was the last time I tried to wash my cushions.

We soon moved out of that apartment, taking our furniture and all the plastic decorations we'd bought at Honest Ed's. We'd found an apartment on Lakeshore Boulevard in the back of Crawford's plumbing shop. The owner, Mr. Crawford, was a great fellow who helped us in many ways. Yet the apartment wasn't much to look at when we arrived. It was down a short alley and through a yard full of junk from years when it had served as a trash heap. When we moved in, I cleaned that yard. It was unrecognizable when I was finished, with a grassy lawn newly seeded where the trash heap had been.

In the entry, which was a porch, there was more trash, which we had to wade through to open the door. We cleaned this up too, and it was completely transformed when we added bamboo blinds and some plastic flowers in a vase on a table. Inside, there was a small kitchen, two bedrooms, and a living room. The back wall of the living room divided our apartment from the plumbing shop and if Mr. Crawford sneezed the wall shook. It was still our own special place and the landlord was very impressed with our hard work.

Now that her two sons were in Canada, David's mother, Lillian, decided to move to Toronto. She came to live with us. My first impressions were vivid: she wore a flowered dress and horn-rimmed glasses. She was strong and independent, and she spoke her mind. We exchanged a few pleasantries and then she looked around the living room.

"Your furniture," she said, "needs a little rearranging. I could do it tomorrow if you'd like."

"Well," I said dubiously, looking around. The furniture looked fine to me.

Lillian wanted to help from the beginning. She immediately took to Laura, cuddling and rocking her. She'd brought up four children as a young widow in England and told me stories of some of the difficulties. They'd all had to work hard during those times. She and I went shopping together, and once we went to have our fortune told. It was an interest of hers, because she read tea leaves herself. The fortune-teller, a native Indian, examined my cards closely.

He looked up. "I see lots of fame in your cards."

◆ ◆ ◆

It wasn't always easy living with my mother-in-law. She must have found it just as hard with me, because we had our own ways of doing things. Once I was cooking sausages and she remarked, "That's not how David likes them." Another time I bought a gold-colored dress, which cost twenty-five dollars. It was too much to be spending, she told David. She complained to him behind closed doors and then I did the same. He was getting it from both sides.

"There was nothing wrong with that dinner," I told him.

"I know," he told me. "I liked it."

"Well, I just have my way of cooking and she has hers."

"I realize that," he sighed. "Don't worry about it."

"You can understand, can't you?"

David nodded. We were all quietly becoming more and more frustrated.

I went back to work at Eaton's for a while, since Lillian offered to take care of Laura for me, and I was also working and singing at the Legion every Wednesday night. They had amateur night and sometimes talent contests. I entered every one of them without winning once, but I kept entering them because I thought that one day I might strike it lucky.

One night we saw smoke coming from the apartment next door. Fire had broken out there, and David raced over and tried to get up the stairs, until the smoke was too much for him. He kept yelling to find out if anyone was inside, but didn't get an answer. The fire engines came soon after, sirens blaring, and David retreated so the firemen could do their work. Afterwards, they discovered two small children at the top of the stairs who had died from smoke inhalation. A pot had been forgotten as it simmered on the stove: the cause of the fire. David felt terrible about it later, wishing that he could have saved the children's lives. Yet he'd done everything he could.

◆　◆　◆

Then our lives took another turn. David's sister Brenda decided to come over to Canada and she stayed with us as well. I liked her immediately. She was a warm, talented woman, an accomplished horseback rider and a self-taught painter. Like me, she had schemes for the future. She had boundless energy and a vivid imagination. She wasn't with us long before I became caught up in her dreams.

"Can't you just imagine a farm?" she asked, eyes sparkling. "Not far from here, you know, with a few horses you could train."

I envisioned some sleek Arabian stallions prancing around a green field.

"There's land here—it's the sort of thing you could do here, but it would be too expensive in England," she went on. "Wouldn't it be great?"

"There must be some place just outside Toronto, David," I said.

"We could look in the newspaper," he said. So we began looking at listings of farms, each of us caught up in the enthusiasm of the moment. None of us really knew much about farms, but it wasn't going to stop us.

"You could keep working in the city," I said to David. "Brenda could train horses, and I could sing at clubs and bring in some money."

"It'd be nice to have a bit of land," agreed David. "A place of our own."

"And we wouldn't have to rent."

So, very impulsively, we went out to the country to look at farms. We quickly found a place in Dundalk, about eighty miles north of Toronto in Grey County. Dundalk was not a large place; in fact, it was a village. And though we were not aware of it at the time, it was situated on the highest land mass in Ontario, in the snow belt, so the winters were harsher than they'd been in Toronto. Blissfully ignorant of the step we were taking, in the summer of 1968 we signed our names to a seventy-eight-acre farm with a house badly in need of repair. All this for a mere $14,000. It doesn't seem like much now, but at the time we were probably paying thousands more than we should have. Still, we were delighted. Everything would work out just as we'd imagined.

We went back to Toronto and gave notice to Mr. Crawford, loaded up David's old car and a U-Haul we'd rented, and went back to Dundalk. David's mother wisely decided to stay in the city. It was summer and all things seemed possible. There was work to do on the farmhouse and the barn, but we could manage it. We ignored the fact that the dirt road to the farm was five miles long. The driveway itself was a quarter of a mile long. The old gray farmhouse stood in the midst of weeds and wildflowers, neglected for years. It would be a wonderful place to raise a child, we thought, because here she'd have space to run and play.

It was evening when we arrived. We entered through the porch, where there was an old hand pump. This was where we'd have to haul water. The porch led into a spacious kitchen, similar to ones I'd known in Big Pond, and against one wall stood an old woodstove that also burned coal, with four burners and a warming oven. Like my grandmother's kitchen, it had a small pantry adjoining it. There was a large living room downstairs and three bedrooms upstairs. There was no bathroom—no indoor plumbing at all—only an outhouse in the weeds outside. There were layers upon layers of old wallpaper that had seen better days. Flowered wallpaper covered striped, which covered another pattern beneath. Every inch of that house needed work. The place was filthy too, which didn't help matters. At least there was electricity, because now the daylight had faded altogether.

The house was already inhabited. It seemed something was nesting in every corner. I hadn't seen them in the daylight, but in the night the whole house seemed full of living things. I opened the door to the back porch and suddenly realized there were hundreds of bats against the wall.

"Oh, my God," I screamed, quickly slamming the door shut.

There weren't hundreds of bats. There were thousands.

Well, I'd just take another path to the outhouse. Better yet, maybe I'd find something to use as a chamber pot and then I wouldn't have to go out at all. Who knew what lurked in the outhouse? It was probably full of snakes. Maybe I'd just let it wait until morning.

It was like a house of horrors. Mice were scurrying around behind the baseboards. Something was in a closet, but I dared not open it. And upstairs, when we were putting our bed together, the window started to move. It literally seemed to be coming unstuck from its frame and moving away.

"The window," I cried.

It wasn't the window itself, it was thousands of flies stuck together that were suddenly coming to life. The two of us crowded into bed together with Laura between us, and I waited, eyes wide open for hours listening to every sound. There was definitely something trying to get in the door. No doubt there were skeletons in that room downstairs off the kitchen. There were probably ghosts climbing the stairs. Finally my exhaustion got the better of me and I fell asleep.

The next day we all began the task of transforming that place. David had sworn he was up to the task, while Brenda had talked about how the barn could be made to accommodate horses, and I was just as eager as the two of them to do my bit. Armed with a mop and pail, I was going to clean the house from top to bottom. No feathered or furry creatures were going to be able to live in any corner when I was done with it. I was armed for battle. Nothing would stand in my way.

I scoured the floors. I washed the walls. I attacked the windows. I was mistress of my dominions.

By afternoon I was flagging. I realized Laura had disappeared. She had been sweeping busily, but she'd wandered off somewhere. When I couldn't find her in the house, I ran through the fields, shouting her name. She could be anywhere on that farm. I raced into the barn, still calling, and looked up through a hole to see her sweeping the floor above me.

"Come down, dear," I said, gently. There were holes everywhere; she could fall through at any moment. She looked so tiny, batting her little broom back and forth and raising clouds of dust. I climbed the rickety ladder.

"I'm helping you, Mommy," she said, in her high, clear voice.

"That's wonderful, dear. What a good job you've done." I tried to keep my voice calm. "Come on over here and Mommy will take you inside and get you something to drink."

She started over to me.

"Not there, honey. Go over there and come around."

When she got to me, I clutched her tight and helped her down.

"I was helping," she proudly informed me, still holding her broom.

"Yes," I said, giving her a kiss. "We'll wait until Daddy fixes the barn before we clean it. We need you to sweep in the house now, because you're so good at sweeping."

Meanwhile David had been busy in the yard, trying to clean it up. He began mowing the lawn, but it wasn't a lawn. It was more like a hay field. He was undaunted.

He mowed.

He mowed some more.

He mowed up. He mowed down. He mowed in circles.

Finally, the cord snapped on the mower and hit him in the mouth, knocking out a tooth.

This was the luxurious farm I'd described to everyone at home.

"So Rita, how's the ranch?" my sister Ann asked when I called. "Have you got horses yet?"

"We've got mice," I said. "Mice with saddles."

◆ ◆ ◆

Up at five, David drove the eighty-mile distance to and from Toronto to go to work. He put in full days there, came home, and immediately began working on the house. He had to repair things. Or he had to knock things down and start from scratch. One room off the kitchen was too much for us to tackle so we simply closed the door and left it as it was. We all painted and wallpapered. David built a scaffold so we could wallpaper the high places in the stairway. He did most of the bigger jobs, though. Soon we had a new bathroom, complete with toilet, tub, sink, and fixtures. He did some wiring. He replaced windows. The most difficult job of all, though, was replacing two new supporting beams in the basement. We couldn't really give him the help he needed, and since he was not a big, hefty man it was harder for him to manage. Yet he was determined. He never complained, though he worked long hours in the basement.

Sometimes it was too much for him, and once I saw him so tired that he cried. It was more than he could manage. I was touched by his devotion to us, working as hard as he did.

While David worked on the house, I was usually busy with cleaning, cooking, and looking after Laura, who was rapidly growing. Brenda got to know the farmer next door, and he sold her a horse for $150. It could only be described as a work horse. Later she discovered that it wasn't his horse to sell, but finally that was all straightened out. She trained that work horse to jump, with jumps she had set up around the backyard. It was not the vision I'd had of groomed, shining horses being led through their paces around a perfect ring. Nonetheless, Brenda worked hard, took it to horse shows, and began winning all kinds of ribbons, which were proudly displayed in the house.

During the day the horse left piles of manure outside the back door, and the odor wafted in through the window. If it wasn't the horse surprising me, it was cows. We didn't even own cows. Yet one day I looked up and saw four of them standing in the back porch. They mooed woefully.

I broke into peals of laughter.

◆　◆　◆

I talked to my mother every week.

"I'm great, Mom," I lied. "The music is going so well."

I was singing the odd time at the Legion. I knew that I was not doing what I'd intended. I felt guilty. I was unhappy. And I'd become disillusioned about our dream of living in the country.

From time to time, friends drove out to see us and stay the weekend. It was good to see them, but on Sunday after they left I cried my heart out. We lived in such an isolated place. In the winter, the visits tapered off. There were dramatic snowstorms there and sometimes we spent days digging out. We had someone plough the driveway, but it was still hard for David, who had to go to work. The days were short and I was cooped up in the house with a small child. Each day I would look out on the fields, brilliant with snow, and wonder what had ever possessed us to buy the farm in the first place. Certainly we would never have bought it in the winter. Not only was I lonely and unhappy, the place scared me. Brenda was usually gone in the daytime and so was David; I was terrified to be there by myself. I slid gradually into depression.

In the summer, I became pregnant again. I was sick right from the beginning, vomiting incessantly. There was still work to do around the farm though, and animals to be taken care of. As well as her own horse, Brenda was boarding one. Once I went out to the field to give it some hay. It wheeled around and kicked me in the stomach, sending me flying through the air. I got up gingerly, one hand on my abdomen, wondering if I'd lose the baby. Luckily I didn't, but I continued to feel very sick. I had to go into the hospital occasionally, as I had with the first pregnancy, to be put on intravenous. Around this time Brenda left and the horse we'd been boarding went back to its owner. She took her own horse with her though, figuring she might be able to show it in the United States. Eventually, my condition forced us to move to Toronto for a while during the winter of 1970, where we stayed until our son was born at St. Joseph's Hospital on April 30th.

It was a much easier birth than the first. I was worried it would be the same dreadful experience all over again and I cried when I talked to the doctor. He ensured that it wouldn't be so bad: my water was broken and I was given an epidural. The baby was born within eight hours.

"Is he all right?" I asked, just as I had with Laura. "Does he have a cleft lip?"

He was fine. I was very excited holding him. He seemed a healthy little thing, but I noticed his skin had a slightly dark, yellowish cast. David came by that evening, as delighted as I was, but a little shy to hold him at first. We decided to call him Wade. However, my fears about his skin colouring were justified, because it turned out he had jaundice and had to be kept in the hospital longer.

Though I was depleted from the pregnancy and birth, as well as depression that left me feeling empty, we still had to go back to Dundalk afterwards. We had no choice. David was the only one bringing in an income. I wasn't happy about going back because I knew that I'd sink lower with depression, especially now that I had a baby and child making more demands on me. At least friends continued to visit us. At one point, hearing that some prisoners had escaped from a penitentiary, some friends taught me how to shoot a rifle. We used the outhouse as a target. I never really learned to shoot a gun very well, but the outhouse looked a little different by the time we were done with it.

My sister Ann and her husband Gerald came by for a short visit, as did my brother Neil. They wanted to see our new baby. One night when Neil was there, I heard the sound of wailing. I was with guests and asked Neil if he'd mind bringing the baby down to me. He went upstairs to the alcove in our bedroom where Wade's crib stood, and soothed him back to sleep. Seeing one of Laura's dolls, he thought he'd play a joke on me. There was no grate over the heating vent in the bedroom and he wrapped the doll in a blanket and told me to catch it.

"No," I cried.

"It'll be fine," he said, disregarding me. "Just put out your arms and catch him."

He dangled the doll in the blanket through the hole.

"Neil, don't—"

"Here he comes!" cried Neil.

Down dropped the bundle into my arms.

"There," he said, "I knew you'd catch him."

One weekend a couple came to see us, and while we chatted I rocked the baby in my arms close to the stove. A friend put some gas on it to get the fire going. The next thing I knew my hair was on fire, and that was enough. I was ready to leave.

"We could cut our losses and put it up for sale," suggested David.

I jumped at the idea. "Do you think we'd find a buyer?"

"Well, we might as well try to sell it now. People might look at it in the summer."

"We could move back to the city," I went on. "You wouldn't have to do the drive every day."

"If we spruced it up a bit, we might get back what we put into it," he mused. "Maybe even a little more."

So we listed the farm with an agent. Every day I prayed for a buyer. In the meantime, I was battling weight gain from the pregnancy so I ordered a track suit from a catalogue. Every evening when David came home, I put it on and went out to run around the field. The suit was a metallic grey that glittered in the light.

The farmer from next door called up. "You folks know what's in your field?"

"No," said David.

"Well, there's a person running around down there and I just thought you'd want to be aware of it. Wearing some kind of space suit."

◆ ◆ ◆

We stayed into the autumn, waiting and hoping for someone to buy the farm. David did more work on it, trying to make it look appealing. One day a young couple—Mr. and Mrs. Gano—came by for a look. They wanted a place where they could relax and do a bit of snowmobiling in the winter. They were impressed by all the work David had done, especially the beams in the basement that he had replaced, and they decided they wanted to buy it. I almost brought the walls down with whoops of joy when I heard, and my poor children had no idea what had happened to their mother. When I talked to the real estate agent later I told her about David's hard work, spending hours in the basement until he cried with exhaustion. The agent was in tears. I was in tears. Yet I was still jubilant, because all of David's hard work had paid off. I felt as if a great burden had been lifted from us.

We sold the farm for $17,000 after having been there two years. The Ganos were pleased with their purchase, while we had made a small profit, which seemed like a fortune to us. By then the snow had begun to fall, but the Ganos lent us a snowmobile to load things in the U-Haul. They also invited us to supper at their house in the city, so after we moved into a friend's place we went over. They lived in a beautiful house in Mississauga. One of the rooms had white furniture and a white rug; there was a white velvet rope across the doorway. Downstairs was a built-in bar, and we were so relieved we'd sold the farm that we probably drank too much rum that night. The Ganos may have been a little taken aback, but we couldn't tell them how happy we were that we'd sold the farm.

We stayed with our friends for a while, deciding what to do next. David wanted to rent an apartment, but I was adamant that we put a down payment on a house. We began to search for one that would suit us. One evening, we went to look at a house on Horner Avenue in Etobicoke and liked it right away.

"Well, it's solid," observed David. "And well built."

"It's perfect," I said.

We put in an offer immediately. It was accepted at midnight. Imagine our surprise when we went to see it the next day and realized that the white stucco exterior was pink! Yet the house itself was everything we wanted. There was a small kitchen, bathroom, living room, and dining room, as well as two very small bedrooms upstairs. There was also a partially finished basement. And it had a fenced back yard where the children could play. I was delighted with it. It was so much better than living at the farm.

We went to second-hand stores and found all kinds of bargains that we'd never be able to find nowadays. At one store we found a couch that was ivory with a design of purple flowers with matching purple piping. We bought a couple of end tables and some lamps, and put up macramé hangings. And we had a deep pink rug in the living room. One day we discovered an antique clock—an eight-day grandmother clock—which David was able to get working again. He refaced the kitchen cupboards with pine paneling and put black handles on them. He also made some shutters for the kitchen windows. And he made a Colonial lamp with glass shades which hung from the ceiling. The kitchen sink was pink, the fridge green, and the cat white.

Our neighbors were good to us. The woman who lived behind us used to give me boxes of dishes. Once she gave me a box with Fiesta plates, large green and blue plates, which delighted me. The neighbors on both sides were very kind too. There were two older sisters who lived on one side and a couple, Ted and Ruth, who lived on the other.

David continued to work, without having to make the long drive, while I had the odd temporary job. Laura was settled into the school on the same street and Wade was at home with me or with Lillian. We even managed to save enough money to make our annual trip home in the summer to see my family. I tried to work at music for the most part, and managed to get invited to many of the small outdoor festivals, which was a real boost. Perhaps I could get my music career off to a start now. Yet I couldn't shake the gloom I'd felt in the country. What was missing?

# $\mathscr{B}$ORN A WOMAN

I was growing more and more restless. I'd heard Christina Kaminski talking about a women's group at a friend's house. She was talking about demonstrations these women had been involved in, and how some businessmen had jeered at them when they were at city hall. The others didn't see anything wrong with this; in fact it made them laugh. I didn't laugh. And when Christina called to invite me to go to a meeting of the Toronto Women's Caucus, I went with her. It took some persuasion on her part.

"What will I wear?" I asked.

"It doesn't matter what you wear," she said. "They won't pay attention to what you're wearing."

"Really?"

I didn't go out much then, so I was scared going with her, climbing the dark stairs to the warehouse room where they met. I'd been together with women for wedding and baby showers, card parties, or hen parties. This was different. I thought there would be about four or five women talking in a circle, but there were more than fifty. I went in there with Christina, sat down, and just listened. They were all fired up about something new that was going on in their lives. It turned out they had just come back from a demonstration at Parliament Hill in Ottawa—two busloads of women had gone. They were strong, aware women, who thought about issues I hadn't considered before. I'd never really imagined that the situation of women could be addressed in these very political terms.

"The only way they're going to pay any attention to us is if we're right there in the middle of things," one was saying. "They can't ignore us when we're on Parliament Hill."

"They try."

"Well, sooner or later they have to start paying attention. If they want to treat us like we don't exist, they've got another thing coming."

It was my introduction to the women's movement. It had been there, growing, but in 1971 it burst into my consciousness. It began that evening sitting in the circle, not saying anything, but listening to the others talk about how things needed to be changed, about the fact that women, not politicians, ought to be in control of women's bodies, about how they had to organize further to continue their protests. It made sense to me. Women had always been the ones in my life to give me strength. Yet they lacked a voice. I lacked a voice. It was like a light went on and my whole life was lit up by it.

All my life I'd pushed things to the back of my mind, like the fact that my mother had scrubbed the floors only to have my brothers walk across it in their muddy boots. My brothers weren't aware they were doing it, but I knew how hard she worked. When we were children, the boys were always the first to sit at the table. Then the girls sat down to the leftovers. It was simply the way things were done. When women were talking and men came into the room, the conversation changed. Men had authority; women did not. Though I didn't question it as a girl, it had troubled me from time to time since then. Girls were taught to be helpless and boys were taught to be assertive. It continued when girls grew up. Women talked about men, while men talked about things they were doing in the world. Sometimes during a hen party, I'd be disturbed by the dissatisfaction of the women in the room. Worse than that was an occasion at another party David and I attended. Some bad jokes were made at the expense of women, and it seemed to me that was where it all started. If someone made a joke about a woman, he wasn't treating her as a person.

I went to several meetings, taking the streetcar to King Street and then walking to the building where we met on Adelaide Street. The women at these meetings seemed to be able to discuss what was going on in their lives, and indeed what was going on in all of our lives. I listened to them without speaking, but it was generally accepted that each of us would have a chance to speak. I asked if I could sing about my feelings instead of talking about them. That was fine with the others. I went home to Horner Avenue, sat down and wrote a song. I had written songs before, but I didn't know where this one came from. The cat came and purred close to me as it poured out. It was called "Need for Restoration," and while it wasn't hit-parade material, it was honest and real.

At the next meeting, I stood in the middle of the circle and belted out that song. It was a departure for me, but it felt like it had been there all along:

> So I found me a man in the good old tradition
> Being conditioned as I was.
> But when it came to making big decisions
> I found he overlooked my mind.
> And there was unrest and a need for restoration
> To fill the needs in me.

Before I finished, I could tell it had hit home. The women stamped their feet and applauded wildly. It was exhilarating.

I loved those meetings and I kept on going month after month. It was as though I'd discovered a place where I could really learn something, like a university where the women were my professors. We talked about everything, from women as leaders to women as mothers. We talked about keeping the spirit of our children alive and not quenching it. We talked about ourselves. We talked about our bodies. We talked about our souls. And we did it with a sense of humor.

At one meeting we discovered there was a bat in the room, and we all began to flutter, ready to panic. One calm woman named Mary spoke up.

"Don't everyone start screaming. There are fifty women in this room. Surely fifty women can handle a bat."

We settled back in our seats. Why did we think we couldn't handle a bat? The bat was freed and no one panicked.

One of the women whom I admired was a teacher with a great skill for helping to organize others. "If you want to demonstrate, that's a good thing," she observed, setting down her knitting as she spoke. "Some people are good at that sort of thing. But if you'd rather not, there are all kinds of things that can be done besides going out and waving a placard. We need people to make phone calls, for instance. We need somebody to set up a car pool. We need a few to take care of people's kids while they're demonstrating." She sat back and looked around the room. "There now. That's what we need." She picked up her knitting again.

Within the hour a list of those making phone calls was drawn up. A car pool had been arranged. A list of babysitters was circulated.

Sometimes we talked about our children. One of the reasons I kept coming to the meetings was that I wanted to be a better parent.

"What is it we're teaching girls about their bodies?" said a small woman with red hair. "We teach them to go on diets, to look slim and beautiful. We're not teaching them to cultivate their minds."

"Well, what about boys?" asked another. "If we're teaching girls then we have to teach boys."

It was true. I thought back to the times in A. A.'s store when the girls had always been the ones chosen to be Indians while the boys were cowboys. The girls always died early on in the fight and the boys were victorious. It happened over and over.

At some meetings we talked about our relationships. We mentioned what was going on in our marriages. We discussed sex.

"So many women pretend that sex is great and it's just not," said a woman with a direct gaze. She wore a red peasant blouse with embroidery on the yoke.

"Things just aren't working between Jim and I," said someone else, flicking her blond bangs out of her eyes. "We haven't had sex in months. Now it's become an issue with us. I get tired being with the kids and then he comes home and I'm supposed to switch it off and suddenly be romantic."

"It doesn't work," said the woman in the peasant blouse.

"Well, maybe if you're Barbie and Ken."

Though I didn't say anything, it seemed to me that with these women I was allowed to feel unhappy about my marriage. As I went home that night, I weighed David's expectations against mine. I'd begun to dislike physical intimacy. It was something that seemed to be expected of me whether I wanted it or not. Every time we made love, I couldn't help but recall the trauma of my childhood. I thought of Uncle Angus undoing the buttons of my blouse. I thought of his hands on my skin. I pushed the thoughts away, but they just came back.

I continued to write songs. I wrote another one in 1972, specifically to protest a Miss Toronto Pageant, called "Born a Woman." It was hard to believe that I had the nerve to sing it, standing on a street corner, having people boo and throw things at us. Meanwhile, beautiful young women were arriving, and rushing out of cars into the building, trying to pretend they hadn't seen us. I had nothing against those women; no doubt they felt honored to be a part of it. What I was protesting, along with everyone else, was the fact that they were being put on display simply for their looks:

> And it was more than a feeling,
> It was more than in my mind,
> To be born a woman, you quickly learn,
> Your body will be their first concern.

I was learning that I did have an intellect, that I could write, and that I could say something that made sense to people. Wherever there were protests, there I was, with women singing and clapping along with me. I went to community colleges, universities, conventions, and rallies, where I sang my heart out. I felt very strongly that things had to change for women. In support of this cause, the shy little girl from a village in Cape Breton was transformed into someone who could actually move people with songs. I became known among a small group of women trying to make change. They were the ones who invited me to sing at different demonstrations or events. Afterwards I'd go home and wonder how I could go on in the confines of domesticity when the top of my head felt as though it had been blown off with so many new ideas.

"Look at these magazines, David."

"What?"

"Well, look at the way they show women." I pointed. "Like objects. I mean, what are they really selling?"

He flipped through a couple of them.

"Look at that one. Are they selling the car or the woman?"

He studied the advertisement. "Well, I see what you mean."

He told me that if he were a woman he wouldn't have been able to put up with it. Yet he couldn't put himself in my place. I was the one who did the laundry and cleaned the floors so that anyone could have eaten off them. And I didn't just clean at home. With Laura at school and Wade with Lillian during the day, I got a cleaning job at the Odeon Theatre.

When I went in on Monday morning, the entire theatre would be littered with the remains of the weekend crowd. First I went through the rows picking up hundreds of popcorn boxes and drink containers. Then I got the broom and dustpan and began sweeping up the popcorn and candy wrappers. The aisles had to be vacuumed when that was done. Then I went up and cleaned the stage. Sometimes I'd stand in front of the velvet curtains and sing to the empty seats, using my mop as a microphone.

Then I went upstairs to do the balcony, something I didn't like to do because of the dark. I'd get a light out of the projection room so I could see to clean and then I'd go through the process again, cleaning up boxes first, then sweeping up popcorn. I wiped the white plastic marking on the stair treads. Then I cleaned the men's and women's washrooms, and finally mopped the floor of the foyer and washed the windows, making sure they were gleaming. Afterwards, I'd take out the thirty or forty bags of garbage that had accumulated. I did a good job and was proud of my work there, knowing I'd earned my five dollars an hour. I didn't complain about it, nor did I view it with contempt. It seemed to me that the jobs that women did, like cleaning, were tasks that were always devalued.

I was still writing songs. I soon realized that my creativity came at a cost. On the one hand I was highly stimulated, on the other, I was lethargic and depressed. When David came home, he didn't know what to expect. How would I be that night? Would I be in tears? The more he wanted me to show physical closeness, the more I balked. And while I wanted him to talk about his feelings, he couldn't deal with mine. Could I stay in this marriage? Could I just get up and leave when we had two small children? I didn't know. My only solution was to write more music and sing whenever and wherever I could.

It was around this time that my mother was diagnosed with throat cancer. I was devastated. And in my unbalanced state, I went home to be with her. As I look back I can see that I wasn't a help to her. I acted like a spoiled child. I also tried to block out her condition. It was hard for me to imagine that I was losing my mother, so I chose not to deal with it. Instead, I sang my new songs to her and to my father, and they were both bewildered. My life had been changed radically, but they had no way of relating to it. I had even written about safe abortion in one of them, and they responded with shock. How could a daughter of theirs be singing about such things? They had brought me up as a good Catholic and here I was singing about women's liberation. Yet I wanted so much to reveal some of the excitement I felt in being part of this group of women. I'd been enriched by it.

When I went home I wrote a song called "Warm and Cold," which helped me sort out the warmth I felt when my family saw me and the coolness with which my new ideas were being received:

In three short years, I've changed my views,
And I've seen what the change has done to you,
In the way you act, and the way you feel.
And when I go home for the very last time,
We will say hello, we will say goodbye.
And the feeling will be warm and cold,
And the feeling will be warm and cold.

It was not the time to be sharing what was going on in my life. My mother was dealing with an illness that would eventually kill her. Sometimes she would sit looking out the window and cry. And I had to leave her and go back home. I saw her again after that, and by that time my parents had moved into a low-rental apartment that had recently been built in Sydney. My sisters and brothers had gotten together to buy them a red couch, black end tables, and a black coffee table. They'd also bought her a black nightgown, but it looked stark against her white skin. And she couldn't eat; instead she had to be given a feeding tube in bed.

By 1972, the disease had gotten worse and she went into the hospital. My father went every day to be with her. For all that it had cost them to be together, all the years they'd been married, this seemed to bring them closer. I flew home once more and was distraught when I saw how my mother had wasted away. I sang for her just as I had when I was young, and it was like singing in the kitchen at Mechanic Street. It touched her when I sang the "The Green Grass of Home." She was so proud of me. She still believed I was really something when it came to music.

"If you just stick with country and western, you'll be all right," she told me. "You have such a gift."

She had such faith in me, even then. But it was terrible to see her in such a frail state. The hospital room was spotlessly clean, the sheets so neat over her thin body. She was in great pain, and at one point my brother went out and demanded that she be given a stronger dose of morphine, because she wouldn't have asked for it herself.

I wasn't there when she died. Her last words were whispered to my father: "Neil, I hear beautiful music."

St. Mary's Church in Big Pond was filled to capacity for her funeral. I got up to sing and my aunt was confused about what I was doing. She reached out her hand to grab me and pull me back. If people sang in church it was always in the choir loft, so she had no idea what I was intending to do. With my hand on her coffin, I sang "Bridge over Troubled Water." I also sang a song I'd written, "Who Will I Go to See?"

> Who will I go to see after you're gone?
> I'm very fond of Mary and I'm very fond of John
> And I truly care for all the rest and I hope they do fine.
> Who will I go to see after you're gone?
>
> It wasn't the place I know that kept me coming home
> Just to know that you were there was worth the miles I'd go
> Yet I truly care for all the rest, and I hope they do fine.
> Who will I go to see after you're gone?
>
> This may be the last trip home and the longest one I'll make
> And I'll watch the lines and the mileage signs; I pray I'm not too late
> Yet I truly care for all the rest, and I hope they do fine.
> Who will I go to see after you're gone?

It was very hard to sing and I really don't know how I managed it. Afterwards at the interment, we stood watching as her coffin was lowered into the ground in the small cemetery. It was already cold; soon winter would come. They shoveled earth over the coffin. We were all crying, but my father was weeping as if his heart would break.

I went back to Toronto, taking her small ornaments with me: the two ceramic houses and the little boy with his geese. I was overcome with grief. She'd been an anchor for me. I went back to work, but sometimes I'd be down on my knees cleaning the toilets at the Odeon and stopped what I was doing, still kneeling. I couldn't stop crying. How many times had I seen her unhappy? Had she ever found any peace in her life? I'd never found out the answers. I wouldn't be able to call her, or go back and see her in the summer. She was really gone. I wrote a song in the midst of that pain, as a kind of tribute to her, called "Rene," though her name was actually Catherine:

> Rene wore a dress of white,
> White was her colour.
> And on her face
> She wore a smile
> I've seen on no other.
>
> And when she danced
> She was dazzling
> And when she smiled
> She was pretty.
>
> Any way you looked at her
> She sure was a beauty.
>
> And the life she led
> And the dreams she had
> Were like so many another
> Rene in your dress of white
> It may soon change its colour.

I cried day and night for her. And my sorrow drew me further into depression. I really hadn't been well for a long time, yet it got worse. Now it was a deep heaviness, like a weight on my soul. I was under a doctor's supervision, with prescriptions for anti-depressants that didn't seem to help. I started to drink as well. Not only was I desolate about the loss of my mother, I was dealing with a marriage that wasn't working out. I didn't go out much either. Where was I to go? The little house that had seemed so perfect in the beginning now began to seem like a prison. I stopped doing things. I sat at the kitchen table drinking beer, or crying, and wondering how I would ever get through the days.

Things went from bad to worse, until I hardly noticed what was going on at home. I began singing again at conferences and rallies, but everything else was in chaos. And at a time when I most needed to talk, I couldn't get David to open up. I was unable to offer him the solace of embraces and he wasn't able to give me the understanding I needed. Feelings were private; they were kept hidden. Mine were spilling out all over. He went down to the basement to work for hours on projects. I wanted the two of us to go for counselling, but it wasn't something he was comfortable doing. So we went home in the summer of 1974 as usual: things looked bleak in our marriage, and I was still in a very low state. My sister Mary offered to take Laura for part of the year. And Lillian helped with Wade when we got back to Toronto, since it was clear that I was in no shape to be caring for either of my children. I went to therapy when it seemed that the pills weren't working.

"We'll try to work through a process, Rita," the doctor told me.

She directed me to lie down on the floor.

"Now think of this pillow as the things that are oppressing you in your life right now," she explained. "I'll push this pillow against you and you push it back."

She pushed the pillow roughly against my chest. I pushed it back half-heartedly.

"You've got to push the pillow away."

I couldn't. I didn't want to hurt her.

"Come on. Push harder."

I really didn't see how pushing a pillow was going to help me. Perhaps I'd be better off struggling along on my own.

I gave up on the therapy.

At the same time, I was being tested at the hospital for an array of things. During that time David took me to see a heart specialist who informed me that I had Wolfe Parkinson White syndrome. The idea that something was wrong with my heart was frightening. The doctor told me that I had an extra connection between the top and bottom chambers of my heart, which meant that the heart could beat very fast or irregularly at times. It was one more thing that worried me.

I was fortunate that friends decided to get together and raise money to help me cut an album. Certainly it was not going to rescue me, but we went ahead anyway, recording it at the Manta Sound studio on a shoestring. Judith Lawrence was the producer; she was a graying woman with an enthusiastic personality who worked as a puppeteer on television. Lois Pearson, a music teacher, had also worked in television for years. Both of them were very excited about my music and determined that it would see the light of day. They spearheaded the project and Jim Pirie was the musical director. He was a slight man with dark hair, whose manner was consistently gentle. He could always get the best out of people, allowing them to be creative. Without these three people, the album never would have happened. Instrumentation was added on some songs but many were sung a capella. I was terrified, but we were able to do each song without having to go back and re-record much. We did it within the space of a few weeks, working hard on it. Eventually we were able to produce my first album: "Born a Woman." The songs on that album were songs of hope, of protest, of home. It was picked up by Boot Records, some copies were sold, and I was launched on the folk circuit for the next five years.

I sang at the Mariposa Folk Festival, which was the first big one for me. I sang at the Multicultural Festival in Ottawa, Sudbury's Northern Lights Festival, and the Kootenays Folk Festival. I sang at the Festival of Women and the Arts at the St. Lawrence Centre and twice at the Status of Women Conference in Toronto. And I sang at the Riverboat and Cafe Taresse. I went to any little festival to sing. And I almost always sang unaccompanied on stage.

When I went to the festivals, the first thing we did was find out the schedule for the day or the few days we'd be there. Generally, the big name performers were on the main stage in the evening. I would be told I'd be on stage during the day with others who sat in on my set, as I did on theirs, on chairs in a row right on stage. That was the way I met some of those wonderful people, like Valdy, Stan Rogers and his brother Garnet, Marie-Lynn Hammond, Connie Kaldor, and Jane Siberry.

While all of this created excitement, it couldn't cure the problems in my marriage. In one last attempt to save it, David and I decided to move to Cape Breton. It was 1975. We sold our home on Horner Avenue and I went ahead with the children by train while David drove a rented truck with all our belongings. He was full of hope and determination, having no doubt this would work. We arrived in Big Pond, where my father had moved after my mother died, and stayed with him briefly. David got a job in Sydney, and soon we were able to buy a small piece of land with a trailer on it. We had plans to build a house, which David started. The children were both at MacDonald Consolidated School, where my cousin Jackie was the principal. I was back in Big Pond, which I'd always loved.

Our new life began there, but moving hadn't really solved the underlying problems. We had just brought them with us. We hardly had any kind of relationship. And I was sliding in and out of depression. On the surface, everything seemed to be going well: I had two beautiful children and a husband who wanted to make things work. Yet I couldn't go on. The day came when I had to leave.

"Why?" asked David. "We're just getting going."

"I have to go. I just can't do it any more."

"But you wanted to come home to live. What is it you want?"

"I don't know." I said, tears rolling down my cheeks. "I just can't stay."

I knew in my heart we hadn't sorted out the things that needed to be resolved. We might be able to build a house together, but we couldn't build our relationship all over again from the ground up. It was agreed that I would leave the children with him until I got into music, or got myself a life, or both. Neither of us really imagined that this meant a long-lasting separation. I thought I would be coming back, but I just didn't know how long it would take. The night before I left was very sad. I cried and so did David. We talked about it, but I'd made up my mind. And as I went down the hall to go to bed, I heard Wade, who was five years old now, talking to his teddy bear.

"Could you get Mommy to stay?" he was saying to it. I dissolved in tears, listening.

The next day, David drove me to the train station in Sydney. He looked stricken, his face pale, but he didn't try to stand in my way. He watched the train pull out and for eight months lived in a state of upheaval, wondering when I would return. He continued to work during the day and build the house in his spare time. The woman across the road looked after the children when they were finished school. She told them things that weren't true.

"Your mother left because she doesn't love you."

They looked at her in disbelief.

◆ ◆ ◆

Meanwhile, I was in Toronto, living with a friend. Beverly was on social assistance at the time, while I was grabbing odd cleaning jobs, or temporary office work, and singing at pubs and festivals to keep going. David provided me with a little support or I would not have survived.

One day I saw an advertisement in the *Toronto Star*: a music agency was recruiting new talent. That same day I went there, nervous and hopeful at the same time. I went into the studio and sang "Bill Bailey." I sang my heart out. The two men listening to me seemed pleased and told me to come back every week and sing. They could probably get me some bookings.

"Think about losing, say, thirty pounds," one of them told me. "Oh, and you could do with less conservative clothes. You want things that look a little more trendy—you know, shorter skirts. Maybe a pair of boots. See if you can change your image a bit."

"You've got a good voice, though," said the other. "You just want to look the part."

I nodded happily, overwhelmed with excitement. I was allowing myself to fall into the trap of trying to look attractive to promote my singing career, but for about three weeks, I faithfully kept myself on a strict diet. Then the story broke in the *Toronto Star* that young women were being lured into stripping joints by an agency purporting to recruit singers. Several men had been charged in connection to it. It was the same agency to which I'd been going, but I'd had no way of knowing it wasn't legitimate and I was just very lucky that things didn't end up differently.

Undaunted, I still tried to get into the music circuit. I sang at several universities, and there were always concerts here and there. Bev and I went to a pub where they played country and western music, and from time to time I would get up and sing; the response was warm and exciting. It was really the only time I was in control of my life, though. The days passed in a haze of anti-depressants and alcohol. I also started to date an Italian. I'd met him at the bar and he reminded me of someone I'd known in another lifetime. It was as if all the things I'd learned in the meetings with the women had been swept out the window. I punished myself with that relationship. All it really did was undermine my self-esteem.

Once, after I'd sung at Mariposa, I went out with him. My cousin came along with us.

"Wasn't Rita's singing great?" she remarked.

"She doesn't have the class to be a singer," he said.

I should have gotten myself out of the relationship then and there. Things got worse, though, and while he'd been verbally abusive before, he now got physically abusive.

I phoned Mary and it was a cry for help. "I'm still a mess," I told her. "I don't know what I'm doing."

"Oh, Rita, come home."

"I can't," I cried. "I just can't."

"You've got to get yourself together."

But I couldn't.

One evening he beat me. He knew what he was doing, because he didn't touch my face, only my body, which was covered with ugly bruises. Like a sleepwalker who'd come up against a wall, I woke abruptly from that surreal nightmare. I knew the life I was living was all wrong, and that if I went on like this I would ruin everything I had going for me. I had to think of my children, because they needed me.

In the spring of 1976 I went home.

# CHAPTER FOURTEEN

# DEPRESSION

When I came back I knew that it was just to take the children and leave. I would stay a couple of weeks, but my mind was made up.

I didn't realize just how hard it would be to go. David had bought a new washer and dryer; they were tied with a red ribbon. He'd done a lot of work on the house. All of this made it harder for me to make a clear break. I told him that I was in love with someone else, although the truth was that I was still depressed, and locked into old patterns of dependence on pills and alcohol. I think part of him died when I told him there was someone else. We were both so sad.

Laura was very pensive then, trying to adjust to the idea of moving. She didn't want to leave all her friends in Big Pond, but she didn't want to be parted from me. Wade didn't want to be without me either. Neither of them wanted to leave David, of course. And at one point when he and I were talking, Wade took our hands and put them together.

"This is how I want it to be," he said, looking at both of us.

It was a terrible time for everyone. So it was made all the more difficult when Mary and Johnny came the night before we left and tried to get me to stay. David was listening, but he couldn't bear the thought that I was really going.

"Rita," pleaded Mary. "Don't do this."

"I have to," I said, doggedly.

"You have a home here, the kids are in school, David has a job—"

"I know."

"And how will you support the kids?"

"I'll get work."

"You have nowhere to stay."

"I've got a friend we'll stay with for the first bit."

"And then what?"

It went on and on, until we were all crying. I knew one thing: I had to leave and I had to take the children with me.

David drove us to the train station the next day. How many partings had there been from that station? Yet this was the most wrenching one of all. My cousin Jackie came to say goodbye to us too, and slipped a hundred-dollar bill into my hand. Then we were off. I felt terrible, as though something had been torn apart. A friend approached me shortly after we got going, though, and it turned out she was going to Ottawa too. We went to the bar car to talk some more. When I finally got back to the children, I saw their small, trusting faces looking up at me. Things had gotten to a low point, indeed. I resolved to take care of them the best way I knew.

When we got to Ottawa, we went to stay with a friend of mine, Sheila Coe. She had a big, pleasant house, where she was living with her children after her own separation. It seemed to me they had a good relationship; she was very loving with them. I felt it was the best place to get a start of my own. She showed us up to the third floor where we'd be staying and we slept that night on army cots. Mine kept folding up with a loud bang throughout the night.

The next thing I had to do was get the children registered in school. It was all right for Wade, who was six, but Laura, at ten, found it harder. They had both been uprooted before, but this time there was a lot of adjustment. She had to try and find her way in a school that was very new and different, and for a time she got lost in the shuffle. They both missed David, who could now only father them by telephone. And they missed their friends.

Soon after they'd started school, Wade had an accident in the schoolyard. I was out with a friend who wanted to show me some places I might be able to rent. We looked at one on Lorne Avenue in the heart of Ottawa, a duplex on a street with a familiar, open feeling about it. There were people there much like myself, from all walks of life, who lived from day to day as we were doing. I met the landlord and made arrangements to rent it, elated that everything had worked out.

When we got back to Sheila's, we found her out on the sidewalk.

"Quick, Rita," she cried. "Wade had an accident and they've taken him to the hospital."

It seemed as though all the blood drained from my body. I felt sick at heart. We ran to Sheila's car and she sped to the hospital, telling me along the way that she'd met the children after school as planned, but that Wade had been playing on the climbing bars. He'd fallen and hit his head, cutting it through to the bone. I found him in Emergency, where a playground supervisor from the school had stayed with him. They had stopped the gushing blood, and I held his hand as they stitched up the wound.

It was at times like that I wondered if I was really doing the right thing, trying to look after them on my own. I thought we'd be fine, but sometimes it was all too much for me, and there were moments when I felt desolate. It was extremely hard for me to go on social assistance, for instance, since the process of going on welfare is so demeaning. Perhaps without even meaning to, the clerks in the office looked down on people like me. I could hear it in the tone of their voices. I was just another in a long line of those in need.

"Did you fill out the form?"

"Yes," I answered.

"Well, take a seat over there."

If the people in that office were indifferent, friends and acquaintances who knew my music were very encouraging. They helped me get cleaning jobs, by getting me to clean their homes and telling their friends I needed work. And we prepared to move into the place on Lorne Avenue. I told the children, who accepted it, but once again it meant changes for them because they'd have to go to a new school. I went with them to clean the house, taking a mop and bucket on the bus and asking the driver if he went close to our destination. He told me he'd let us off close to it. Then we sat down, and everyone in the bus stared at the mop and bucket. I was determined to clean the place though, because I'd seen how filthy it was. The driver let us off as close as possible to the place we were going and we set off. We wandered around for an hour.

"Where is it, Mom?" Laura asked.

"I don't know," I said. "None of this looks familiar."

I had only enough money for a return trip on the bus, but I used some of that change to make a phone call to a friend. I started to cry in the phone booth as I fumbled with the coins, and Laura and Wade looked up at me with frightened faces.

"Where are you, Rita?" asked my friend.

"I don't know."

"Well, what's behind you?"

I looked. "A big grey building. It's huge. And it has a fancy green roof."

"Oh, my goodness, Rita," she told me, "you're on Parliament Hill."

"Well, I'm here with the two kids. And a mop and bucket."

"You wait right there. I'll come and get you."

We were all relieved to see her when she pulled up by the curb. She took us over to our new place and once we were inside the door I pulled the children close and the three of us cried together. In so many moments of my life, they have been like a light to me.

We all cleaned that place together. We even had a good time doing it, in spite of our rough start. Downstairs there was a hall with a living room, small dining room, and narrow kitchen with a few cupboards and a sink, and upstairs were three bedrooms. Mine faced the street, Laura's was in the middle near the bathroom, and Wade's was at the back. It took hours to clean it since it was so dirty.

We had nothing to start with, but people who knew me brought all kinds of things to get us going. They gave us an old record player and a box of records, a huge bean bag chair that we put in the living room, a small table with a couple of chairs, things for the kitchen, and beds for each of us. Soon we were established better than we'd expected, all thanks to those friends who were so good to us.

The next step was the hardest. I took the children to get them registered at Centennial Public School, all of us dreading it. Yet it turned out to be fine, because it was an inclusive, stimulating place, and the children felt at home almost immediately. The principal, a woman, had many innovative ideas she had put into practice. For instance, there were other children in Laura and Wade's classes who were physically challenged and they were soon learning sign language and trying to teach me at home.

"Look," said Laura, crossing her hands over her chest.

"What?" I asked.

"That's the word for love."

They both made friends quickly at that school, and at the same time they learned something about trying to understand others and being compassionate. I had friends, fairly steady work, children who seemed to be adjusting to the changes in their lives, and the support of women who were inviting me to sing at rallies and offering me help at the Ottawa Women's Centre. Yet I always made sure I was home in time for the children, even if I had a big cleaning job to do. My favorite time was listening to their stories of what had happened in school that day.

My weight was an ongoing problem, fluctuating up and down. I could never seem to get to a weight that was right, but I found a great place to get our clothes. I got them free at the women's centre. I went down to the basement where there were bins of old clothes, and like everyone else, I helped myself. Once I even found a second-hand bathing suit and started to swim every day during the lunch hour at a place called the Plant Bath. I did it faithfully for months until I got some weight off. Gradually I lost about fifty pounds until my weight was steady at about 135 lbs. I seemed to have control over things for a while, even though it didn't last.

Money was always scarce, but I bought groceries at the IGA on Bank Street, trundling back with my cart loaded with food for the week. And every Saturday we walked to Neighborhood Services where we were able to buy things at bargain prices. It was a wonderful place that sold toasters, shoes, kettles, couches, chairs, dresses, lamps, and beds, as well as all kinds of other things. The place was chock-full of stuff that people had given away. There was a table by the front door, where we'd line up to buy cushions at the cushion bin. For only a dime we could buy bright, colorful cushions and pillows. Because Wade was small, he used to nip to the front of the line and see what he could find. By the time we got to him, he was loaded down with cushions. (Over a few months we bought over three hundred and fifty of them, which we put in the centre of the living room, where they formed a wall or a pile where we could flop.) Laura would go immediately to the clothes section, and pick through the offerings, very selective even then about what she chose. By the time we left, loaded down with our purchases in plastic bags, we had usually spent less than five dollars.

It was still very hard trying to make music at that stage in my life. I still wrote my own songs and once I contacted a musician to help me get them on a tape. I already had the song lyrics and melodies. He agreed to do it as long as I gave him co-writer status on each song. That didn't sit well with me, and thank goodness I said I wouldn't do it! Sometimes I managed to go to a few coffee houses and festivals. When I could, I'd take the children along with me and they'd sit at the foot of the stage and listen as I sent my songs out across the fields where people sat on picnic blankets or in lawn chairs. When we went home in the summer I sang at the Big Pond Folk Festival, although the response to my songs about women's rights was lukewarm.

I saw David when I was home in Cape Breton. He was excited to see me and showed me all that he'd done on the house. He was hoping things would change between us, sending out Christmas cards with both our names on them. Seeing him made me grieve all over again. I went to a dance with him at the parish hall, because he urged to me to go. There my father cornered me and told me to give my marriage another chance, but it was long past the time when I could have done that even though everyone wanted me to give it a try. Couldn't I see what a fine man my husband was?

"How about a dance?" asked David. He was as reserved as if we were on a first date.

We danced, but my heart ached, because his hands trembled as he held me. Had I really caused all this pain? I left after a short time in Big Pond, but it seemed like a lifetime, because all the old hurt had come back, trapping both of us. I couldn't bear it any longer and neither could he.

When we went back to Ottawa I felt that I was no closer to my dream than I had been before, and sometimes it seemed more distant than ever. Was I any further ahead? I cried when I thought of how difficult it all seemed. If it hadn't been for the children, I don't know how I could have kept going at those times.

David continued to call each Sunday.

"Hello, Rita."

"Hello."

"How are you doing?"

"Okay."

"And the kids?"

They'd tell him everything that was going on in their lives, and I watched their young faces light up at the sound of his voice. He missed us all so much.

I knew I couldn't have stayed with him. Yet after each of his calls, I would hang up the phone and cry. For him. For me. For the children. How did things come to this?

◆ ◆ ◆

Some days were fine, but others were miserable. I went for counselling at the Eccles Street Community Centre every Friday afternoon, talking constantly about my failed marriage and my children. I felt the guilt of leaving David so keenly. And I worried so much about my children.

"So how did this week go?" asked the counselor.

"Oh well, it was all right," I said. "I talked a bit more to David when he called."

"And how was that?"

"It was—" I started to cry. "It just all hurts so much."

"It's all right to cry."

Yet my despair was not something I could communicate. I didn't seem to be able to free myself from it. Walking home after one of those sessions, I cried. I couldn't stop. It just all seemed so very futile. I thought about Cape Breton. I thought about Laura, about the look in her eyes, the flicker of sadness that I was certain I saw there. I thought about Wade and how the break-up must have changed his childish world forever. In both of them I saw what my father had seen in his mother's eyes: little shadows of pain in her gaze. Life had scarred her too. I thought about where we were living and it seemed the most desolate place on earth.

When I got home, I went to look in the mirror, thinking about the mess I'd made of everything. Overwrought, I opened the bottle of sleeping pills I'd been prescribed and put them in my mouth. By the time the children came home from school, I had taken all of them. I was completely incoherent. I couldn't talk to them, but as I lay on the bed I made movements with my hands. Then I blacked out. The children were both beside me on the bed when I came to, never having left my side.

"Mommy, you were asleep so hard we couldn't wake you up," Laura said.

There were bits of pizza crust scattered across the blanket from the children's supper, which they had eaten sitting on the bed beside me. It was cold in the room.

"How long was I asleep?" I asked. My mouth was dry, my heart racing.

"Since yesterday afternoon."

"What day is it?"

"Saturday."

I'd been unconscious for more than twenty-four hours. God forgive me. I felt shame sweep over me. Here were my two beautiful, trusting children, who knew something was wrong with their mother. Worried, they had stayed close by me. What would have happened if I'd died?

I sat up slowly. My head felt strange. Still in a daze, with the empty bottle in my hand, I went outside to a neighbor's place two houses down the street. I was in my bare feet, but I didn't notice. I was still in shock. I managed to tell her what had happened and she helped, coming with me back to our place and encouraging me to tell a doctor about it.

◆ ◆ ◆

I lived through it. I did go and see a doctor, who gave me a complete check-up, but it wasn't the doctor who helped as much as the realization that I couldn't descend to that point again. It was probably the most important wake-up call of my life. I had to take care of myself, but I also had to keep the children first in my thoughts. They had been through so much already.

Unfortunately, the house we were renting was sold, and we had to find a new place. The next place we lived was a long way out on Medford Avenue in a new low-rental unit. I was still trying to get myself back on my feet, feeling very fragile. We all tried to adjust to this new place, but none of us liked it very much. It had no fridge and stove for one thing. I had to put things out on the window ledge to keep them cold, but they would freeze. I phoned the St. Vincent de Paul for help and they sent two workers who gave medals to the children. They wished me luck. But I still needed a fridge and stove, so I phoned the Salvation Army. They found both appliances right away and brought them over. Now we were in business.

Once again, the children had to change schools, but now Laura simply refused to go.

"I'm staying at my old school," she informed me.

"How can you do that?"

"I'll take the bus."

"There's no school bus."

"Well, I'll take the other bus."

"Public transit?"

"Yes."

She was only around ten, but she looked so determined, her childish face so set.

"All right," I said. "But it'll be a long ride each way."

"I don't care."

She had made a big decision. I was proud of her.

Wade, now seven, would be transferring schools, so I took him to be registered. He was immediately placed in a slow learner class. I wasn't aware of this at the time, and it was only when they'd taken him out and put him in a regular class that I was informed. Apparently the school authorities thought he was a slow learner because we were on social assistance. What right did they have to think that? Here was a bright child and they had made their own assumptions about him.

I enrolled in a secretarial course at a community college. It was through an arrangement with Manpower, so I received ninety dollars a week as long as I continued. It would be better than cleaning toilets and floors, though I couldn't see myself doing speed typing and shorthand either. I was frightened getting started as a student there, fearing failure. And the classes themselves were tedious.

"Hands on the home keys," said the instructor.

I put my hands on the home keys.

"Arch your hands, like so, with the ball of each fingertip resting lightly on the keys."

My fingers were arched and resting lightly on the keys.

"Make sure you do not look at your typewriter," she told us. "You will lose points."

I tried not to look at the keys, but I was never quite sure of the semi-colons and quotation marks. Or the numbers, for that matter. I'd even have trouble keeping my fingers on the home keys. I'd get "s" when I wanted "a," or "k" when I wanted "l."

"Do *not* look at your typewriter as you are typing," she reminded us.

All around me, briskly efficient women were learning not to look at their typewriters. I wasn't brisk. I wasn't efficient. I looked at the keys when I typed.

"Now, class," said the instructor. "We will learn the proper format for the business letter."

I could manage the business letter, but shorthand stymied me altogether. I couldn't get used to all the squiggles. I tried hard, but within six months I quit. I was simply not cut out to be a secretary.

What was I cut out to be? My social worker sent me to Carleton University for a career assessment, something which was commonly done then. I was given a test to find out what career would be the most appropriate for me. I wrote down the things I most wanted to do: singing, of course, and teaching children.

Then I was given an interview.

"You say you like music?"

"Yes."

"Can you read music?"

"No."

"Do you play an instrument?"

"No."

"What do you do?"

"I sing."

The assessment revealed that I had little or no aptitude for a musical career, nor should I follow a teaching career. Instead, I would be much better off working in health care as a nurse's aide.

◆ ◆ ◆

One day someone knocked on my door.

"Are you Rita MacNeil?" he asked.

I tried to think which bill I hadn't paid.

"Yes."

"I heard a couple of songs from your 'Born a Woman' album on CBC radio."

"You did?" I was relieved and surprised at the same time.

"Yes," he said, warmly. "You do some great work."

"Thank you."

"I'd like to come in and do an interview with you if I could."

"Well, certainly," I said, overcome, "but it's a mess in here."

He sat down. "If you don't mind my saying so, I find it strange that you're not out there along with your music."

"Well, I have two children to look after and I'm really just trying to get by."

He left after he'd asked me his questions, still a little perplexed that I wasn't doing more music. Clearly, he thought I belonged in that world. On the other hand, I found it wonderful that my songs were being played on the radio.

Soon after that I was asked to play at the Major Hill Park Festival in Ottawa, which delighted me. And I went to the Mariposa Festival in Toronto again. Maybe things were looking up after all. In 1978, the last year we were in Ottawa, I started doing more work, singing at a CUPE Benefit, at Convocation Hall in Toronto, at an INCO Wives' Benefit at Le Patro, and at Patti's Place, Chez Nous, and Elaine's. I was invited to another Status of Women conference, this time in Ottawa. I went to the New Democratic Party Rally in London, Ontario. I sang in libraries and community centers, whenever and wherever I got the chance. Yet I was still trying to reach some kind of emotional equilibrium, dealing with ongoing depression. Each time I sang I had to be persuaded to get up in front of audiences. At one of the outdoor festivals, I went and hid in another building when it was my turn to perform and someone had to come and coax me to come and sing.

My counselor took me to the Ottawa Hospital to see some doctors there. They wanted to admit me for a few months, but I didn't want to go. What would happen to the children while I was gone? I phoned Sheila and told her what had happened.

"You just hang in there, Rita," she told me. "I'll come and get you."

Within an hour she had borrowed a van and come to get us.

"You're not going in there," she said firmly. "It would be the end of you. You're coming home with me."

So we loaded up the van and left. For the rest of the time we lived in Ottawa we stayed in that warm, lively neighborhood, with a few more moves. Once again we all had to get used to a change, but this was a positive one. The children were happy to be back in that part of the city.

Early in 1979 I was asked to perform for International Women's Day in Sydney, Cape Breton. I was very excited about it, buying a black granny skirt with French lace and blouse, as well as a red hat that I got for a dollar at Neighborhood Services, one of the first times I'd worn a hat to a performance. It later became a good-luck charm for me, and I began wearing it to each event until it was ruined after a car accident. I was scared to death, but I was helped by the fact that I rehearsed with two local musicians, Joella Foulds and Jerome Aucoin. Joella was a slender woman with clear, pale skin, and brown hair. Her eyes were like dark pools. Jerome had thick dark hair and a full beard; his eyes were warm behind his glasses. They both grounded me, and when I sang I felt strong. We sang in a pub in Sydney and there was a great response to my music. It was really the best medicine for me. Not only that, it was a turning point. It allowed me to see that maybe I could do my music in Cape Breton.

◆　◆　◆

It was spring when I got back to Ottawa. All the tulips were blooming and the trees were bursting into leaf. It was beautiful, but it wasn't Cape Breton. Like never before, I heard the call of home and I knew we had to go back there to make a life for ourselves. David needed to see the children, for one thing. And I couldn't exist doing cleaning work and getting by on social assistance. I had to do more. I would just have to try singing at home, and that was all there was to it.

I waited until the children had finished out their school year and I had the fare to get us home. It was time to go.

# CHAPTER FIFTEEN

# PART OF THE MYSTERY

We arrived in Big Pond in the summer of 1979. David was still working on the house, finishing a big stone chimney. He had worked so hard on it and done a remarkable job, but it was clear we were not going to live there as a family. We decided to get a divorce and sell the house to my brother. David gave me a lump sum from the sale, which helped to get us established, and he also gave me child support every month.

We stayed at my brother's in the basement, where we'd set up a couple of beds, but I soon found a bungalow to rent at a hundred dollars a month. Now we had our own space, though we had to move carefully or we'd knock something over, because it was really just one big room. It was heated by an oil stove, and it had a bathroom with a shower and toilet in one corner, which also served as the kitchen, since it had a sink. It was also my bedroom. There were two other small bedrooms for Wade and Laura. Later on, David rigged up a shelf hinged to the wall so that Wade could have a place for his train set.

That first summer I played at the Savoy Theatre in Glace Bay to an audience of a little over a dozen people. I walked on stage with a tambourine.

"I don't play the tambourine," I told the tiny audience. "I just brought it out to look good."

Peter Gillis was playing the piano and I made as if to sit down beside him. "Move over, honey," I said. "Isn't there room for me?"

I had fun with that performance, singing my heart out. The response from those few people was wonderful.

◆　◆　◆

Laura was now thirteen and Wade was nine. Both had had to make new adjustments to school and friends, but at least there were familiar faces. They went to MacDonald Consolidated School, where they'd been before. My cousin Jackie was the principal, working along with two other teachers. Because of the distracting view of the lake, the children were always looking out the windows instead of concentrating. The Bras d'Or stretched out for miles, dark blue on some days, misty grey on rainy days, or piled up with ice on others. Jackie turned the desks away from the large windows, so that more work could get done.

At that point Laura had a boyfriend from Big Pond.

"That's the second outfit you've put on today," I remarked.

"Well, I like this one better," she said.

"Does he notice?"

"Yes," she said. "He does."

"You've done your nails too."

She splayed her fingers so I could see her brightly polished nails.

It had to be love, I thought. Puppy love.

I was able to keep things going from the sale of the house, and I began writing more. I had the inspiration of a place I'd always loved. I wrote in the bungalow, or down by the Bras d'Or, on the black rocks, watching the wind riffle over the water. "Black Rock" was written then, a song about rediscovering a place I loved:

When I saw the black rock,
The first thing that I thought
I'd fill up with sadness and cry
But I sang
And the blue sky hung over
The fast moving waters
And I stood on the rocks,
And the memories began.
Can you imagine to overcome sadness
A trip to the black rock is all that it takes
And the waves will wash o'er me
And the black rock will hold me
And keep me from drifting away.

Down on the black rocks
I take all of my thoughts
And I hang them to lie
On the wind and the waves.

Now the rock has been worn down
By time and by water
And I have been worn down
By time and myself...

I worked every weekend possible, so the children went either to stay at Mary's, Ann's, or David's place. It seemed that I might be able to make a career for myself, now that I was concentrating on music. But it was still very difficult to go up on stage and sing. Once I got going I was fine, always wearing my hat as I stood in my bare feet and rocked to the music, but there were times that I'd have a couple of drinks before I was ready to go on. It helped to get me up on the stage, but it wasn't a healthy way to do it.

"Rita, it has to be you and only you up there," a friend told me.

"What do you mean?" I asked.

"You don't need to have a drink or two before you go on. You can't have the help of anything else but yourself."

I took those words to heart, and tried to adhere to them. It was true. I couldn't be one of the people in the pub if I was going to perform for them. I had to stay on top of things. It was difficult because I did a lot of pub work then, but it helped to recall that advice from time to time.

Now I was working with other musicians too, so I had to take on more responsibility. I'd performed with Joella once or twice, but when I was singing at the College Pub at the College of Cape Breton one night, she was in the audience. I shared my songs with a full house, singing without accompaniment. At the end of the night I sang "Amazing Grace" and I heard a voice singing along with me. It was the clear, sweet voice of an angel.

It was Joella.

It was shortly afterwards that we began working together, along with Jerome Aucoin and Dougie Johnston. It turned out Joella worked for CBC Radio as a broadcaster and writer, and she was married to Jim Foulds, a pro-fessor at the college. They lived in Boularderie with their two sons, which meant that she had a long drive in to work every day. How she managed it all, I don't know.

Jerome and Joella were with me for the longest time, but Dougie Johnston, a ginger-haired guitarist who also played mandolin, was with us at the beginning too. I shared new songs with them at rehearsals like a kid with candy and they responded by spurring me on to write more. We did a lot of gigs in the College Pub and the Crow Pub in Sydney as well as other bookings nearby, and we also worked at Ginger's and some other pubs in Halifax from time to time. When we went to Newfoundland we played at the Five Fishermen in St. John's. Everywhere we went the audiences seemed to be turning out in good numbers. It seemed to me that the audiences really listened and cared about what I was doing. They gave me the reassurance that I needed, not unlike a family.

Years later I wrote a song about those years, called "Troubadours":

Oh, Jerome I heard you play last night
And you took me back to the corner pub
Where I saw the faces of the ones I love
They were waiting to surrender
*Mo chridhe agus m'anam.*

To the music of a thousand nights
Where we held our court on Friday's time
Where we missed our cues, but we made it right
We were all troubadours then.

And we heard the words *o cia mar a tha thu*
And we answered with a quick *glé mhath*
They were phrases from another time.

Some were passed around and some survived
But we knew their heart and we knew their pride
We were all troubadours then…

We were gradually getting off the ground. At one point we hired a manager—Peyton Chisholm—who received the grand sum of thirty dollars a week. We really didn't know what we were doing when we hired him, but it soon became clear that we had no money to pay him. I was the one who had to call and ask him to meet me at Jasper's Restaurant in Sydney. I'd never fired anyone and to get up the courage to do it, I ordered a drink.

"Make it a double," I said.

Peyton appeared when I had nearly finished my drink. His red hair seemed even bushier than usual.

"I've got something to tell you," I said, after he sat down in the booth.

The light glinted on his glasses. He waited.

"I—we—we have to let you go." I started to cry.

"Why?"

"Well," I spluttered, still crying. "We just can't afford it."

"Oh, now, Rita," he said, comforting me. "It's all right."

After that, if I ever suggested going to Jasper's to the band members, they'd start to chuckle, asking me who was going to be fired.

◆　◆　◆

It was always the audience that mattered most to me. I tried to give them new songs during every show. It wasn't always easy to make the band members understand how important it was, because they didn't necessarily see things as I did. Yet I knew that they needed to feel special. Each audience was unique to me and I gave them everything I could, straight from the heart. Sometimes people would come up to me afterwards and tell me how much a song had meant to them.

"I loved that last one you did," a woman told me. "It really got me."

"Well, thank you."

"And the one called 'Black Rock,'" said an older man with glasses. "I liked that one a lot."

"You're really amazing, Rita. It's great."

The things they said brought tears to my eyes. People related so much to the music, and it was as if we all shared something together. I'd always had a fear of performing, but somehow with this Cape Breton crowd, it was different. I knew the response would be good. Even though it was emotionally draining, I felt a real joy when I performed for them.

While I had been writing the songs for "Born a Woman," I had been interested in writing about other things besides the struggles of women. At that time, I wrote "Rene," "My Island," and "Brown Grass," among others, which were songs that spoke of family and of Cape Breton. I wanted to sing for all kinds of groups, not just women, though I identified deeply with their struggles. When I came home to Cape Breton I did more songs that had as much to do with the place where I was living and the people I loved as anything else.

One of the people I wanted to write a song about was my father.

Each spring Mary and Ann had cleaned his bungalow in Big Pond. They did the floors, beat the rugs, and washed the windows. They cleaned the curtains and rehung them. They scoured the kitchen. By the time they were done, the place looked neat as a pin. One year just after they'd finished their usual spring cleaning, Ann was at the Big Pond firehall for the Firemen's Lobster Supper and heard that Neily's place was burning down. The firemen all went directly from the fire hall and by the time Ann got there, all she could see were flames and smoke pouring out of what was left of his house. She found him with people who had been taking care of him, but he was very disoriented. It was discovered that there had been a fire in the chimney; sparks had set the attic on fire. The house was almost completely destroyed, but my father later rebuilt it, not an easy task considering that he had Addison's disease. He took medication for it, but it still affected him. We helped as much as we could, but he liked to be independent.

Once when I was driving through Big Pond I started thinking about how many houses my father had built, repaired, or renovated. He had worked so hard all his life, but in the years after my mother died he was very lonely, and he used to get up early in the morning and walk miles along the road. He seemed troubled sometimes and yet he had grown gentler over time. "Old Man" is his song:

> It must be something while driving through
> And you suddenly see a piece of wood
> And you know you drove every nail
> To make a place for someone to stay.
>
> And it must be something to realize
> That somebody else now lives inside
> When you know you were the first to walk within.

And it must be something to rise at the dawn
You travel the road and you're all alone, oh
Old man, what have they done to you...

And they hold up well and they stand up strong
And to think, my God, you did it all
With these tired old hands that are now holding on
To what's left of your life...

It must be something to rise at the dawn
You travel the road and you're all alone, oh
Old man, what have they done to you...

◆   ◆   ◆

At one point in that time I went on a tour of the Princess Colliery in Sydney Mines where I wrote "Working Man." The men who acted as our tour guides had been miners themselves and they talked about it in a way that made it all very real to me. We got into the cage and went down a long way in the dark, with one guide telling us stories of hardships the miners had faced. He talked about the fact that men travelling in the rake, or the trolley that moves along a track, couldn't stand up. When one miner did so, he was decapitated.

The worst accident in that mine was in 1938, when the haulage cable holding the rake snapped, and men hurtled to their deaths. The rake went down a long slope with a ten per cent grade, but this was no ordinary descent. The twenty-six cars on the rake, holding two hundred men, gained speed as it flew downwards, and dust billowed up on all sides. Some of the men jumped almost immediately and many of them lived, but those who waited had to make a critical decision when to jump. If they timed it badly they hit the wall or the roof and were flung back under the cars of the rake. If they waited until the rake came to the curve in the slope, they would certainly die, because the walls narrowed beyond it. Finally the rake crashed into the wall at the bottom of the slope. Twenty-one men died and eighty were injured that day.

I found myself moved to tears by these tales as we went down dank tunnels that went under the Atlantic Ocean, and the walls seemed to close in on us. Though I'd known men who were miners it had never been as real as it was then and I suddenly realized what it must have been like to work there day after day. Our guide had throat cancer and I remembered my mother's struggle with it. As he talked, the melody of "Working Man" began in my head, complete with lyrics. It came about as simply as that.

It's a working man I am
And I've been down under ground
And I swear to God if I ever see the sun
Or for any length of time
I can hold it in my mind
I never again will go down under ground.

At the age of sixteen years
Oh, he quarrels with his peers
Who vowed they'd never see another one
In the dark recess of the mines
Where you age before your time
And the coal dust lies heavy on your lungs…

At the age of sixty four
Oh, he'll greet you at the door
And he'll gently lead you by the arm
Through the dark recess of the mine
Oh, he'll take you back in time
And he'll tell you of the hardships that were had…

When I began singing "Working Man" in pubs everyone seemed to sit up and pay attention. They appeared to be riveted. Once when I sang it in a Sydney pub, a few miners in the room got up, fists raised in salute. Perhaps it was the monumental struggle of miners that drew people to the song, but it seemed to strike a chord even in those who hadn't known such hardships. After I'd been singing it for a while, I was approached to sing it with the Men of the Deeps, an all-male choir of miners and retired miners. Under the direction of John O'Donnell, a professor of music at St. Francis Xavier University, the men had been singing together since 1967. The choir was originally begun in Canada's centennial year to keep alive songs like those that conveyed the experience of coal mining. We sang "Working Man" together for a special hospital benefit event at the Savoy Theatre, which was a very powerful experience. The song became like an anthem when the men sang with me.

In the summer of 1980, I performed with the Rise and Follies of Cape Breton Island, a wonderful home-grown show produced by Kenzie MacNeil that played at the College of Cape Breton in Sydney through the summer. It was the brainchild of Harry and Liz Broadmore who were teaching at Xavier Junior College. Their students were writing pieces at the college and then they'd perform them. It really all began with a cooperative approach; the students doing their comedy sketches interspersed with music. Gerard Morrison did a rendition of an old man; Maynard Morrison, wearing professor's robes, gave an account of Cape Breton Island history; Bryden MacDonald acted the part of a lady going to visit a fortune-teller; and Max MacDonald got laughs just with a pause and a pointed glance. One of the highlights was Kathy MacQuire Lamey, who did a comic portrayal of dealing with her children while on the telephone. This was the grassroots beginning of the Cape Breton Summertime Revue, which is still going almost twenty years later.

Ralph Dillon was the musical director and I got to know him a little better there. I knew him from Buddy and the Boys, a group of Cape Breton musicians. A good-looking man in his early twenties, with thick, light-brown hair and round wire-rimmed glasses, he was eager to collaborate with me. I was happy that two of my songs were showcased there: "Working Man" and "Old Man," both recently written. The response was very good for my confidence, because the crowd loved them. I really felt as though I soared when I sang those songs to them. And there was good press for the songs too, in the *Cape Breton Post*, and later in the *Chronicle Herald*, when we took the show to the Rebecca Cohn Auditorium in Halifax. While I did the Rise and Follies for most of the summer, I also worked at the Atlantic Folk Festival. I sang at various conferences for women, and at the New Democratic Party leadership convention in Halifax. And I appeared on the CBC for "Take Thirty" and on Sylvia Tyson's show, "Touch the Earth." It was shortly after that show that I met Noreen Basker.

Noreen had heard a few of my songs on the radio, when they taped a Big Pond concert, and she found out that I was going to be on "Touch the Earth." She had a keen interest in music herself, as did her husband, and she liked to pick up the guitar and play occasionally. At the "Touch the Earth" concert, I came out with Joella and sang "Working Man" and "Old Man." Noreen didn't know which one of us was Rita MacNeil until later. The audience clapped and clapped, wanting more, but the show had to continue and we didn't appear on stage again.

Noreen was determined to know more about me. She and a friend drove to Big Pond and found out where I lived. They were nervous about going to the house, but finally Noreen went up to the door. When it opened, she was a little taken aback, but she wasn't one to lose her nerve.

"Is this where Rita MacNeil lives?"

It was. And Noreen was soon one of my closest friends.

◆  ◆  ◆

Ralph Dillon joined our band after the Rise and Follies, on keyboards. He gave a hundred per cent of himself since he truly believed in my music. I would sing my songs and he would play the chords on the piano for the other musicians. Then the song structure was worked out. It was never easy to get all my ideas across to someone else so they could play what I heard in my head, but Ralph came very close. He really became the driving force behind the making of the next album, "Part of the Mystery," which we worked on during 1980 and released early in 1981. Jerome Aucoin, Dougie Johnston, Joella Foulds, Berkeley Lamey, and John Alphonse all worked on that album. I had twelve songs that I'd been singing regularly and we decided to put these out. Of them all, "Part of the Mystery," "Old Man," "Black Rock," and "Working Man" were the most popular songs. We rehearsed in the old parish hall in Big Pond, and eventually we went to Halifax where we recorded the album at Audio Atlantic Studios. We didn't have much money to do it, but our spirits were high and we had lots of support. Ralph went around Cape Breton to encourage investors to back it. They donated money, though it wasn't until "Flying on Your Own" came out that I was able to pay them back. Like "Born a Woman" this album was another grassroots project, requiring the efforts of people who believed in it.

The title song, "Part of the Mystery," was close to my heart.

> I don't know what I'm gonna do
> When all of my travelling is finally through
> And I'm home on the rocks with my thoughts and memories of you
> The medicine woman she gave me the warning
> Wear only the colours that heal the soul over
> Stay out of the colours where evil will penetrate through.
>
> Did you ever feel like a wick in a candle
> Part of the question and part of the answer?
> Part of the mystery far greater than me or you.
>
> I don't know what I'm gonna do
> When I'm flying so high and away from the view
> And the storm clouds they paint me a different image of you
> My thoughts and my feelings are caught in the middle
> I'm holding together like some kind of riddle
> Now I'm needing answers to questions and I'm turning to you...

On the cover of the album is a picture of the group of us, taken at Jerome's house in Sydney. I had long hair, my trademark red hat, and a serious expression on my face. Dougie Johnston, Joella Foulds, and Jerome Aucoin look as solemn as I do, standing behind me at the table. Behind us the window is filled with plants. My antique eight-day grandmother clock—the same one that David and I bought years before—is on a shelf. It seems like another era entirely.

We were sent the first 250 albums from Toronto, and then two days later we got a call from the manufacturer who told us that there had been a problem with the pressing on one side. It was a flaw on the "A" side. We tried to recall the ones we'd distributed but they'd all sold out. We offered a refund or exchange for those people who bought the record, but no one returned one. We had formed Big Pond Publishing and Productions Limited in 1980, in an effort to manage our affairs. We tried to be professional, but it was mostly a hilarious family endeavor. My sisters, Mary and Ann, and a third party got involved. Mary looked after the money, Ann was the secretary, and I took minutes.

The minutes of one of our meetings, on June 2, 1981, reads as follows:

A third party arrived late. Spoke strongly about merits of sinking company into debt.

Mary argued against such action.

Ann counted monies.

Rita smoked cigarettes.

Laura arrived uninvited.

A third party reopened discussion on company debt.

Mary asked Ann to help with discussion.

Ann said, "You have to spend money to make money."

A third party expressed the need for an accountant to keep on top of things, saw no reason for not going for a loan (small loan) to keep on top of things, and mentioned a need for a salary.

Mary and Ann vetoed talk of receiving salaries.

A third party emphasized need for salary.

Ann agreed to hiring accountant.

Vote taken on hiring accountant.

Three parties agree on hiring accountant.

In a subsequent meeting, we got a little further:

Ann agreed lunch was in order.

A third party vetoed such action and went on to say he wanted a
salary of $200 a week.

Mary said it was outrageous.

He felt it was reasonable, not outrageous.

Mary left to get pizza.

A third party put forward an idea. After five minutes of talking we
asked him to run it by us again.

Ann seemed to understand his plan.

Mary arrived with pizza.

The point was made that a third party had agreed to a monthly
salary. Now he would not be receiving a monthly salary.

He expressed sorrow.

On June 17, 1981, we held another meeting:

Mary excited by prospect of new deposit in bank account which
turned out to be an old deposit, long since gone. She recalled the
fact that we had nearly gone under and that we were still not out
from under.

Dog peed in filing cabinet placed on floor.

Discussion turned to food.

Mary mentioned a loathing for spinach.

Ann noted that oysters were not good for sex drive.

Meeting adjourned at 2:30.

Our meetings may not have gotten us very far, but we had faith in Big Pond
Publishing and Productions, which is still in existence. And as a helper, my
brother had creative ideas and an eagerness to learn. He tried to get us to
Boston in 1983, for instance, and did quite a bit of paperwork to try to
arrange for help with funding. One of the things he took on was the pro-
motion of a concert at the Savoy Theatre. There were a lot of skeptics who

believed he couldn't pull it off, but he did. He had to get some promotional photographs, so he set me up against an old black coat and took the pictures. One was used many times and no one ever realized the backdrop was an old coat. He promoted our show well, because he packed the Savoy. It was sold out! Hundreds of people bought tickets while only a few had purchased them for my first show there a couple of years before.

Mary distributed the albums by going around to different places where we left them on consignment, and she also collected the overdue payments. She was braver than the rest of us and over time, some albums sold. The rest of that year proved to be busy, with the acclaim we were getting from "Part of the Mystery."

The summer of 1981 was packed with appearances, from a Canada Day booking at the Garrison Grounds in Halifax to various folk festivals, like the Sudbury Folk Festival. We also did more television and radio work. In the fall of 1981 we appeared as guests on The Entertainers, as well as the odd news item for the CBC. Yet money, or the lack of it, continued to be a problem. One day I went to the mail box and found a royalty cheque for $38. I jumped for joy. I'd written some children's songs when I was in Toronto—"My Special Room" and "Cardboard Box"—and was fortunate to have had them performed on "Sesame Street" and "Mr. Dress-Up." I had forgotten all about them, but thank goodness someone had been keeping count.

That week we had money for groceries, but usually it was necessary to talk to Mary each week.

"Is it okay if I write a check, Mary?"

"Well, don't make it out for any more than forty."

"Didn't you say that we're solvent this week?"

After talking to Mary, I'd phone my father and ask him what he needed in town. I'd drive to MacLeod's Grocery in Big Pond, which had been our old store, and write a cheque for thirty dollars, hoping that it wouldn't bounce. I drove from there to Sydney for groceries at Sobeys, and to go to the Credit Union and the liquor store, always the same one. After that I'd drive home and make something for whoever was at home, like special club sandwiches for Wade or a spaghetti supper for some friends.

One day I saw a For Sale sign on the old school house. It was not the same one my father had built; instead, it was the larger one at the other end of the village. The asking price was $35,000. I would need three thousand dollars for the down payment and I certainly didn't have that kind of money, much as I wanted that school house. I approached my brother-in-law Gerald.

"Do you think you could co-sign a loan for me?" I asked. I hated to ask him, but I needed help.

"Sure, Rita. When?"

The next day after his work he met me at the Credit Union in Sydney River, and signed the forms without batting an eye. Now I could buy the school house. It was all very exciting and scary at the same time. What if I couldn't keep up with the mortgage payments? Well, I would just have to manage. My father came over to see it and looked at me with tears in his eyes.

"It'll be a good place for you," he said.

It was.

# CHAPTER SIXTEEN

# *I'*M NOT WHAT I SEEM

I loved that school house. It was painted yellow with brown trim and it had a pitched roof. It was really one big room downstairs, with the old coal room made over into a galley kitchen. There was a bathroom under the stairs, and three bedrooms and another bathroom, with a tub and shower, on the second floor. The window in my room looked out over the front yard and the trees, a hawthorn and a linden, that had been planted by the superintendent in 1939. It reminded me of the scenes in that old Stephen Foster songbook that I'd adored when I was a child.

It was heated by a woodstove, and soon Wade had taken over the job of keeping it going in winter. Our water came from a well, but it was faulty, which we didn't discover until later. The lines had holes in them and the foot valve was broken. The water would be muddy or we wouldn't have any at all. Discouragement set in time after time. David tried to fix it, but it was a big problem, and I finally capitulated and got people in to try to repair it. They charged me $150, money I could not afford, and when they left the water was as muddy as before. I cried with frustration. Finally I got them to come back and see if they could do a better job than they'd done before, but it was an ongoing nightmare for a year. I used to spend nights listening to the pump, trying to figure out if it had shut off.

Because money was so tight, I would put a For Sale sign on the front lawn whenever I felt I couldn't cope. When things got better I would throw it in the back yard, ready to be set up again when things were difficult. Sometimes I had yard sales to make a bit of pocket money. To get people to come in from the road, I'd put out an antique hat rack on the lawn as a lure. There was a little Sold sticker on it, but they didn't see that until they'd come in and parked. Then they'd usually stay around and buy a few dishes or plant holders. We made enough from these sales to hold us over for a bit.

I was still writing songs then. Once, when the children were at school, I put on a pot of tea and sat down at the kitchen table. There was wind blowing from the southeast and it got me started on a song:

> David and I collected old bottles,
> Ladderback chairs and broken-down rockers.
> When we first came together
> We had such ideas
> Full of the future and full of good feelings.

I didn't ever think we'd be divorced. And now here we were, living in different places with our belongings divided between households. I put on another pot of tea, and then sat down and wrote some more:

> David and I gathered up our belongings,
> Parted the ways when the dreams started falling.
> We visit the children on separate occasions
> And justify loneliness whenever we're able.

It took a long time to get over the heartache of that divorce; it still haunted me. Yet I wasn't dealing with the same deep troughs of depression as I had in Ontario.

There were many times when I depended on my family for support. My father would often come over on Sunday to see how the gigs had gone on the weekend. His visits were always brief, but he was pleased I was doing so much singing. My sister Ann, who was always the one to sew me a new outfit for my gigs when one got too worn out, often called me for a poker game. We took turns having these, and Laura, a good player who often went with friends to the card games in the firehall, was usually there with me. My father protested at this, but I told him we were in the country. It wasn't as though we were throwing away money at casinos.

It was 1982. Laura was growing up as quickly as Wade, and my sister Ann gave her a party on her sixteenth birthday. Now she was taking on all kinds of odd jobs to make a little extra money, working in MacLeod's Grocery for a while and even teaching aerobics. She was always innovative in the things she did. They both did consistently well at school, and while Laura liked to be out doing things, Wade was just as content at home. At twelve, he was interested in music and showed real curiosity in what I was doing. He began to listen to my stories after I'd been working.

"I was tired last night," I told him.

He got me a cup of tea.

"I was off key with 'Old Man.'" I sipped on the tea. "And we came in too fast on 'Part of the Mystery.'"

"Did they notice?"

"No," I said, and smiled.

I was gone from the children more than I liked though, especially since it was turning out to be a busy year. We did the usual pub work at places like Maloney's in Halifax and the Crow in Sydney. In the winter of 1982 we were taped at King's College for "Ryan's Fancy," a television show in Halifax, getting some good press in the *Chronicle Herald*. Then we played at the Rebecca Cohn Auditorium in March. The first time I ever sang there in a solo performance, my friends Marg and Eileen bought me a red dress that cost them a hundred dollars. They knew I had no money to buy a dress for myself. I was very touched by that gift and wore it with pride, along with my hat.

In the summer there were folk festivals, some of which were great, like the Winnipeg Folk Festival and the Mariposa Folk Festival. And I was still getting exposure from the CBC, with appearances on "Summer Magazine," a television program, and a radio segment taped live at Mariposa. My brother was still involved, and from time to time he lived with me. Once I came home to find him hard at work on a concoction with his friend. All the sugar was gone in the house: he was making beer. Within hours of brewing it, they tried it out.

"This stuff is terrible," he pronounced.

"It's okay," said his friend.

They both downed quantities of the stuff and then the two of them had to run back and forth to the bathroom when it gave them diarrhea.

Not only was I constantly battling weight gain, I was having trouble with chest pains then, and though I'd been to different doctors, none of them seemed to be able to diagnose it. Many nights in the schoolhouse, I'd stay awake pacing the floor, worrying about the pain. I tried to sleep, but it often kept me awake. I lay awake drowsy with pain sometimes, and in a half-wakeful state one night I heard voices outside.

"It's open."

"And the keys are inside."

I looked out the window to see two teenage boys trying to steal my car. It was the Dodge Dart that I'd bought from my friend Eileen and it worked like a charm.

"You leave that damn car alone," I shouted.

They'd already started it and were backing down the lane.

"It's all I have," I screamed.

I raced down the stairs and out the front door in my nightgown, chasing after them.

"You can't take my car," I yelled. By now they'd turned onto the main road. "Leave it alone."

I ran down the road after them, flying after them like an apparition in my old nightgown. They were quite a distance ahead of me by then.

"Stop."

Magically, they stopped. They'd gone into the ditch, and then they scrambled up and ran off into the bushes.

I had my car back. It had run out of gas!

◆　◆　◆

From about 1980, we'd had a friend in Mark Andrew Cardiff, a CBC Radio producer who played my songs. He was able to get funding to produce a CBC transcription album, which we worked on in March, May, and December of 1982. We recorded it at Solar Audio in Halifax. Like the other albums, it was done fairly quickly because of limited studio availability and a low budget. Our distribution, no longer something to be managed by Big Pond Publishing, was taken over, after a delay, by the College of Cape Breton when the album was released in 1983.

Joella Foulds and Ralph Dillon continued to work with me, along with Scott Macmillan, who was the principal arranger. We had violinists for some of the cuts and a cellist for a few others. With the flute, saxophone, and violins, it was another sound altogether, a departure from what we'd done before. It contained some songs that I'd been writing about different stages in my life. "Southeast Wind" was one of the songs on that album, about David and me. "Some of Us Slide" was for my brother. "Ninety Percent Stoned and Ten Percent Blue" was really about my time in Ottawa, when I'd just managed to get along by the skin of my teeth. One song had to do with someone sending me a Stephen Foster songbook, which I hadn't seen since I was a child. The title cut, "I'm Not What I Seem," had to do with different perspectives people had about me. As a performer, I seemed like one kind of person to them, but I wasn't always that person:

> I'm not what I seem and I'm not what you're seeing
> I'm a re-creation of somebody's dream...

◆　◆　◆

We continued to work. In 1983, we did some radio work for the CBC, called "The Ocean Limited," which was taped at the Rebecca Cohn Auditorium. The pace had been steady before, but now it was starting to be hectic. In January, after working the Cabaret at what was now the University College of Cape Breton, we went to Ginger's in Halifax for a week-long stint, followed by a week in February at the Crow in Sydney and another four days at the Stag and Doe. In March, we were at Mount Saint Vincent University for Women's Day, followed by work at Ginger's, and then back to Cape Breton to work at the Corral and then the Crow. It continued like that into the summer, always one of our busiest times. We did the Great Canadian Folk Music Express, a sort of travelling folk festival show that toured the Maritimes, beginning in St. John's, Newfoundland, and ending up in Summerside, Prince Edward Island. Connie Kaldor, Garnet Rogers, Chris Whiteley, and Valdy were among the musicians who played with us on that tour. Even when we finished that exhausting schedule, we turned around and played another festival in Cape Breton. No work was too much; I never stopped singing.

Soon we came to the attention of a manager who was keen to work with us. She had a strong, charming personality, convincing us she enjoyed our music. More important, she had good contacts in the music business. I felt a burden lift from my shoulders when she took over. We still did a lot of singing in small community halls, where we'd be lucky to get something to eat. Sometimes we were snowed in and we had to stay overnight; this happened many times. Yet I felt someone was in charge of things, even though I was still approached directly about lot of gigs.

Ralph Dillon and I were invited to do school tours around the Maritimes. It wasn't always easy for me to do the schools; I was reminded too much of my own ordeals when I was young, knowing how cruel children can be at that age. We'd go into the gym during the lunch hour and I'd sing while he played the piano. There were times when it went over like a lead balloon and other times when it went well. It all depended if the groups were interested or not.

One of the strangest incidents during that time was an occasion when

I sang at a school in Sydney. I gave a workshop in the music class. When I was finished the teacher passed out forms to his students.

"Now," he said. "I'd like all of you to rate Miss MacNeil."

"Should we fill it in now, sir?" asked a student.

"Yes, I'm sure she'd like to know how you viewed her singing."

I was appalled. It was like an exam. I had come to help out in the school and had no idea I was to be evaluated by the students.

We went to schools from Mabou to Musquodoboit. We had very little money and stayed wherever we could. Eventually, we scraped enough money together to buy an old Econoline van for $1,200 to take our lighting and sound equipment and other gear. After that particular tour I realized we'd made no money out of it. The cost of brakes for the van cut into any profit we made. I swore that I'd never do another schools tour, but a few years afterwards there I was doing another one. Call me crazy.

We still went to any little pub or bar that would have us. One gig we took was the MacBouch Tavern in St. Peter's in Cape Breton. Ralph and I were to meet there at seven o'clock; it wasn't a long drive from Big Pond. I headed out in plenty of time with Noreen, who was always willing to give moral support. We were ready to take on the jokers and beer drinkers who went to these bars; as always, we were on the lookout for deer that might leap onto the road. We arrived in good time and the tavern owner showed us where we could wait in the back, apologizing because there was no room to sit down. I spotted an empty beer case and sat on that, taking my coat off.

"Oh, my God, Noreen, this dress is attacking me." It was a red polyester number that I had bought for half-price. Now I knew why.

"It's static," she said.

"Yes, I know it's static. What am I going to do about it?"

The dress was clinging to me: I tried pulling it down but it had taken on a life of its own. Where, in that village, would we find a spray to remove the static? Noreen went on a hunt for a convenience store and came back quite soon after with a small box of Bounce. I rubbed it all over the dress and ten minutes before I had to walk out to the piano, my dress settled down.

Sometimes my father was sick, but he always seemed to pull through. He was slowing down now. I regret that I didn't visit him as often as I should have. Whenever I dropped by he was always pleased. He missed my mother a great deal, and talked about her often; when he did, he would often fill up with emotion. He tried to get all of his children together for Sunday dinners, perhaps trying to re-create those memorable meals my mother had made.

He always wanted me to learn Gaelic, but I never had.

"You could do just one song in Gaelic," he told me.

"Oh, well, I do my own songs."

"It wouldn't kill you to do one."

I wish I'd listened to him.

Once I sang him "Old Man" and he looked at me after I'd finished with tears in his eyes. Neither of us could say anything.

In the spring of 1984, Laura was now ready to graduate from high school. She'd just turned eighteen. I couldn't believe that she'd grown up so fast. Always one to succeed at what she did, she'd applied to go to St. Francis Xavier University in Antigonish in the engineering program.

"What am I going to wear to the graduation dance?" she asked.

We asked my sister Mary for help.

"What about my wedding dress?" she said.

"You're kidding!" I said.

"Well, why not?"

It fit perfectly when Laura tried it on. She was slim and lovely.

"We'll fix it up so it doesn't look like a wedding dress," said Mary. "You could have a sash."

Laura looked beautiful in it on the night of the dance. Around her tiny waist was a red sash and she had a red ribbon in her hair. She stood beside her boyfriend, who was wearing a white tuxedo, for a photograph. Her brown eyes sparkled.

"Have a wonderful time," I told her.

Yet I felt empty after she'd gone. My daughter would soon be a woman; she'd leave home and go her own way. I had just turned forty myself, and it was strange to think that my youth was behind me. I thought back to the times I'd held Laura as a baby and here she was, ready to fly. It was hard to know where the time had gone.

She reminded me so much of myself at that age, when the whole world lay before me.

# CHAPTER SEVENTEEN

# FAST TRAIN TO TOKYO

J oella and I often made plans as we toured around the Maritimes and one of them was to pack the Rebecca Cohn Auditorium. We were certainly doing that by 1984, when I sang there twice. The winter was full, with gigs from Newfoundland to Fredericton. By June we were doing the folk festival circuit again: the Northwind Folk Festival in Toronto, the Edmonton Folk Festival, and the Vancouver Folk Festival. I was finding that Joella was spreading her wings; at the Edmonton Folk Festival she had a solo performance, along with work she was still doing with me. Things were going well for her and she was on her way to developing a name for herself. She was already promoting her own work with tapes that she passed around at the folk festivals. I'd begun to realize it during the Great Canadian Folk Music Express tour, when she'd done some work with Connie Kaldor. She was very drawn to Connie's music, like all of us.

I talked to several people about the fact that Joella was becoming more independent. She seemed to want to be on her own, yet she was still working with us. Perhaps the time had come for her to go solo. Ralph and I were going to sit down and talk to her about it at one point, but it never happened. I've never liked dealing with these things, yet I was the one who had to do it. On this occasion, it must have seemed like I was dropping a bomb on Joella. She came to Halifax to sing with us at a pub, I discussed my feelings with her, and the next day she drove home. No doubt she was hurt by it. I felt badly about it for a long time, because she had given a great deal over the years, and I respected her as a person and as a musician. We'd done so much together and had some wonderful times.

I was still singing most often at pubs, and the Ladies' Beverage Room (called the "LBR") at the Lord Nelson Hotel was one place where we used to get bookings quite often, doing a six-day stint there from Monday to Saturday. I enjoyed this gig because when it was over each night all I had to do was take the elevator up to my room on the seventh floor of the hotel. When I was finished singing, I'd go up and settle in for the night. I had one black dress that I'd worn for at least a hundred shows, and every night I'd hang the dress by the open window to air it out for the next performance.

About three o'clock one night I heard a commotion outside. When I looked out I saw fire trucks. I went back to bed, but after a short time the fire alarm went off. Frightened, I grabbed my teeth from the table and headed for the hallway where smoke was billowing out. I had visions of fire blazing through the building, and like the others, I fled down the stairs. I found myself in the lobby wearing one of those ratty old nightgowns that I'd meant to throw away, but never had. I also had on a pair of big, old slippers. In the corner of the lobby was a woman who had passed out in a drunken stupor. She came to suddenly, surprised by all the noise, and looked at me.

"Those are my slippers," she bawled, looking at mine.

"No, they're not," I told her.

"Yes, they are." She staggered to her feet and pointed. "She's got my slippers."

"I do not." Everyone was looking at me, no doubt scrutinizing the worn nightgown.

"You give them to me."

"Listen, ma'am—" said a man, but she interrupted, cawing like an old crow.

"Goddamn it, those are my slippers." Now she was trying to take them off my feet.

I was almost ready to give her the slippers by the time they arranged for buses to take us to another hotel, where I stood in the line-up with the others to get a room, decked out in my lovely attire.

At least I had my teeth!

◆　◆　◆

We were able to do several showcases that our manager had arranged: one in Vancouver on one occasion and another date in Toronto, together with another gig in Ottawa. The showcases were important for any musician, because people in the industry got a chance to hear the music and decide whether to book a band. Our showcase in Vancouver was received very well and lots of people approached us wanting to know more, in order to book us at cultural centers.

I hadn't been feeling very well throughout that year, with the same chest pain complaint, but doctors still told me that it was nothing to worry about. It might be a problem with my weight or it might be just my nerves. However, when we reached Toronto to do a showcase there, I felt terrible. I could hardly move from my bed and I was in excruciating pain. What was wrong with me? The showcase was at the Constellation Hotel near the airport; I managed to get through it, but the next stop was Ottawa. We were scheduled to take the bus from Toronto to Ottawa, but I knew I'd never make it. Instead, we flew, and even then I didn't know if I'd be able to get up and sing. Even when I was backstage, lying down, I remember thinking: "What if I pass out on the stage?" I was afraid because I didn't know what was happening, or whether I'd be all right, and there didn't seem to be anything that could alleviate the pain.

I got up on stage and started to sing. So long as I was singing I seemed to be able to forget the terrible pain, but as soon as I went backstage for the intermission, I collapsed. I thought I was dying. When I got home to Sydney the doctor wanted to do some tests, but it would be almost a week before the results were known. That was too long to wait. I knew something had to be done before that. I was very, very sick. Finally, Noreen Basker called the doctor and said she'd be taking me in to the hospital. She wanted a doctor to be sure to meet me there. It was fortunate she did, because the doctor checked me and immediately decided to do an emergency operation. It turned out I desperately needed my gall bladder taken out. For some reason, this was the cause of my chest pains. If the doctors had waited any longer there could have been much more serious problems, since the gall bladder had slowly been poisoning me. It was a potentially fatal situation for me, and it took me some time to recover.

As for the showcases, we had been very excited about our prospects, but our manager soon informed us she was pulling out of the music industry altogether. She had met someone on the elevator and had fallen in love with him there and then. We were left in the lurch, losing the contacts we'd made. It was difficult not to be discouraged. It would be a few more years before we'd be able to try the market in British Columbia again. If anyone had told me then that we were on the brink of success, I would have laughed it off, but in a year or so everything changed.

1985 was a big year for me. I seemed to be getting more attention, after years of working the pubs. In February of that year I signed with Brookes Diamond, a manager in Halifax. A direct man, with graying blond hair and penetrating eyes, he spoke with great authority. For many years he was responsible for the Atlantic Folk Festival. When he took me on, he created new excitement because he was so committed to my music. He had boundless energy too, and the fire that was needed to get us noticed.

I was now working with Ralph on piano, Allie Bennett on bass guitar, Scott Macmillan on guitar, and John Alphonse on drums. It was a good combination, but I still often played with only Ralph. In March, he and I went together to Yellowknife to sing for International Women's Day. We were in a cargo plane, in which there were few seats and a curtain partitioning the cockpit from the passengers. Shortly after I got on, I felt very strange. Then I knew it was the problem with my heart that the doctor in Toronto had told me about: it was Wolfe Parkinson White syndrome. I was paralyzed with fear as I felt it coming on, yet I wanted to jump up and run, as if it would help me escape. There was nothing I could do in the plane but wait until the sensations passed. I felt like my life was slipping away. It seemed as though my eyes were spinning in my head, and there were flashes in my mind as I thought I was losing hold on things. I had the feeling that if I gave in to it, I would drop into oblivion, not unlike the feeling of clinging to a window ledge at the top of a high building. It lasted only for ten minutes, yet when I came out of it I felt I was coming back to life. I wanted to rest, but of course there was no time for that. I had a show to do at the theatre in Yellowknife; people were depending on me. I gave the show, but I was still terribly worried that the symptoms might recur.

I should have taken it as a sign to slow down, but there was no chance to do that. We were busy throughout the spring, doing the Rebecca Cohn Auditorium once again, the Middle Deck in Halifax, a school tour, then some more work at the LBR in Halifax. I also did a CBC special from Glace Bay, backed by the Men of the Deeps. Whenever they sang with me, I was always moved by them. In the summer, the pace picked up enormously.

The best booking Brookes got us at the beginning was the job at Japan's Expo '85. With Canada Council funding, we were invited to sing at the Canada pavilion. It was a great opportunity. We went straight from another gig to the Halifax airport to fly to Tokyo. I had to wait for my luggage at the conveyor belt, and I saw that one of my bags had gotten stuck. I waited, but nothing moved it. Finally I looked around and tried to grab it, but since I'm short the reach was more than I could manage, so I tried a bit harder and found myself on the conveyor belt along with the bags, going around in a circle. I was embarrassed, knowing that I'd never be able to get out of the situation by myself. I needed help. Around I went. Finally someone stopped it and gave me a hand.

We were off. Only Ralph Dillon and I went to Japan, and we were paid a total of five hundred dollars each, playing four shows a day for over twenty days. After a long flight we got to the hotel ready to drop. We stayed in a hotel near Tsukuba where no one spoke any English. We spoke no Japanese. Slippers were placed at the door where we entered and we realized that we were to remove our shoes and put them on. The rooms where we stayed were very small. The bed was right by the door and it was narrow; it occurred to me that people my size wouldn't survive long in this country.

The first morning I went down for breakfast, I was horrified because I didn't see any food that was familiar, not to mention the fact that everyone was using chopsticks. I sat down in silence and watched as everyone else ate with great gusto. The next morning when I went down, the people working in the restaurant realized that I'd had trouble the day before and brought me a bowl of rice and an egg. I was so excited to see an egg! Then my waitress proceeded to break the egg, which was raw, and pour it over the rice. She smiled at me. Then she mixed it up. I was still perplexed about the chopsticks and she showed me how to use them too. I was immediately converted. And the rice and egg tasted wonderful. From that point on, I tried a wide variety of very good foods, some of the healthiest I'd ever been offered.

Brookes had also arranged for a film crew to do a documentary of us while we were there. Lulu Keating and Chris Zimmer of Red Snapper Films in Halifax were the best people we could have asked for. We all had fun doing that documentary. One day I wore a green caftan made to fit my ample size and I looked very much like a caricature of myself. When the cameraman followed me around there were stares on all sides, because none of the people knew what we were up to. We must have seemed like oddities to the Japanese.

After breakfast we were driven to the Expo site. It turned out that we would be singing outside the pavilion, not inside as I'd imagined. I was disappointed, but I was there to sing and so I gave it my all. There was a huge Jumbotron screen behind us and when we went on breaks, there would be an image of me that would fill up the screen. Our audience was a constantly changing one: Japanese people who were queuing to see the Canada pavilion. They understood nothing of what I was singing about, but they were all very polite and they seemed to respond to the emotion in the songs.

There were two tiny women who came to do the cleaning at the pavilion each day and afterwards they would come up to me, put their arms around me and smile. They wanted photographs of themselves with me too, and motioned to me to explain what they wanted. The man who was head of operations at the Philippine pavilion next door to the Canada pavilion came over to laud my singing too, bowing and nodding as he did so. Though people didn't swarm me, it was clear they were interested in what I was doing.

After Ralph and I had been at the hotel about a week, we both wanted to order more than just individual items on the menu. Taking out his glasses, Ralph scanned the menu while the waitress stood at our table.

"Supper," said Ralph, pointing to the menu. "Sup-per."

The waitress nodded and bowed. We nodded and bowed.

"Supper," said Ralph again, not knowing if she'd understood.

"Sup-per," she repeated.

She nodded, bowed, and disappeared.

Ralph took out his magazine.

The waitress came back bringing several dishes, setting them down on the table. Each one was exquisite, prepared with delicate care, with tiny garnishes along the side of the plate like twists and curls of a vegetable, or miniature umbrellas decorating the food. It was artfully done. I leaned over to look at the cleverly-made rolls, stuffed with raw fish, the rice dishes, and the array of vegetables on another plate.

The waitress returned. Ralph glanced up from his magazine as she set down more dishes, each one quite small, and every one as beautifully conceived as the one before.

"Should we start?" I wondered.

The waitress returned again, setting down more little dishes. She brought fish. She brought vegetable tempura. She went away and came back again. Ralph put down his magazine.

"How do we tell her to stop?" I looked at Ralph in consternation.

"I don't know," he said. "Maybe she misunderstood us and she's bringing everything on the menu.

We glanced around the restaurant, thinking we might find someone who could help us. It was a place that had some low tables, where Japanese customers sat on cushions, and another section for tourists with higher tables and chairs. Everyone was calmly eating.

Finally the waitress stopped bringing the little dishes. There must have been more than twenty-five or thirty plates on the table.

"Sup-per," she said, smiling.

We smiled back, a little faintly.

◆　◆　◆

One Japanese man worked at the Canadian pavilion as head of operations. He always spoke in a gruff voice, and I thought he simply had a difficult personality. However, I soon found out that he was really very different. One night we all went to a karaoke bar, where people took turns getting up to the mike. The man from the Canadian pavilion was one of those to get up, singing a song he had written for his daughter. I couldn't understand any of it, but his depth of feeling was clear to everyone. His voice became softer as he sang, entirely unlike his speaking voice. Afterwards he sat and talked to me through an interpreter. He loved the sound of my voice, even though he couldn't figure out the words of my songs. He took my hand in his, turning it over and studying it. Then he took my other hand. Through the interpreter he talked about the configuration of the stars and my sign, and how I had a good moon over my head, which apparently meant wonderful things.

"You have a special gift," he told me.

I was moved by our meeting, which I enjoyed immensely. And out of it came a new song, "Fast Train to Tokyo," which attempted to sum up my encounter with him.

> ... That night you sang in that karaoke bar,
> The words were new but not the heart.
> I crossed a path you walk upon;
> We shared a moment through your song
> And I believe we're all part of the temples
> That move our lives in different directions.

In the College Pub in Sydney, Rita sings favorites like "Old Man" and "Black Rock" in the early 1980s.

This promotional shot of Rita, taken by her brother (against the backdrop of a coat), shows her singing in Big Pond (c. 1980-81).

After the ground-breaking album "Flying on Your Own," Rita was certainly flying on her own by 1987.

At the turning point of her career, Rita and the band perform at Expo '86 in Vancouver.

Rita and Laura on the set of "Once Upon a Christmas" in 1993, when Laura played a young Rita for the television special.

During a tour of Australia in 1992, Rita pauses to view the magnificent Sydney harbor.

Filled with pride, Rita sings the Canadian anthem prior to Game Two of the World Series at the Toronto SkyDome in October 1993.

When the 1987 album "Flying on Your Own" went gold, Rita and the band (Ralph Dillon is second right at rear), along with manager Brookes Diamond (second left at rear) and producer Declan O'Doherty (right at rear), marked the occasion with a party.

Rita sings with the Men of the Deeps at the University College of Cape Breton (UCCB) in the late 1980s.

As host of the CBC television variety show "Rita & Friends," Rita is delighted to invite Joni Mitchell to perform.

Another guest on "Rita & Friends," Ronnie Hawkins gives Rita a bear hug.

Rita with the inimitable Rankin family of Mabou, Nova Scotia, on "Rita & Friends."

When Rita received the Order of Canada at Rideau Hall in 1992, it was a highlight of her life and a "moment in time not to be forgotten."

A signed poster of Rita, from the early days of her career, with a verse from "The Lupins."

In front of the Tea Room in Big Pond (before renovation) in the early 1990s, Rita celebrates with family and friends.

Rita making tea at home in 1992: "This is my kitchen in Sydney."

From Rita's home in Big Pond—the old MacLellan farmhouse—the Bras d'Or Lake is a welcome sight (1994).

We pass on,
We pass on.

Fast train to Tokyo,
You're still a memory on your own.
Fast train to Tokyo,
A night remembered long ago.

The old ways among the new
You hold the key I turn to you
You touched my life while passing through
You bend, you bow, I honour you
And I believe we're all part of the temples
That move our lives in a different direction...

There was little time to see the country, but on one occasion Lulu Keating, Ralph, and I went into Tokyo late in the afternoon. It was a completely new world for me with the many high-rise buildings, the traffic, and the crowds of people. Everywhere we went we caused a stir. Lulu is a tall, strikingly attractive woman, has wild red hair, and wears bright clothes. The Japanese couldn't stop looking at her. They looked at me too, but I wasn't as exotic as Lulu. They invited her to be in photographs with them and she graciously stood while they snapped her with first one person, then another, then a small group. Each time she laughed and tried to communicate with signs.

We went to a few department stores where we bought trinkets, and to our amazement everything was beautifully wrapped, like works of art. While I was in one of the stores, though, I had another turn with my heart problem. Again I felt as if I were losing touch with everything. Soon I came out of it, but it was terrifying, just as it had been on the plane to Yellowknife. Then we had lunch at a small restaurant where we pointed to pictures of food that we wanted which were displayed in the windows. Everywhere we went people were unfailingly gentle and polite. They would bow their heads, we would bow ours.

They bowed.

We bowed.

They bowed.

We looked at each other and tried to stop giggling.

We bowed again.

They bowed.

At the end of the evening, worn out, Lulu and I plunked ourselves down on the curb outside the train station to wait for Ralph. There were crowds of people all around us passing back and forth, pausing when they saw us. Who were these two women sitting on the curb? We bought two watches from a street salesman just before we caught the last train back to Tsukuba. I watched as the many lights of Tokyo faded into the distance.

It was a long time before I was really able to let that whole experience sink in, though I kept on thinking of it. On the way home from Japan, we stopped off in Vancouver to do a gig at the pre–Expo '86 site, since it had already been arranged that we would sing there the following year. It was a far cry from Japan. The grounds hadn't been officially opened yet so we sang at the entrance gates, outdoors, to an audience that didn't exist. The odd person would stroll by, umbrella in hand, but most of the time we sang to ourselves. Ralph was very sick then, but he kept going somehow and never missed a beat. He had developed flu-like symptoms that left him weak and drained, but Ralph, being the way he was, always rose to the occasion and was always an inspiration to others.

"If this is what singing at Expo is going to be like, then I don't want to go," I told him. If I'd had any idea how things would turn out at Expo '86 I never would have believed it.

We did a cross-Canada tour that summer, with a short break back in Nova Scotia before we were out on tour again, doing shows from Vancouver through to St. John's. The month of September didn't allow for much rest, though, because I did a CBC taping, called "Celtic Fantasy," a one-hour special, and a show at the Rebecca Cohn Auditorium. Then we were due to play in a town about an hour from Halifax, staying in a place the promoters had picked for us. It wasn't the best choice. We left for the gig in the evening when it was still light, but when we returned at midnight, we couldn't believe our eyes when we switched on the lights.

"Oh, my God!" The room was swarming with crawling insects. "What are they? Cockroaches?" I ran to the bedroom to get my suitcase, hoping they hadn't invaded it.

"Here," said one of the band members. "This'll get rid of them." He poured dish detergent into the sink, apparently to keep them from going into hiding.

"I'll never be able to sleep in here," I said, but I was exhausted. It was out of the question to go to another hotel; there was simply no money for that sort of thing.

I lay awake all that night, wondering if they would crawl over me in the bed. At dawn I got up, discovering that what I had imagined to be cockroaches were really earwigs. Earwigs weren't much better, but at least they weren't cockroaches.

The next morning we were all looking forward to spending the following night at another town only a half-hour away. We left bright and early, thinking longingly of hot baths and decent rooms. When we arrived at the next place, Ralph went in to register all of us. We were told our rooms were up on the hill, so we went there. All we could see were old trailers. Surely they didn't intend us to stay in them. We went back to the office.

"We can't find our rooms," we told the desk clerk.

"You saw the trailers up there, didn't you?"

"Yes, but—"

"That's where you stay."

Our hearts sank. We went back to the trailers and I went inside. Gone were my dreams of a hot bath; there was only a shower stall in the corner. The single beds had no coverings and the mattresses were stained. There were cigarette burns on the pillow. An elderly woman appeared at the door with her mop and bucket, and sheets over one arm.

"I won't be staying," I told her, feeling as though I were insulting her personally.

I needed a better place to stay. I'd had enough.

It took years of such frustrations to get my band the very best accommodations they could be given. Eventually they were staying in four- and five-star hotels, where there were no cigarette burns on the pillows, only mints underneath them.

◆ ◆ ◆

In December of 1985, my father visited everyone in the family. He even made a trip to Halifax to see Neil and his family. One Friday night, not long afterwards, he went to Ann's for a brief visit, but she was going out that night, so he said he'd return home. Early the next morning Ann woke knowing something was wrong. Gerald went over to my father's place, but got no response. He went back home to get Ann, and the two of them returned. This time Gerald climbed in through the window and opened the door. My father was in bed, lying as peacefully as if he were sleeping. He'd died in the night. Ann immediately called a nurse to verify that he was dead, and then phoned for a priest, eventually finding one in East Bay who said he'd come. Then she began phoning the family. She called me in Sydney.

I thought she told me that his body had been taken to the hospital morgue in Sydney, and so I called Noreen to ask if she'd drive me there. Realizing that he wasn't there, we left, and with the ambulance just ahead of us the whole way, we drove as fast as we could to Big Pond. I went through the house, past the chairs he'd managed to cover with burn marks because of his smoking, and went into his bedroom by myself. I cried when I saw him. He looked small and slightly shrunken, alone in that bed with the blankets loosely covering him. I went over to him and touched him, rubbing his forehead. He didn't feel cold, just somehow gone. It seemed to me that he died a lonely man, yet I knew that I loved him very much.

That night I had a gig in Englishtown, and Ralph Dillon and Allie Bennett were backing me up. I didn't say anything about my father's death. I simply did the show. When I started singing "Old Man," it was as if my father was with me in that place. I felt him close by. All the things I wanted to say to him came through in that song; it was my way of dealing with his death.

At his funeral, I wanted the church to be full, but some of his family and many of his friends had already passed away. Somehow I felt that he'd given so much of himself to the village through his hard work that I wanted to see him remembered. I sang his favorite song, "Danny Boy." And I also sang "Old Man." When they lowered his coffin into the ground, it made me very sad that his grave was at a distance from my mother's. It didn't seem right. I thought of all the times he had encouraged me to sing, and how he'd watched from the audience, with that slightly embarrassed, yet deeply proud expression on his face. He'd seen me through the pub days and had even seen me once at the Savoy Theatre in Glace Bay, overcome that his daughter had finally made it.

Christmas that year was very quiet. I wanted only to be surrounded by family. It seemed to me that the year had been long and extremely busy; I needed time to rest and absorb the loss of my father. My sisters and brothers were always near when I wanted to see them, but first and foremost that Christmas, I wanted to be with Laura, now nineteen, a free spirit after my own heart, and Wade, who at fifteen was steady and always ready to listen. I drew great strength from both of them, especially then. I found it hard that both my parents had been taken from me before I really got going in my career. I so wanted to share with them all that was beginning to happen to me. My father was at least able to go to Scotland when Malkie and Ruth took him over there for a trip. He loved being there, but I think he would have been proud to know that I was able to go there and sing. I wish he and my mother had lived long enough.

# $\mathscr{F}$LYING

s usual, I was very busy in 1986, working around the province throughout the winter and spring, and joining in the Cape Breton Summertime Revue in June and the first part of July. To make things a bit easier for rehearsals and shows, I took a one-bedroom apartment on George Street in Sydney so we wouldn't always be driving back and forth from Big Pond. The apartment, above MacLeod's Denture Clinic, wasn't big, but both Wade and I loved it. From the big windows, hung with bright cotton curtains Ann had made for me, I could look directly out onto George Street and see the action. I had a great time that summer, acting as Mitzi, Cecil's wife, in a skit with Maynard Morrison. Of course I was there to sing, too. As soon as I was finished with the Revue, I had to move immediately into the next event: Expo '86.

Of all the things I had done up until that time, the turning point was really Expo '86, but I had no way of knowing that before I went. I took the band with me, but I went with mixed feelings, thinking of how difficult things had been the year before. I travelled light, bringing only a flowered jacket in pastel colors that Ann had made for me, and a few dresses. I had some beads and a straw hat, and it was all I needed.

"Do you think they'll come to see us?" I asked Ralph.

"Well, this is different than last year," he said. "It's the real thing."

As usual, there was stage fright to contend with on the first night. Would anyone come, or would it be a repeat of the year before? The stage at the Canada pavilion was small, but on the roof above us was a huge, fantastically carved totem of a bird—perhaps a raven—dramatically painted in white, brown, and black. Its wings hung down on either side of the roof as if it were embracing it. I was on cloud nine when I discovered that the first show there was sold out. Three hundred and eighty-five people were in the audience, and while it was a venue where people could sit down and watch or wander away, the bulk of the audience stayed. Even if it was hard to walk out on the stage, I was very heartened by that night. People wanted to listen to the music; they were receptive to it.

Everything snowballed from there. We were there for a number of weeks in late summer, enough time to become known. We played every available venue: the theatre at the Canada pavilion, the Xerox International Amphitheatre, and the Folklife pavilion. Everywhere we went, people came to hear us. The Men of the Deeps were also performing there, and occasionally we'd get together and sing "Working Man." As always, it was magical working with them, and the crowds loved it. I also had the chance to perform with the RCMP Concert Band when we played at the Xerox amphitheatre, which worked very well too. We worked hard there: we had three or four concerts a day for a total of more than eighty concerts, and though it was tiring we were stimulated by the audiences.

Soon people were hearing about us by word of mouth. We became, almost overnight, something of a hot item. That was very gratifying, because we'd worked so many years for this moment. In the Vancouver *Sun* on August 20, Denny Boyd wrote:

… for God's sake, you must hear Rita MacNeil. See her at Expo this month so you can talk knowledgeably when she becomes a star.

I was thrilled. In the same article, he suggested that I should receive an Order of Canada award "for all that she has done to illuminate her part of the nation." Such high praise had never come my way before, even if the notion of the Order of Canada seemed a little far-fetched. He was alluding to the fact that I had written a song about Nova Scotia, "She's Called Nova Scotia," because we were at Expo '86 during Nova Scotia Day and I wanted to share how I felt about my province with the people of the west coast.

So walk through her green fields,
Go down to the sea,
The fortune in your eyes
Is more like a dream.
She's called Nova Scotia
And she so makes you feel,
You've discovered a treasure
No other has seen.

The song, which was simple and direct, took me a night to write. It sounds easy, but I often spend hours working on a song. As with my other songs, the lyrics and melody were inseparable. I had a feeling that it worked once I'd finished with it, and when the band was able to score the chords so that it seemed right we tried it out on the audiences. At each concert after that I explained why I wrote the song and I felt people really understood what I had done. We included it in our repertoire for almost forty concerts. I became very close to them by sharing that song, and I met a lot of people after the concerts whose comments encouraged me immensely. Some things they told me had a lasting effect on my life and my career.

I took in as much of Expo as I could while I was there. I loved the crafts and art exhibits, the costumed characters, the pavilions, the boats moored at the docks, and the fireworks that seemed to bloom in the sky every night. People were in a festive mood and it was catching; everyone seemed in high spirits. When I had some extra time I went to Chinatown to shop. I felt on top of the world, delighted with the way people had responded to the music as well as the glowing reviews in the media. One highlight before I left was a Labor Day concert with Connie Kaldor, Ferron, and Heather Bishop, all terrific musicians I admire very much. We had a great time doing that! Then, sadly, it was time to say goodbye to it all.

We had two shows to do at Toronto's Horseshoe Tavern, both sold-out events, and then it was time to go east again, to do a show on Prince Edward Island. We were met at the Charlottetown airport by the town crier.

"Hear ye, hear ye," he bellowed, walking towards me.

I didn't know what to expect.

When I realized he was there to offer congratulations from the people of Prince Edward Island, I was truly touched. After a show at Stanhope Beach I finally had time to return home and have a five-day break with Wade; I hadn't seen him in a long time. Laura had moved from Antigonish to Halifax by this time, since she'd transferred from St. Francis Xavier University to go to Mount Saint Vincent University, working her way through school by taking various part-time jobs. She worked at Sears Canada, waitressed at the Five Fishermen, and bartended at Cheers.

There was just time to pay the bills, get some groceries, and feed the cats, and then I was to go back to work again. What I didn't know was that plans were afoot in Big Pond. I went over to my brother's house, having no idea they'd planned something, and when I went through the door, the place was strung with balloons and a banner that read "You Did It, Rita!" Mary and Johnny were there as well as Ann and Gerald. Wade was smiling from ear to ear. The whole family had gathered and I was overcome. It was true that Expo '86 had been a special time, and now it was clear they'd been with me in spirit.

◆ ◆ ◆

One of the things that happened early in the fall was that CBC invited me to host a pilot television show—"View from the Heart"—with John Gracie, a fine singer. I was very excited because this was happening at home. Everyone involved was brimming with enthusiasm and they were at great pains to assure me that all would go well. I trusted them. They made a dress at the wardrobe department and showed me where to stand on the stage; in front of some light curtains that acted as a partition between me and the band behind. I was delighted about it all, working in a lovely theatre with a live audience. After the shoot I felt great. Then I had to take a brief trip to Nashville to record a single: "Flying on Your Own" and "Fast Train to Tokyo," two songs that would be on the next album. When I got back I knew the people around me were upset and I finally found out they were trying to hide a newspaper article from me. Its blaring headline read "Fat Lady With Cleft Lip Not Marketable: So Says CBC Toronto." Needless to say, they never showed the pilot.

Despite that, I was still euphoric about the reception we'd received in the West and it helped me plunge into the next project: cutting another album, to be called "Flying on Your Own." We worked on this for a while in Halifax in the fall of 1986 at Solar Audio. This was a bigger project than any we'd done so far, and it had a more sophisticated, professional sound than the other three albums. Brookes Diamond was the executive producer, but Ralph Dillon was very involved as the producer, assisted by Scott Macmillan. The key musicians were the band members, but now there were a lot of others involved to give the album a polished sound. There was a suggestion as we did it that I should cut "Flying on Your Own" down a bit. I couldn't agree to that and stuck to my guns. It was one of the most popular of the songs I'd sung at Expo '86 and sometimes it isn't possible to compromise on these things. Ultimately, we did it the way I intended and I'm happy now that we did.

> You were never more strong, girl,
> You were never more alone.
> Once there were two,
> Now there's just you,
> You're flying on your own.
>
> You were never more happy, girl,
> You were never oh so blue

Once heartaches begin, nobody wins
You're flying on your own.

And when you know the wings you ride,
Can keep you in the sky,
There isn't anyone holding back you.
First you stumble, then you fall,
You reach out and you fly
There isn't anything that you can't do...

I used to tell audiences that the song was about racing through the toll booth in Halifax when my quarter didn't drop in the bucket. Terrified at the sound of the siren, I put the gas pedal to the floor and sped off before anyone could catch me. It's a good story, yet the song really concerns the struggle to find the courage to do things independently and how we feel when we find that courage.

When Brookes and I first heard that cut, he had tears in his eyes. We were like two children who had been given a treat. I know he believed in my music and he gave it solid support all the time I worked with him. That album came together rather quickly. I knew it was good and I had great faith in it, but the problem was that the major record labels didn't pick it up, even though "Flying on Your Own," as a single, was getting airplay regularly from some stations. Not all of them were playing the single simultaneously, which often happens when there is a hit. Over the next few months, though, more and more started to play it.

Much as we believed in the album, the record companies didn't want it. I still have twenty-five rejections from them. A little dispirited, we decided to release it independently, under the Lupins Records label. We'd received some help from a Halifax investor, and borrowed more in order to do it. It was a wise decision, because the album immediately started selling in the Maritimes.

In the middle of this, I took time out in December to work with Robert Frank, an American filmmaker who once documented the Rolling Stones' cross-American tour. He sent me a movie script and filmed it soon after. It was called "Ain't No Candy Mountain," and while it didn't take movie theaters by storm, it was later shown at a film festival at the Calgary Olympics.

That Christmas, a young man phoned to see if he could come and visit me. Apparently, he had a gift he wanted to give me. When Alan Simper came to visit—a healthy-looking man in his thirties—he was very nervous.

"I want to give you this gift," he said. Then he presented me with a model of an airplane that he'd carved out of wood. He had been listening to the song "Flying on Your Own," and it had inspired him. Not only had it inspired him, he told me, he thought it had cured him of cancer. He had been told that he had gone into remission, and he felt sure that it was because of his faith in the song.

I was very moved. Nothing like this had ever happened to me before, and even though I couldn't take any credit for his apparent recovery, he was still convinced I'd helped to transform his world.

◆ ◆ ◆

As we waited with bated breath to see what would happen to the album, I got phone calls at home in Sydney. First I was told that sales were brisk, then that they were topping the charts. After it had sold 22,000 copies, we were finally taken seriously: Virgin Records Canada together with A&M Records Canada took over the distribution in February 1987. After only five weeks with Virgin and A&M, album sales had topped the 40,000 mark. I'd never been happier. Fifty thousand was a gold record. When sales reached that number we had a big party at my home. The record people were there and I was just astonished to be holding a gold record for the first time. It was a real moment for me and the band. Declan O'Doherty was the producer for two of the cuts. He was amazing to work with. When we went to Nashville to cut "Flying on Your Own" and "Fast Train" I was able to hear these songs with Nashville's finest musicians; I felt that I was peeking in on a part of history—involving *my* music!

Ralph, after all his years of hard work as arranger, sound man, booking agent, and lighting man, now had his first gold record. Declan and Ralph had brought their total commitment and heart to the project, surrounding my songs with sounds that let the lyrics live in a safe place forever.

By the end of 1987 the album sales had reached 75,000, but that was just the beginning.

Then I learned I was going to be given the Most Promising Female Vocalist award at the Juno Awards in March of that year. I was thrilled about it. It was good to be recognized nationally, even if there was an ironic side to the Most Promising Female Vocalist award. I would soon be forty-two and I'd been singing for years, but it was true that my career was just taking off in a big way.

My sisters were all at the O'Keefe Centre to support me, as well as Brookes Diamond. When they announced my name as a winner my sisters leapt from their seats, barely able to contain themselves. It was very exciting for them to watch me go up and accept the award. They loved everything about the awards ceremony, from the cocktail party to the feast that came afterwards.

I didn't expect what happened when I went backstage to be photographed first and then taken to a room full of thirty or forty journalists. I sat down behind a table on a raised platform. I felt bulky in my blue dress and I was worried about questions they might ask me. I tried to prepare myself, smiling at everyone.

I waited.

They waited.

No one asked me anything. I stared out at the sea of faces. They thought I would speak and I thought they were there to ask questions. Finally, after a long awkward pause, one of them spoke.

"Rita, how does it feel to win Most Promising Female Vocalist after all these years?"

I bravely smiled, but I was at a loss as to what to say. I could see they were wondering about me. Who was this woman? And how had she made it to where she was, when she didn't look the part? She didn't seem to fit the part either.

"It feels great," I told them. Then I rushed from the room.

It did feel great, but I couldn't tell them how it felt.

In early April I sang at Convocation Hall in Toronto, where the audience was very receptive to the songs. I was flying that night for sure. The audience was electric during "Flying on Your Own" and "Working Man" and the place was aglow with lighters that people had brought just for those songs: it was like a room full of candles, a room full of love. By then I had written a song called "Still the Music's Going Round Again," which was a song of revisiting a place after a long spell of being away.

> Standing on the balcony
> On the eighteenth floor I can see
> Old haunts and memories
> The city skyline staring back at me.
>
> And this is where my song began
> I tried to hold you, you weren't ready then.
> And now I come back as a friend
> And still the music's going round again.
>
> Holding on to history
> On the eighteenth floor I can see
> New ways, a different scene
> The city skyline reaching out to me ...

So much had happened in Toronto. I'd begun singing there as a girl fresh from Cape Breton in the days when I worked at Eaton's. Then I'd sung my protest songs for women. And now here I was again, in yet another phase of my life. Everything had changed and yet the music was still there, just as it had always been.

Around the corner was another prospect, both exciting and intimidating: in April I went to the United Kingdom, where I opened for Steeleye Span at several venues. It would be a first crack at a new market, all because "Flying on Your Own" was doing so well there. It wasn't easy to do, because I had to go on before Steeleye Span, the band that audiences had paid to see. These were sell-out crowds, too, and they didn't know much about me. I sang in big theaters at two places: Worthing, which is a big resort on the coast, and Lewisham, in suburban south London, as well as a few other places. The people at Nova Scotia House were particularly good to me, and some of them appeared at my concerts. On the whole, the audiences were warm and welcoming.

If it was difficult to appear before strangers in another country, it was a relief to tour Canada. No more did I have to put up with catcalls from the back, like, "Hey, why don't you go to Weight Watchers?" I had to contend with the odd snide remark in the press, but the audiences were enthusiastic, generous, and loyal. And I was receiving tributes, such as a nomination for Rising Star at the Canadian Country Music Awards. I was also named Honorary Citizen of Sydney and given the key to the city. When my home town recognized me, it was very special. Another outstanding occasion was the tribute to Rick Hansen at B.C. Place in Vancouver in May. A crowd of more than 50,000 people celebrated the end of his Man-in-Motion global journey by wheelchair. I was as emotional as everyone else in the crowd as I belted out "Flying on Your Own."

One of the greatest highlights of 1987 was going home to Big Pond. They were ready for me. At the firehall I was treated to a heartwarming welcome, where people had prepared a sit-down turkey dinner and ceilidh, all in my honor. Laura and Wade were there, as were all the members of my family. There were hand-made signs and balloons decorating the walls. The tables were set, the china laid out, and plates loaded with steaming hot food. Friends had made a big cake, others gave me gifts. I was offered a huge painting of the black rocks, commissioned from an artist. And I was also given a tartan blanket. Roses were put into my arms.

It was a sweet moment, after all those years when success had seemed so far away.

While 1987 was a blur, 1988 was no better. It seemed to me that I blinked and it was gone. I hardly had time to be at home, let alone spend any time with Wade, who was now at the University College of Cape Breton, studying business. Laura had gotten a full-time job with the Archives of Nova Scotia, but told me she'd go back and finish up her degree.

Though it was busy, it was very important to make time for a real honor in the spring: a doctorate of letters from the University of New Brunswick. I was very excited to be in a place where so many were graduating, having fulfilled the requirements for degrees. It made me feel humble to be among them. Like them, I wore a cap and gown. It was a real gift to me to be included with those who had studied so hard, and to be in the presence of the other luminaries receiving honorary degrees: Reuben Cohen and Frank McKenna.

If there were moments like that, the rest of the time we seemed to fly around the country on tour, barely stopping to breathe. Not only did we tour, we cut two albums: "Reason to Believe" and "Now the Bells Ring," banking on the same sales we were continuing to have with "Flying on Your Own."

I had written the title track of "Reason to Believe" for my mother, quite a while before we recorded it. I was driving to Baddeck in Cape Breton and recalling the times when she asked me to sing in the kitchen. It was really the only thing she ever asked of me. Daily now, I thought of how much she would have loved to see me touring the country on concert stages.

I've been going over my life
And I feel you in the breeze
You're a constant reminder
Of what used to be
And I know you walk beside me
On the earth beneath my feet
And though you're only a memory
You still give to me
A reason to remember
And a reason to believe.

I've been going over your life
And I've seen you on your knees
You so wanted favours bestowed upon me
And I know that in our distance
You were never out of reach

And though you're only a memory
You still give to me
A reason to remember
And a reason to believe.

And the love that you gave me
Is the reason I feel
Why the heart needs affection
And the soul needs the peace …

It had taken me a while to appreciate her great faith in me. Now I understood. We were to perform in Baddeck and before I went on stage, Scott Macmillan and I practiced it. That night I sang it to the audience and there was an immediate response. They seemed to really like it.

Another cut of the "Reason to Believe" album was the remake of "Working Man," because I felt strongly that if we did a newer version with the Men of the Deeps it would get airplay in Canada. Brookes agreed and we enlisted the help of the Men of the Deeps, recording the song at the Glace Bay Miners' Museum. Working with them was always a highlight for me, because it brought home what we were really singing about. A lot of the men in that choir had experienced at close hand the tragedies of mining. One man had lost his son in an explosion and another had lost his father. It seemed to me that these men deserved recognition for the troubles they had endured. Though I didn't get to know each and every one, I was fond of them all, particularly Tommy Tighe, who was one of the older ones.

We recorded that album in various places: Inception Sound in Toronto, Ocean Studios in Vancouver, and Solar Audio in Halifax. Things were changing too, because now the entire album bore the stamp of Declan O'Doherty's producing work, though Ralph Dillon produced one of the cuts, "Causing the Fall." Many new musicians worked with us, and the sound was clean and fresh. My voice sounded clear as a bell, a change from some of the very early recordings. I was pleased with it and so were Declan and Brookes. By now "Flying on Your Own" had surpassed sales of 120,000, which was high for the Canadian market. It had achieved platinum status.

When "Reason to Believe" came out, it sold very well. Released in the summer of 1988, it had gone platinum by November of that year. By the end of the year Brookes expected the total sales from the three albums to top the 400,000 mark. As well, I was given the Procan award, a music industry tribute. I'd never imagined such success. It seemed only a moment ago that I'd been singing to people sitting on the grass at folk festivals and now everything was different. Brookes had moved into the World Trade and Convention Centre in Halifax now and whenever I went to see him, he put everything aside and treated me like royalty.

"Rita, how are you? It's great to see you." He pulled up a chair for me. "How about a cup of tea?"

"All right."

His office was spacious and comfortable; there were photographs of me on his walls. I felt assured that he wanted only the best for me. And each time he was asked to talk about my work in the press, he was effusive. I was special, my music was special.

We were all winning from the sales of my albums. No longer did we have to stay in dirty hotel rooms with insects crawling on the floors. No more did I have to buy a few groceries to save money, putting them outside on the window sill of my room (I'd done that in the past and one morning found pigeons fighting over the spoils). Now we were touring a great deal and we all had the best of everything. We travelled in a bus that had a complete video and sound system. In hotels, we didn't share rooms. We chose hotels with gyms, always close to the heart of the city. There were hot meals before the shows. There were drinks, there were fruit trays, there were rooms with good views. I was making very good money then, and felt that I should be more than fair to those who worked with me. When I saw the receipts later on, I was aghast at the way money had been spent. Things might not always be so rosy.

I hopped continents that year from Scotland and Sweden as far as Japan. One great opportunity was going to Brisbane, Australia, for Expo '88, where I was invited to sing with Andre-Philippe Gagnon and the RCMP Concert Band. People didn't know me there. Apparently some in the audience were asking, "Who is this Rita person?"

They soon found out.

◆ ◆ ◆

We put out another album, "Now the Bells Ring," distributed by Virgin/A&M Canada especially for the Christmas season. This time, Ralph Dillon wasn't on keyboards, nor was he producing the album, though he arranged one of the cuts. Again, there was a crystal-clear sound to each of the songs. I loved doing that album, which Declan O'Doherty produced as he had the previous one.

We did a number of my songs as well as some traditional favorites. As I wrote the songs, I went back in my mind to Big Pond to the time when I was a child. Christmas is really a time for children.

I thought sadly of my friend Everett Gillis, too, and wished that he could have been there. I had met him in late 1986. He was a sweet child with golden-brown hair and pale skin; it seemed unthinkable that he had to endure cancer at such a young age. He lived in New Waterford and we heard that he was one of my greatest fans. I invited him over and he came with his father, who waited downstairs while I took Everett into another room to sing to him. I'd sit him beside me and sing anything he asked to hear.

"What next, Everett?"

"'Working Man' again."

"Again? Aren't you sick of it?"

"No. It's a good one."

He invited me to his birthday party when he turned eleven. The house was decorated with balloons, and there was a little heap of presents, but only two of his friends were there.

"I didn't want to have anybody else, Rita," he confided, "because I knew you're shy."

I smiled.

When I was told of his death in August 1988, I cried and cried. If anyone ever taught me the meaning of struggle and courage, it was Everett. I dedicated the Christmas album to him because of it.

# CHAPTER NINETEEN

# WHIRLWIND

It was a special privilege to be able to have the Men of the Deeps come to the O'Keefe Centre in Toronto for the Juno awards in 1989. All day we were getting ready for the event, and while we were rehearsing it was hard not to feel excited. People kept coming into the theatre to see what was going on, because only a few knew what we were going to be doing that evening. No one could make out why there were so many men with me. The miners themselves had a great time of it. When they went in to get their makeup on before the show, they joked around, having a great time. There had never been such hilarity backstage.

We were to perform "Working Man," which was not so much entertainment that night as a kind of paean to the mining life. It was moving for me to watch the men walk down the aisles towards the stage in the darkened hall, bearing themselves with pride, the lamps lit on their helmets. People in the audience had to look around to see why the theater lights had been dimmed. My sisters Mary and Ann were there watching, along with my friends Elaine, Janice, and Lois.

Then the men filed up onto the stage, each giving me a wink that the television cameras didn't catch, standing in tiers behind me with a reddish glow of lights in the background. The presence of those men always has the effect of bringing the audience to their feet, and it was the same that night when the song was finished. People in the audience later told me that everyone was moved by it, but I knew it already. I was moved as much as they were.

Afterwards, k.d. lang came up to accept her award with tears in her eyes.

"It's tough standing up here," she said, wiping her eyes, "after listening to that."

There was no question that it was an unforgettable evening.

After a busy spring tour through northern Ontario, then to Winnipeg, Regina, and Saskatoon, and finally Montreal and Boston—my first time in the United States—I wound up with a tour of the Maritimes. Then I was honored with a doctor of letters degree from Saint Mary's University. Again, I was struck by how gracious everyone was to me. Yet I hardly had time to digest it before I was off again. Throughout the year I was as busy as before, but I was determined to have more time to myself in the summer and a bit of a break around Christmas. I really needed a good rest, though it wasn't likely I'd get it. Brookes had another album planned and the tours went on, show after show.

I always felt that when it came right down to it, the audience was most important. I gave to them as much as I could. And they always gave back to me. Sometimes on tour I was so loaded down with things that I'd have to buy more luggage to take things home with me. They would bring portraits of me, wedding photographs of themselves, teacups, plaques, stained-glass ornaments, baskets of soaps and lotions, and bouquet after bouquet of flowers.

If some people wanted to give me things, others wanted to take things. Noreen, who had been my personal assistant for some years, seemed to have a sixth sense for that sort of thing. Once, in Moncton, she was hanging up some things in the wardrobe case, which is like a huge trunk, too big to haul up the stairs to the dressing rooms. It was after the show and people were lined up the stairs to get autographs. One woman noticed the dresses in the case.

Noreen went away to get some shirts and when she brought them back to hang in the case, one of the dresses was gone. She came to tell me.

"Rita, I think someone took your dress. Maybe she wants you to autograph it."

"Well, give her a pair of earrings instead," I said.

Noreen went out to check the people in the line-up, and found the woman who'd taken it.

"Darling," she said, "You're going to have to give that back. That dress was custom-made for Rita."

The woman glanced at her friends, who were looking at the ground.

"Come on, dear," said Noreen. "Hand it over. I'll give you these earrings if you give me the dress."

Embarrassed, she pulled it from under her coat and Noreen gave her the earrings.

Another time a woman wanted my hat, which I needed for the performance, so I politely refused. When we went out to the car one of the hubcaps was missing. The hat cost $5 at Zellers while the hubcap was a much more expensive $83 at the car dealership. I should have given her the hat!

As if dresses and hubcaps weren't enough, someone wanted my shoes. I kick them off during many performances and once a woman made off with them. Noreen had to go after her and drag the shoes out from under her car.

Other fans made comments to me that I found delightfully comical. One woman once asked if I'd sing "The first time ever I heard your face." I laughed and complied with the request, changing the words a bit. Someone else told me he loved my "Song for the Mira," which is actually a song by Allister MacGillvray. Another woman wanted me to sing "that Anne

Murray song, 'Flying on Your Own.'" ("Flying" was covered by Anne Murray, and when I heard her singing my song I could not believe it. I will never get over that feeling—to hear someone who picks her songs so carefully wrapping her golden voice around each phrase of my song—it gave me inspiration, and helped to once again believe. It only got better after that. She also covered one of my Christmas songs, from "Now the Bells Ring.")

Some fans wanted things, while others offered the gift of their hearts. I got hundreds of cards and letters and did my best to answer them whenever I could. There were people who were overweight, people who were shy, people who adored my music, people with cleft lips or cleft palates, people with terminal illnesses, people who had found love, people who said I'd changed their lives forever. Some fans sent photographs, while others sent entire albums, complete with clippings and photos. It was amazing to me that so many lives had been touched.

The most moving encounters with the public were those who were dying. In New Brunswick once when I was on tour, a priest came into the hotel and dropped off a note for me. It explained that a young man, sick with AIDS, wanted desperately to see me. He had wanted to go to the concert, but was too sick. If there was any chance I could go and see him it would make him very happy.

I went to the hospital with Noreen, asked directions to his room, and walked down the hall. On the door to his room was a sign that read, "Family only. Do not enter unless you are wearing a cap, gown, and rubber gloves." I knocked and went right in, straight to the young man's bed, and I sang to him. He was attached to several IVs, but I didn't care. Then I sat beside him and sang him songs he wanted, like "Working Man" and "Flying on Your Own."

Noreen, waiting outside, had watched me go in to him.

"How are you doing?" she asked me later.

"I'm glad I went."

I simply went out there and sang my songs, never knowing the impact it would have.

Whenever I extended the invitation for people to come and see me in Cape Breton for a cup of tea, they came. I'd had an idea in the back of my mind for a long time: the dream of opening a tea room in Big Pond. I'd been considering it since 1980 or 1981 when we were in Newfoundland. I talked about it with Ralph then, and I kept notes in a little book. Later, I talked about it with my sisters.

"We could serve soup and sandwiches," I suggested.

"Well, Rita," said Ann, thoughtfully, "you're always saying to people when you're on tour that they should come to Big Pond for a cup of tea. Why not call it a tea room?"

Why not?

The three of us had meetings on the deck of the school house in Big Pond in the spring of 1989. Ann would be the manager. My older sister would be in charge of all the baking. We could get local people to wait on tables, and have a gift shop too. We could give the school house a makeover, and with a new coat of paint it would look great. First we had to get the place rezoned, which was time-consuming, and we were facing a deadline because we wanted to open it that summer. We had nothing to get it started so I took my Zellers card and went shopping. I bought up a storm: plates, teapots, utensils, tables, chairs. The works.

I bought white wicker chairs and five glass-topped tables for the tea room, and five more plastic tables with chairs to go on the deck. Ann made pink and white curtains. We made a small gift shop on the other side of the house. The kitchen and washroom were both tiny, but we could make do with them.

On the opening day in early summer we were all prepared for our customers. The school house was now a fire-engine red and the trim had been repainted with fresh white paint. A little shed had been repainted at the back so children could play in it. There were blue or yellow umbrellas above the tables on the deck. By the road was a brightly painted sign advertising Rita's Tea Room with a picture of a red hat and a cup and saucer. Inside we were all set, with my sister's fresh biscuits, oat cakes, and cookies. Now where were the people?

We'd heard the skeptics say that it was a crazy idea and that no one would stop in a little place like Big Pond. Well, on that opening day we wondered if they might be right. We sat outside under one of the bright umbrellas and watched the cars go by.

"It's too early yet," I said.

"It's after eleven," said Ann.

We waited some more.

"Where's Mary?" I asked. "And Wade?"

"I don't know," said Noreen. "They were here a minute ago. Maybe they're doing crowd control."

Suddenly people descended on us. After a morning of getting discouraged we were running in circles trying to keep up with the demand. At the end of the day, we sank into chairs with big grins on our faces.

The first weekend, no one was able to predict the demand. Ann had gone into Sydney briefly and when she came in the mid-afternoon, Wade could hardly wait on tables because he was so swamped with people. Hundreds of them came. There was no baking for them. There weren't enough teapots. There weren't enough teacups. And there was no room for them, so they waited outside until tables were ready. They sat on the steps of the deck, but the line of people stretched almost to the road.

That day Ann decided that they needed more help, and the next week she interviewed people and hired staff. My older sister was kept busy with the baking, a big task. As the manager, Ann was at the Tea Room from early in the morning until late in the evening. The kitchen was clearly unsuitable: it was so hot in there that I went out one day and bought fans at Canadian Tire. Sometimes the well gave up the ghost and there was no water.

Without the help of friends, and especially my sister Ann, the Tea Room might not have been the success it was. It was common for one of them to offer a hand in the kitchen and then wash dishes for two or three hours at a time. Many gave willingly of their time. And we put out the word that we needed teacups and people came by with all kinds of them. Some were delicate, the china so thin we could almost see through it. Others were covered with tiny flowers. Some were painted gold, some pink, some blue. There were real treasures among them, but more precious was the fact that people gave them to us so freely. I still have some of them on a shelf in the Tea Room, but others were used so much that they broke. In those days we flew by the seat of our pants, though we had a good time doing it.

I wasn't always there, but some Sundays I'd go out and visit. I helped by singing on the deck to give the staff inside time to clear the tables. People would request songs and I'd sing them. I was very happy that the whole thing was actually working and that we'd made a dream come true. On each tour after that I talked about the Tea Room and how people would be welcome there if they ever went down east to the Maritimes. They took me at my word.

Not only did we open the Tea Room that summer, I also did a special with CTV—"Flying on Your Own"—in Cape Breton and Prince Edward Island. Cliff Jones was producing it, a good person to work with, and I had the pleasure of Loreena McKennitt's company, a wonderful harpist. The Barra MacNeils, Terry Kelly, and Hal Bruce and the Hired Hand Band were all part of it too. Though the days were long, doing takes and re-takes, one of the best times was driving Loreena around in a red convertible while she played exquisite music and sang in that angelic voice of hers. It's a moment in time that I held dear. The conclusion of the special, also one of the highlights for me, was when all of us got together for the finale to sing "We'll Reach the Sky Tonight." It was a song I'd written for the opening of the SkyDome, and though it wasn't accepted it was still a joyous song to sing, particularly with others joining in.

It never seemed there was enough time: we had to record the new album, so we flew to Vancouver where it was to be recorded. Again, it was produced by Declan O'Doherty and we did another album to be proud of. Several of the songs on that album had stories behind them. I wrote "Anna I.O.U." for Anna Kaminski. When I sang that song in Toronto at the O'Keefe Centre, I arranged for her to be driven there in a limousine so she could hear it live:

> …And Anna I owe you one
> For taking me under your wing
> I was a stranger to you

And you were like family
Your country was lost to you then
And I so needed a friend
Whatever the reason we met
You're someone I'll never forget.

The few years that I stayed
I learned to love your ways
Your Polish heart so full of love
The wisdom that you gave us all
And how your children loved you
Those were years of few regrets
You seemed so ageless in our time
Your future never crossed our minds
Now looking back at photographs
Anna, I owe you.

Anna came backstage after the show and gave me a big hug.

"I got your lovely roses today," she said.

"Do you know I drove by your house today, but I wouldn't go in?" I told her. "I was too shy."

"Ah, Rita," she laughed. "You're as silly as ever."

She was delighted by that evening, just as I was.

Another song on the album, "I'll Accept the Rose," was one I wrote to give something back to the fans. It was a way to thank people for coming to the shows and showing their faith in me. I actually wrote it long before I recorded it, but I was a bit scared to sing it in public. I'm glad I finally got up the nerve to do it.

I'm so afraid of losing you
I don't know how I'm holding you
I can't believe you love me
After all this time.

For you're the kind you look up to
I know you say that of me too
And of all the loves that walked with you
I'm glad I'm walking now.

So I'll accept the rose tonight
The one you give with so much love
You've taken all the fear inside
And right before my very eyes
You turned it into love...

I began singing it wherever we went. I wasn't quite prepared for the stir it provoked. When I sang it, people wanted to jump up and give me roses. In fact, at one concert in Ontario, a young man actually leaped from a low balcony onto the stage.

I stared at him, paralyzed with fright.

"Rita," he said. "I just wanted to give you these." He thrust a bouquet of flowers into my hands.

It took a few moments to compose myself after that.

On another occasion, when I sang the song in Antigonish one gentleman was very sorry to see that no one gave me roses. He found out that I'd be performing in Sydney the next day and he drove up to see me in concert there, where he offered me a lovely rose. And once at the Centre 200 in Sydney, a little girl gave me a package of cheese and crackers, in lieu of a rose, which she didn't happen to have.

That fall, as usual, we went all over the country. At least I had a chance to get to the celebration at the Savoy Theatre in Glace Bay, where I was included in the "Walk of the Stars." But my schedule for September alone took me all over the Maritimes. By October I had started the tour of Ontario, from National Arts Centre in Ottawa, for the beginning of the Bell Legacy Concert Series to benefit disadvantaged children, to Roy Thomson Hall in Toronto.

Finally, on December 16, I reached Sydney, where I performed at Centre 200. It was a homecoming, and I knew that I could rest afterwards.

So I gave it my best, because I wanted it to go well there. People thought that I was flying in for the performance, but we had actually driven from Halifax, so I was in time for a breather at home in the apartment in Sydney before I went across the street to perform. I could see people buying tickets from my window. I was a wreck, on tenterhooks to see if we'd have a good crowd. When I heard that it was a sell-out crowd, I wanted to thank them all personally and I wrote a song for them.

That evening was thrilling. It was like my Carnegie Hall, right there in Centre 200. Before I went on I could hear the introduction by the master of ceremonies, then the band started and I could hear the sound of feet stamping in rhythm as people waited for me to go out. Out I went, my hat jauntily set on my head, prouder than I'd ever been. I was nervous at the same time, and found that I couldn't walk out on the extension they'd added to the front of the stage. Yet I was determined to sing "Good Friends," which I'd just written for them, explaining that it was from the heart.

It was wonderful to be home.

> Don't forget when the day is done
> Who's around when the morning comes
> Who's always there to cheer you up
> When you're down and out of luck.
>
> Good friends light a candle
> Whenever they're around
> And old friends keep it burning
> They never let you down,
> Oh down.
>
> It's not always rain and shine
> Not always clear sometimes
> But to know when you turn around
> There's someone who's reaching out.

And when my day was darkest
You shone a light for me
And all through the good times
You shared it all with me...

# CHAPTER TWENTY

# FAME AND FORTUNE

By 1990, Laura was working in England. She'd left Canada in the summer of 1988 and now she was working in Leeds for a driving school called BSM. I hoped that she would eventually finish her degree, but for now she was trying her wings. Wade, on the other hand, was still very interested in my affairs in the music business. I was so very proud of them both, but had little time to spend with them. And I wasn't feeling well that year either, since I had bursitis in both my hip and my knee. Travelling was uncomfortable. I had tried different medications and made trips to the doctor, but there seemed to be no relief.

Just before I went out on tour to the West, I fell on the ice when I was taking a pot of spaghetti sauce to Noreen's house. I twisted my knee. What I didn't know at the time was that I had affected something else with the fall. I had a cyst on my ovary and when I twisted my knee, the cyst wrapped itself around my ovary. Because of the pain in my knee I couldn't fly out with the band when they went to British Columbia. Instead, my departure was postponed for two days so I'd arrive on the day of the show. When I got to the airport, we arranged for a Winnebago to take me to the venue. I had to lie down by then since the pain was so severe and I was taking painkillers every couple of hours. I had no idea how I was going to do the shows.

The trip through the Rockies to the first venue in British Columbia was extremely difficult. I had to try to keep my knee iced the whole time. On top of that, it wasn't always the smoothest ride as we wound through the mountains. At the concert, I walked on stage with the aid of a cane, then sat in a chair for the show. The sixth venue on the agenda was Prince Rupert. From there I was to go to the Juno Awards in Toronto and then fly back to pick up with the tour in Terrace.

It was almost too much. My knee was still in great pain as I did the show and then afterwards we had to take a water taxi to the airport. It can be a little unnerving to be in a boat at night, but more frightening was the trip in the tiny rented plane. I felt queasy, as did Noreen, who was with me. I gripped the armrests in the plane and shut my eyes as we took off, feeling as vulnerable as a bird in a storm. We finally got to Vancouver, exhausted, but the next morning we had to catch a commercial flight to Toronto.

We got to Toronto just in time for the Juno ceremony on March 18, though I was running late. Ann was in the hotel lobby waiting for me, as well as the make-up man. They rushed me upstairs, though I wasn't terribly fast on my cane, and in the hotel room the make-up man daubed at my face and then departed. Hurriedly I changed my clothes.

"I look like a strobe light in this thing," I said to Ann as I looked at my reflection in the mirror. I was wearing a brown dress and jacket covered with shimmering sequins.

"More like a spaceship," she said.

We rushed to catch a limousine to the O'Keefe Centre. I didn't want to show up in a white limo, but Ann was savoring this moment and we went right to the door, past the crowds. I wouldn't have been able to walk anyway, had we gotten the driver to let us off somewhere else.

I'd been nominated in three categories: Album of the Year, Female

Vocalist of the Year, and Country Vocalist of the Year. Imagine my stunned surprise, when, during the ceremony I was pronounced Female Vocalist of the Year! I really wasn't expecting the honor. When I got up to receive the award, my bad knee buckled under me and I almost fell.

We had to catch up with the band, now in Terrace, British Columbia, and to do so we had to fly to Vancouver in the morning, where we caught a connecting flight to Terrace. (We couldn't land there because of fog, so we ended up landing back in Prince Rupert where we originally started from and had to take the water taxi again.) At that point we had to drive as fast as we could to the venue, a two-hour drive away, as I tried to keep my throbbing knee elevated. Thank goodness a local performer, Lori Thain, had been entertaining the crowd for two hours before we appeared. As quickly as I could, I threw on a different outfit and went out on stage, but it was all I could do to sing to that crowd.

By this time, more than just my knee was bothering me. Something seemed to be seriously wrong with my abdomen. I got more and more sick, until finally Noreen persuaded me to fly home for the six days that we had off in early April. I could see a doctor there, she told me.

"Look," she said flatly. "You're in pain with the knee and now you're sick. You can't go on like this."

"I'll be all right."

"It'll cost just the same for you to fly home as it would to stay in a hotel for the next week."

I considered it.

"And you may as well fly the band home too, because it'll cost a small fortune to keep them here."

We went home. The first thing I did was go to the doctor, who insisted on an ultrasound. It was a good thing he did, because he discovered the cyst. Emergency surgery followed; I had a hysterectomy and the rest of the tour was postponed.

The minute the press got hold of the news that I was in hospital there were reporters camped out on the lawn of the Sydney Community Health Centre. They tried to get inside the building and they raced to speak with family and friends when they came out. None of them knew why I was in hospital. Then they discovered Ann, who resembles me a bit, in the hospital cafeteria.

"That's Rita!"

"Well, she looks all right."

"No, that's not Rita."

"I'm her sister," said Ann.

"What's the matter with Rita?"

"How's she doing?"

"I don't know," she told them. "I'm waiting to hear myself."

When I was told that people wanted to know why I was in hospital it was clear that we had to let the public know I was all right.

"Tell them I've had a hysterectomy." I said. "Why beat around the bush?"

It was a good thing we did that. After a while the hoopla died down, but nothing prepared me for the outpouring of good wishes, get-well cards, and tributes from fans when I was in the hospital. One card from Halifax well-wishers was approximately eight feet by eight feet, and signed by more than three thousand people! There were so many bouquets that they filled my room. When my room was full, they took them down to the chapel, which was soon banked with lovely blooms. When the chapel became too crowded, the bouquets were put in the room next to it near the geriatrics ward.

"Well," commented one nurse. "All winter we've been trying to get people up and moving. Now all they want to do is walk the hall down to the chapel so they can look at all the flowers."

"The darlings," I said.

◆　◆　◆

"Rita" won Album of the Year at the Canadian Country Music Awards in 1990, a year I also won Female Vocalist and Album of the Year at the East Coast Music Awards. All of these awards were thrilling for me, but didn't change the most important thing: I was there for the people. Awards came second. So it was wonderful that summer to sing at the Big Pond concert, one of my first outings since the operation. The Tea Room was booming too, and we were already thinking about expanding it to accommodate the crowds. And it was time for another album, this time "Home I'll Be." I was happy to learn that we could record it in Sydney because that way I could stay at home. We had special guest performances by the Men of the Deep and the Rankin sisters. There was a host of other musicians who helped, along with the band members. The title track of the album was a song I'd been inspired to write after the death of a good friend, Brother MacDonald. I boarded the plane in Winnipeg that was to take me home and as I looked out the window, thinking of the place I love so much and the people who live there I wrote the song:

I see the mountains, feel the salt air
I have reasons to behold
All the wonders that never cease to be
You're as timeless as the water
You're as gentle as the fields
I caress you, oh Cape Breton, in my dreams.

And you never let the hard times
Take away your soul
And you stopped the tears from falling
As you watched the young ones go
You're as peaceful as a clear day
You're as rugged as the seas
I caress you, oh Cape Breton, in my dreams.

And home I'll be
Home I'll be
Banish thoughts of leaving
Home I'll be.

After a quick tour of western Canada and Ontario, making up the dates that had been postponed when I had surgery, it was time to go back to the United

Kingdom to do some promotional work prior to a big tour the following spring. "Working Man" was the song people seemed to love, and my albums were selling very well there, as they were in Australia. I did a concert and some interviews in London to promote the music, and generally the interviewers seemed receptive, although the *Daily Mail* managed a few pointed remarks on September 19 comparing me to Madonna who was "slim, sexy, and super-confident." I was "short, fat, and painfully shy," not to mention the fact that I had "a double chin and a cleft palate" and that I overbalanced sometimes because I was overweight. The photographs showed me in an unflattering pose, while Madonna, dressed in skimpy rollerblading gear, looked much more fetching. At the end of the article was the comment: "Move over Madonna...or you may get squashed out of the market."

I tried to ignore that sort of press. Between interviews I did a little shopping with Noreen and in one shop I bought a pair of shoes.

"Are you Americans?" asked the clerk.

"No, we're Canadians."

When we got back to the hotel, I realized that I'd been given two left shoes. I called the shoe shop right away.

"I'm not sure about Americans," I said to the clerk, "but Canadians have a right foot as well as a left one."

He laughed.

◆  ◆  ◆

One of my interviews was scheduled for Wogan's, which was a major talk show, as hot in Britain as the David Letterman show in the United States. It was important to go on it and sing "Working Man" for the viewers. So I went, sang the song with a Welsh men's choir, and went to sit with Terry Wogan to be interviewed. Think of my astonishment when I saw Omar Sharif on the set! He was a guest as well. True gentleman that he was, he bent and kissed my hand. Starstruck, I blushed, but I couldn't help looking into those great dark eyes of his. My heart was beating a mile a minute. I was thinking how *Doctor Zhivago* was my favorite movie of all time, and that I'd never dreamed I'd ever meet such an actor.

"That was a wonderful performance," he congratulated me.

"Well, thank you."

Back at the hotel, the band members were watching with glee and when I returned, they laughed, clapped, and cheered.

"Way to go, Rita!"

"I don't care what anyone says," I declared as I danced into the room. "I was kissed by Omar Sharif!"

◆ ◆ ◆

Right on the heels of the brief stint in the United Kingdom was the tour in Australia. My albums, released there by Festival Records, were going through the roof. "Reason to Believe" had won the Number One Award there in the summer of 1990. Even before I went there were phone interviews at home, although I found it difficult to believe I was actually speaking to people in Australia. Then I went over prior to the tour to do the next set of interviews, and again I thought it was curious that they seemed so interested. I knew that "Working Man" was a tremendous hit there; they seemed to be over the moon about it. Yet it seemed an intangible thing to me. Would people come to the shows? That was always the question on my mind.

Once again, my fears were unfounded. The response was wildly enthusiastic and both the band and I fed on the excitement of the audiences. At one point when I was leaving after doing an interview at a radio station we discovered about fifty people outside. I thought they were there for a demonstration of some kind. It turned out there were there for me. Wherever we went there were advertisements for the shows: "For God's sake, see Rita MacNeil." And they came.

We fell in love with the place. I hadn't seen much of it the first time I'd been there and now we were able to enjoy the scenery, which is spectacular. We began the tour in Rockhampton, but we were all too nervous about the upcoming shows and we didn't realize the hotel where we were staying was right on the outskirts of a large city. Only on a later tour did we venture out. Yet we saw a great deal of the country on a tour which took us the length of the eastern coast. We played Rockhampton, Bundaberg,

Brisbane, Tweed Heads on the Gold Coast, Canberra, all the way to Sydney, Adelaide, and Melbourne.

Margaret Kelly, a friend who lives in Brisbane, explained that she hadn't really wanted to see me when I was singing at the Lyric Theatre there. She didn't know me then, but her son Gary had bought tickets, so she went, though rather reluctantly. She spent eight dollars on a program at the door, then sat down to wait for the performance. She flipped through it once.

"Well, that was a waste of money."

"Let's just hope she's not a gospel singer," said Gary.

I wasn't a gospel singer. Maggie told me later that when I sang "Reason to Believe," she was hooked, as was Gary, and that now the program she scorned is one of her dearest possessions.

When we played at the Seagulls Leagues Club at Tweed Heads on the Gold Coast we were all astonished by the large complex. From my room, there was a panoramic view of the Pacific stretching out for miles. I had to pinch myself. Some of us sat together on the balcony, mesmerized by the intense blue of the water. The beach was patrolled by lifeguards and there were nets to stop the sharks from coming in too close to shore. At one point in the evening, a gathering of people appeared. We had no idea what they were doing. Soon we realized what was happening.

"My God," said Noreen. "Can you see that?"

"What?"

"Out there, swimming around."

I looked.

"It's a shark!"

Sharks or no sharks, the place was incredibly beautiful. Each morning the sun shone down in a golden haze in the bluest of blue skies. The beach was a silky white, and the waves lapped lazily against the shore.

We hated to leave, but there was more to see. We went to Sydney and then back up to Canberra, to Mt. Gambier, and then on down the coast to Adelaide. Everywhere we went people wanted to hear the music, and there was an uproar each time I sang "Working Man." In Australia there were many nights when I had to sing "Working Man" three or four times in a show. I had never experienced that before. The song spoke to them in a big way and I as usual was stunned by the reaction. When I got back home so many people kept in touch: Maggie and Gary from Brisbane, Hella from Sailsbury, and miners who appreciated "Working Man." The letters keep coming from that special place. Saisha, another pen pal, sent me beautiful books of scenery and poetry to keep alive my memories.

When we left the Australian spring was glorious and I made a promise to myself to return if I could. How could I go back and do another tour immediately afterwards in Ontario? As always, we did it, but it was the beginning of November when we returned to Canada, one of the gloomiest of months. The touring would soon be over and then it would be Christmas and time for a break, but in my mind I was far away.

How I longed for warm, golden Australia!

◆　◆　◆

Though it was time to come home, I had the pleasure of seeing "Now the Bells Ring," the Christmas special that we'd filmed earlier in Cape Breton, with Gordon James of CTV. I really felt as though we went back in time to capture the sense of Christmases gone by. The inside scenes were shot at Gowrie House in Sydney Mines, in a lovely old inn. The innkeepers, Clifford Matthews and Ken Tutty, were kind enough to let us use the Victorian mansion, which looked appropriately festive. The Men of the Deeps, Matt Minglewood, the Cape Breton Chorale, and four excellent fiddlers were involved in it too, as were members of my family: my nephews and nieces, Wade, some of my brothers and sisters, and Noreen and Val.

On some nights when they had to be on site very early in the morning, members of my family stayed at the North Star Inn, a hotel with an amazing view. They were excited about being part of things and watching how the crew worked. Sometimes they began at five o'clock in the morning and worked straight through until eleven o'clock at night. This went on for two weeks. Sometimes, just to break the tension after people had been working for hours and hours at a stretch, I'd go up and rifle through the costumes, put on a wonderful wig or a crazy hat and waltz downstairs. One of the most moving things was the children's nativity scene. My little nieces and nephews made that a special part of the show. They were so delighted to be part of things and they did their parts very well.

We filmed at Gowrie House, and in Big Pond. One scene showed us setting out in a horse-drawn sleigh, with jingling harness, along the snowy Glengarry Road. Christmas was never quite like this for me as a child, but it ought to have been. We also filmed a segment at St. Mary's, which glowed with that beauty I remembered from the midnight masses of years gone by. Thinking of Hilly singing "O Holy Night," I sang as if my voice would raise the roof.

Many people tuned in to watch it, both that Christmas season and the following one. And Brookes was eager to tell me that the album "Now the Bells Ring" achieved triple platinum status in Canada, while the others from "Flying on Your Own" onwards had gone double platinum. There was more than enough reason to celebrate. Yet it wasn't the record sales that were most important.

Christmas was not a part of all of that, as far as I was concerned, even though it created excitement. It was a time for family and friends, a time to be at home, a time for giving. Our joy in doing the special was evident because of it, and that is what people loved most.

> Christmas has meaning
> For those who have feelings
> Of giving and sharing and love
> Like old songs and good friends
> Small family gatherings
> Bringing us closer
> To remember again.
>
> Some hearts grow softer
> When snow covers rooftops
> And faces of children grow bright
> It's hard not to feel good

When strangers that pass you
Bring you good wishes
Again and again.

So down fall the snowflakes
Out come the keepsakes
The Christmas tree treasures
That fill up the home
All through the season
Good folks keep meeting
And friends round the table
Wherever you go...

# CHAPTER TWENTY-ONE

# WE'LL REACH THE SKY TONIGHT

1991 began with good news: I'd been given the Country Female Vocalist award at the Juno awards ceremony and Female Vocalist, Album of the Year ("Home I'll Be"), and Song of the Year ("Home I'll Be") at the East Coast Music Awards. Later on in the year I discovered I'd been awarded the Socan award, another music industry award for the highest airplay of a song, "We'll Reach the Sky Tonight." I took none of these awards lightly. No one had any idea how little I expected these things.

Everything was in place for a major tour of the United Kingdom. Our work of setting the stage in the fall was very helpful; after a quick tour of Toronto, Victoria, and Vancouver, I went to England, Wales, Scotland, and Northern Ireland in the spring.

Initially, I sang on BBC with British musicians, did afternoon talk shows and other interviews. A BBC documentary was planned during my stay there. That was only the beginning. Next came the shows, beginning at Folkestone in England, then Swansea in Wales, and on to Poole, Nottingham, Bradford, Birmingham, and New Brighton in England. Then we went to Edinburgh and Glasgow in Scotland, a string of English venues in Manchester, Oldham, and Sunderland, back to Wales to do a show in Cardiff, and finally on to London to the Royal Albert Hall. Afterwards we would fly to Northern Ireland to do two shows in Londonderry and Belfast. The shows were the main thing, and I really didn't know if people would come, though there seemed to be interest. I needn't have worried. They came in droves. In fact, at one of the concerts in England they pelted the stage with flowers so that I had to wade through a fragrant scattering of blossoms.

In Scotland I played in Usher Hall in Edinburgh. My dress, covered with black sequins, weighed a ton. Noreen thought I looked like an armadillo.

"I feel like one," I told her.

After seven shows and a lot of travelling, I was tired and sang badly. My pitch was off. I was heartbroken about it, but the fans still came to see me afterwards.

The biggest challenge still lay before me. I had to sing at the Royal Albert Hall in London, where so many famous people had performed. It was a nervewracking prospect. I knew that the hall had a great crowd that night. Brookes came to see me in the dressing room briefly, but he knew it was better to let me be alone. Noreen helped keep things quiet and calm, keeping fans away. Laura had come from Leeds and Wade from Canada, so they were both with me in the dressing room, but I could see they were both a little anxious for me. They left me to go and sit in the audience while I struggled for composure. It seemed to me that this old classic concert hall was filled with all the ghosts of those who had gone before me. Could I live up to such high standards? I died a thousand deaths before that performance, pacing the floor and trembling with fear.

Just before I went on stage I went through some of my worst moments. I knew that both Laura and Wade were in the audience, silently cheering me on, which gave me strength. Somehow or other I got up my courage and walked straight out to center stage. I hoped no one would hear the sound of my pounding heart, as I glanced at the band members for support.

I sang.

I breathed a sigh of relief when the song was over and the clapping began. It was like a roar that filled the hall and when I heard it I knew I'd be fine. I gave the very best of myself that night, knowing the audience was with me. I could feel it. Never before or since have I experienced the thrill of performing in such a venerated place. I realized that there were Canadians in the audience because of the banners and flags, which gave me a lift. By the end of the evening when the audience had called me back three times for encores I was in heaven.

"If you're willing to stay," I told them, "I'm more than willing to sing."

After the performance I was very relieved. It was only then that I could treasure the fact that I'd sung in the Royal Albert Hall. For a moment it occurred to me that it might be my first and my last time there. Then the fans came. They weren't just interested in "Working Man," they were intrigued with other songs. While they didn't always know the names of them, they'd quote a line or two from a song and I'd know which one they meant. It made me realize that other songs besides "Working Man" had made an impact.

I loved having Laura and Wade there with me. Laura was entirely at home in London, where she was quite comfortable driving on the other side of the road. Even though she got lost it didn't seem to worry her. I recalled the time she'd borrowed my Dodge Dart in Big Pond when she and Wade had gone to do last-minute Christmas shopping in Sydney. I'd cooked a roast of beef that night and then paced the floor wondering if the two of them were all right. They were fine. And now here she was driving with ease in another country.

The three of us enjoyed our brief time together. So it was with sadness that I waved goodbye to her the day after that concert. The words of the song "City Child," written for her, were going around in my head:

> She's a City Child
> And there's a crack in the pavement where the grass runs wild
> She sees the beauty on the crowded streets
> In the city subway her heart skips a beat.

She's a lonely child
And there's a tear in her heart that she tries to hide
She knows the strong ones do survive
On the crowded tram-car she holds on tight.

Be there tonight
Oh you know she'll call
Remember how it was when you said goodbye.

The days move on
And there are times she forgets that she's all alone
She talks to people she don't even know
In the hurried city she thinks of home.

She recalls you now
And there's strength in the memory you're there somehow
There's no denying she's tied to you
But like birds that fly, she's flying too...

On we went to Belfast. The hotel where we stayed in Belfast—the Europa—had the dubious record of being one of the most frequently bombed hotels in the city. It wasn't very reassuring. Sure enough, when we were watching television in the evening, a warning flashed on the screen. We had to get out of the hotel as quickly as possible and stand in the street while they combed the building. Similarly, when we went to play the Grand Opera House we were told to leave an hour before the performance was to start. They went in with dogs trained to sniff out explosives. The airport, too, had several tight security checks, gun-toting soldiers, and more trained dogs.

I didn't expect that anyone would know who I was in Northern Ireland, but when I went to a mall to greet a man who had stocked my records in a music store, I couldn't get through the mall because of the crowds. Then I realized they were there for me. It didn't seem possible.

One of the greatest experiences of that tour was going to Barra, birth-place of my ancestors. We flew from the Scottish mainland in a small plane. I could actually look down through the cracks in the floor of the plane and see the ocean beneath. Then we saw Barra: a tiny island that looks like a green jewel set in the blue sea. The plane landed on the shingle at the edge of the water, which served as the runway, and people were there to greet me. I was deeply moved setting foot on the island that my grandmother and father, as well as so many other relatives, thought of as their true home. The people there were extremely kind, courteous, and appreciative that I'd made the trip, just like the people at home. They had arranged for me to participate in a ceilidh, like the Cape Breton kitchen parties and gatherings I knew so well. They had a concert in the community hall. As well, they took me all over the island.

Barra gets its name from the Gaelic word *barr*, meaning point or top. The Norse word for island includes the letters "ay" or "i." So Barra, like a prominent pearl in the string of islands in the Outer Hebrides, was likely a navigational aid to the Norsemen. The interior of the island is mostly moorland, covered with grasses and sedge in subtle colors, and the heather grows wild. There are very few trees on the island, yet it has a rugged, austere beauty. In the sky, the larks dipped and soared. And I was told that there were cuckoos in the glens.

I was shown the stone huts people had lived in centuries ago. These had neither windows nor chimneys, only two round holes in either side to give light, and a roof of turf, bracken, and heather. The holes in the walls were apparently covered with turf when the wind was blowing. Sometimes there was a hole in the roof to let out the smoke of the peat fires, but often the huts were full of smoke. In winter the animals might be brought inside. It was hard to believe people had lived this way.

I was also taken to see the standing stones in different locations. Even now, these stones evoke the mystery of their origins, especially in the midst of that unchanged landscape. And while I was there I sought out the cemetery and spent a long time gazing at gravestones of countless MacNeils. Above all, though, it was the land itself that touched me. The beaches are strands of pure white that stretch for miles. The sky hangs in a silver mist over the sea, and occasionally shafts of light pierce the clouds, making the water glimmer with brilliance. Though I would have liked much more time there, I was still able to walk the pristine beaches and drink the salt-scented wind. It was a time of reflection which inspired me to write "The Crossing."

The past is far behind us now
It was buried in the crossing
We have our place that bears the trace
Of times so long forgotten
We were distant by our broken ties
Made distant by the ocean
I've come to stand in father's place
I heard the night winds calling…

And when the night lies over you
And I lie gently dreaming
Although the candle burns no more
The journey's now completed.

◆ ◆ ◆

It is never easy to be in the music industry. Now I was realizing just how hard it could be. During the tour I was signing contracts when I didn't fully understand their contents. They were all written in legal jargon designed to confuse. Everything appeared to be standard. I was tired and I signed.

Wade had been going through my papers and trying to make sense of them. He spent periods of time in Halifax sorting through files. I came to a crossroads, where I had to make some decisions. However, I still had to go out and work. A tour was scheduled for late June, and in July we had a CTV show to do, which would be filmed in Vancouver. But my mind wasn't on the work. Ultimately, I decided not to renew my contract with Brookes Diamond that summer, but it was agreed in a settlement that neither party would discuss details. I can say only that he gave me great support over the years, for which I was very grateful. On the advice of my legal and financial advisors, I was told it was wise to move on!

It was a difficult fall. When I learned that I had won Fan Choice Entertainer of the Year and Top Selling Album at the Canadian Country Music Awards it was a bright moment in the midst of that darkness. I attended the awards ceremony, but when I won I was completely taken aback. When I went up to receive the award from Christopher Plummer, my eyes filled with tears; it was all I could do to contain my feelings.

Wade received excellent marks on his Christmas exams that year. He was on the dean's list, and in only a few months he would be graduating. I had been without management for some months and he couldn't bear it that my affairs had taken such a turn. Determined to change things, he quit school and took on the monumental task of sorting out the records of my life's work. He wanted to have all the files in the house, where they would be at our fingertips. I was devastated that he was quitting school to help organize things, and felt guilty about it. Nothing I could say would persuade him to change his mind.

"It has to be done," he said.

"Not like this," I told him. "Not with you quitting the program."

"I'll get the rest of the credits later. This can't wait."

It was no use pleading.

With Wade's help, I found a new manager, Cape Bretoner Leonard Rambeau. I first met him at one of my concerts, in awe of him at the time because he was managing Anne Murray. A lean man, with a pepper-and-salt beard and fine eyes, he never spoke ill of anyone in the business. The next time I met him Wade and I drove to Ingonish to see if he would be interested in managing me. Before I left he gave me a hug and told me not to worry.

I had to wait a few months to see if he would take me on. By January of 1992, I was under the Balmur umbrella with Leonard, full of hope. We were able to get the rights to the U.S. market from Polydor and we had high expectations of breaking into that market. So I was very glad to be with them, because Wade and I had been struggling along on our own for a while by that time. Early the same month I got remarkable news: I was to receive the Order of Canada. They phoned to tell me and I was shocked, finding it very difficult to absorb what I'd just been told. Did they really mean me? Yes, indeed. And the ceremony would be in late April in Ottawa. I put the phone down and sat in my rocker, trying to hold onto this marvelous bit of news. I sat for a long time.

In the middle of all of this, I was having a house built. I'd purchased property in Sydney that faced the Sydney River. It was once farmland and there had been an orchard on it, because there were lovely old fruit trees in front. The house was a major undertaking and I had hired an architect to help me with the planning. He was one of swarms of people who worked on it. It could have been the Taj Mahal by the time they were done. It seemed to me that I was living the script of the movie "The Money Pit." All I knew was that I was the one who paid the bills, sometimes twice if the work wasn't done well the first time.

The architect bailed out of the project. But we still had a fellow who was said to be very good at renovating old houses. He was more or less in charge of things, working with a builder who really was topnotch. Yet some things I'd requested did not get done, but I was on tour at the time, so I didn't realize this until later. Mouton bars that should have been put between the panes of the windows were put on the inside of the windows instead, the pool apparatus was put in the basement, and walls were not where they should have been. Money flowed like water: spent on double-wide oak trim, real plastered moldings on the ceiling, beveled glass in the French doors, and so on.

People thought I was building a mansion. According to them it had twenty bedrooms, an Olympic pool, and Jacuzzis in every bathroom. One story was that it had a bowling alley in the basement. Rumors abounded. It was a good-sized house, but not a castle. And it had a pool, though there were many days I rued it. Only now, eight years later, does the pool work as it is supposed to, after many a call to sort it out. It had gotten to the point that whenever I passed the pool, I thought I'd like to blow it up. The air temperature was never right: the windows steamed up like a sauna every time the cover was taken off. And I needed arms of steel to roll the cover out or pull it back. It was all more trouble than it was worth. Finally, an engineer from Moncton figured out the problem within a day. If I'd been at home the day he fixed everything, I would have handed him roses for solving the problems. As well, the kitchen was dark, and I wanted to enjoy the view of the river, so I decided to put a sunroom at the back of it. By the time I was done it had cost me as much as my first house, the schoolhouse in Big Pond. Now I had to contend with the heat: I could fry an egg on the floor. So I came up with the idea of a plywood roof with deflector paper and shingles which cost little and cut the heat by forty per cent. Then I discovered the leak. We had to hire another person to fix it. It reminded me of when we'd moved into the schoolhouse and had so much trouble with the well. All in all, it was not an experience I wanted to repeat.

When I moved in, though, there was much that delighted me. The parlor is one of my favorite places in the house, where I keep a treasured collection of teacups and china sent to me by fans. Sometimes I go in there and turn on the old-fashioned lamps which glow a ruby color because of the red lampshades. The walls are hung with paintings. It is a room that takes me back to the Victorian era.

The house is never more beautiful than at Christmas when it is completely decorated, with garlands up the oak staircase, and Christmas trees in different rooms. I love to open the door to family who have to stamp off the snow from their boots as they come in out of the cold air. The children immediately head for the Christmas village that I set up each year. It is one of the happiest times I spend in this house.

◆ ◆ ◆

In March and April of 1992 I had a tour to do in Australia and I was excited about going. I went initially on a press junket with Leonard Rambeau, who stayed for a while as the tour began. We went into a concert hall together to have a look; it was the place where I'd be performing the following evening.

"I can't believe that tomorrow night this place will be filled and they will all be coming to see me."

"Believe it, Rita," he said, smiling.

Just as I'd imagined, Australia was sheer delight. I was greeted at the Cairns airport in Queensland by fans who had brought flowers for me, which set the tone for the rest of the tour. On a day off in Cairns I rented a sailboat, to take myself, the band, and crew out to the Barrier Reef. The water was like blue Venetian glass, so extremely blue that it hurt the eyes, glittering with the dance of sunlight on it.

Poor Noreen came with us, but she was scared the whole way. She got very seasick, vomiting over the side of the boat even though it was fairly calm. She was sure that the boat was going to sink and that she'd be eaten by a shark. When we reached a certain point far out in the ocean, the boat was anchored so we could go snorkeling. The others went and I decided I wasn't going to miss it either. In the meantime, the boat owners took Noreen to a sandbar in a Zodiac boat, but she was still very sick. They set up an umbrella over her where she'd be safe and went back to the sailboat. She sat in the shade of the umbrella at the edge of the water, a sun hat on her head, clutching the photograph of her grandson to her chest because she was sure she'd never see him again.

I was happily paddling around in the water, which felt silky against my skin. I even went on a deeper dive with some of the others so I could see the bristling coral, which was bright pink, exquisite to look at, though it could scrape the flesh. The fish, rippling past, were a luminous yellow. It was an entire world under water that touched me in a spiritual way, especially when I swam through a school of translucent white fish that parted like a curtain or glided alongside so I could put out my hand to them. We swam for hours, and of course we paid for it later because we got burnt a deep crimson, but at the time it was worth it.

I swam over to Noreen, about a quarter of a mile away on the sand bar.

"Hi, dear, are you all right?"

She was wondering why on earth I'd be swimming all that way, certain that I was going to be eaten by sharks.

"Sharks out there?" she asked.

"No."

"Come for a swim."

"No."

"You're sure you're all right?"

"No."

The boat owners came to get her, but she took one look at the feast spread out on a table, complete with shrimps and other fish, salads, and fruit, and went to the far end of the boat, where she promptly threw up again.

All the time we were there I had the feeling of being in safe hands. As we ate the sumptuous lunch the owners of the boat spread out for us, we saw a grouper go underneath the starboard side. The enormous fish was apparently waiting for scraps of food to be tossed over the side. When we arrived back after that glorious trip, I felt that I'd been to another world in one brief day. Noreen, on the other hand, was deeply grateful not to have been eaten by a shark and swore up and down she'd never leave land again.

"Great Barrier Grief," she said, when any of us mentioned it again.

◆ ◆ ◆

We went back to some of the same places we'd been on the first tour, like Seagulls Leagues Club at Tweed Heads. We had three days there and I found myself looking out at the blue ocean and thinking of home. Somehow the tranquil beauty of the Gold Coast allowed me a space for reflection. I thought about home, I thought back over my life, I thought about Christmas. For some reason, in that warm place I was inspired to write Christmas songs. I wrote nine of them there.

I was able to swim with dolphins in a huge pool at Sea World on the Gold Coast. The trainer explained how dolphins will either take to a person or reject her (as in the case of an Olympic swimmer who had been there the week before). He proceeded to do tricks with the dolphins and then allowed me to swim with them. To me they were almost human in the way they frisked close by, playfully skimming the surface and dipping under the water again. I took to them right away and it seemed they enjoyed being with me; they came up so close that I could even touch them. I was fortunate to have that opportunity. How many can say they've had the chance to swim with those marvelous creatures?

While we were still on the Gold Coast I watched from my hotel room balcony as the band and crew members jumped in the waves. It looked like fun and I went down to join them. Little did I realize the power of those waves. The water is shallow there and one has to walk a long way before the water comes up to the waistline. When I jumped into a wave, it rolled me and then threw me up onto the sand. I was choking and trying to stand when the undertow pulled me out again and the wave slapped me down once again, tossing me about in the water. I was very frightened. This happened three times before I was able to struggle back to safety, sand in my ears, nose, eyes, and all over my body. The band and crew had seen me, but it wasn't clear to them that I was in danger. Noreen couldn't understand why I didn't come out of the water. By morning I was black and blue.

Whenever I've toured, I never wanted to be accused of being late. We used a hired bus once in Australia, and that morning I was the first one on it. I sat waiting for the others, who straggled out one by one. None of them got on the bus. They stood outside, laughing and talking. I began to get impatient. The next thing I knew an orderly file of Japanese tourists was getting on my bus. I glanced over and saw the band members getting on another bus. I was on the wrong one, so I hastily got off, muttering apologies as I went.

Most of the time the band was in one van, and the crew in another, while I was in a car with Noreen and the road manager. We left one city in the car and when we came to the outskirts we saw two women at the side of the road holding up a big sign that read "Rita, please stop." We backed up and I got out of the car to meet them. They must have been holding up the sign to every car that passed, not knowing which one was ours.

It was Noreen's greatest wish to photograph a kangaroo, but they didn't just drop out of the sky. One day, as we were travelling, we came across one on the shoulder of the road.

"I've got to get a picture," said Noreen.

"But it's dead," I objected.

"Well, it may be the only one I get."

She asked the road manager, Lee Stanley, to prop it up against the rail at the side of the road and got her picture, which we kidded her about for the rest of the tour. If Noreen wanted a picture of a kangaroo, I wanted one of a koala bear. I got my wish in the zoo in Adelaide where I was allowed to touch one. It crawled over my chest and snuggled against me.

We played in places with interesting names like Toowoomba, Broken Hill, and Dubbo. In Sydney we played in the Opera House, that fantastically shaped building that looks like a ship with all sails set. That was a night to remember. One song I wrote, "Journey to Australia," shows how I felt about the country:

> On my journey to Australia
> I had visions, I had dreams
> They say that once you walk the land
> You never want to leave.

> And on the way to Bundaberg
> I passed the cane train into town
> There's just a hint of sweetness
> When they burn that cane field down.

> And if you like the city lights
> There's something you should know
> Australia, your city nights
> Are something to behold.

> And how can I tell the folks back home
> Just how great you are
> Did the painter get the picture?
> Can the dreamer catch the star?
> Australia, in your shining sun
> There's one thing you should know
> I will remember you wherever I may go...

◆ ◆ ◆

Back in Canada that spring, Wade came with me to Ottawa when I went to receive the Order of Canada. I listened closely to all the proceedings, watching as the other inductees went up to stand before the governor general. It was hard to believe that such a high honor was about to be bestowed on me. I didn't feel worthy of it, and yet when I stood and went up for my award it was the proudest moment of my life. Who could ever have imagined that Rita MacNeil would ever stand in front of Governor General Ray Hnatyshyn as he offered his congratulations? It was the highest accolade I'd ever received. My heart was brimming. Now the red and white Order of Canada award has pride of place in the Tea Room so that those who come can share in it. As if that wasn't enough, I was asked to sing "We'll Reach the Sky Tonight" on Canada Day at the celebration for the 125th Anniversary of the Confederation of Canada.

We put out another album in 1992, called "Thinking of You," which was produced by Declan O'Doherty, and recorded in Toronto at Inception Sound. I was glad that we were able to put out a re-release of "Old Man," as well as "The Crossing" and "Lupins." Then, of course, we had to tour throughout the fall to ensure the success of the album. I was happy to learn that I'd received the Country Act of the Year award at the East Coast Music Awards early in the fall. And we started the tour at the Canadian Country Music Awards where I'd arranged for a car to pick me up long before everyone else was ready to leave so I could escape the traffic. I was stopped in my tracks when I heard my name. I had the award for Fan Choice Entertainer of the Year. Flabbergasted, I went up to accept it from Garth Brooks, but couldn't speak.

The fall tour took me through Alberta, Saskatchewan, Manitoba, and British Columbia, beginning in northern Ontario. It was just outside of Thunder Bay that we had an accident. A car collided with us and hit the passenger side of the van. My arm was hurt, but of course I realized that it could have been much, much worse. However, by the time we got to Winnipeg, my arm was incredibly painful. Hours later, it began turning color and by morning my upper arm, armpit, and shoulder were black. I had it attended to in the hospital; I had pulled the muscles and sprained the arm itself so I had to wear a sling for the rest of the performances. They were beautiful slings though, always in the same color as my dresses!

That fall I was also invited to participate in a tribute to Rob McCall, a skater who had died of AIDS in the previous year. The benefit, for AIDS research, was televised for CTV and aired in December. I met those who took part, like Kurt Browning and Brian Orser, as well as a host of other very talented skaters. I also had the great pleasure of meeting Toller Cranston. It is difficult for me to put into words how I feel about skating, but it is true that I have a passion for it. I've learned a lot from figure skating, because it seems to me that one performance encapsulates the highs and lows of a lifetime. I likened those performances to my musical career. Sometimes I stumbled and fell when all eyes were on me, sometimes I soared. So I find that skating inspires me, particularly when I see young skaters doing their utmost to achieve their dreams. There are times when I can't watch the skating competitions when they are televised, because I know how much must be riding on it for the skaters. So when I was asked to sing for that benefit, I knew it was something I wanted to do. I went out to sing "We'll Reach the Sky Tonight," walking on a red carpet over the ice. I would love to have skated out there instead. It seemed to me that the song epitomized the highest moments of my life: singing in the Royal Albert Hall in England, and the honor of being given the Order of Canada. Yet it also describes that common joy we all feel when we attain a dream.

> The joys we shared when we were young
> The magic carpets that we rode
> The friends we made, the hills we climbed
> All this and more has shaped our lives.
>
> I know we'll reach the sky tonight
> Look and see how far we've come
> Standing in our brightest light
> This is what the dream has done.

The peace that comes from knowing love
The certain way I see you smile
The happiness we've come to know
Whenever we outride the storm.

And when the night brings on the stars
We'll be there, we'll remember
We've reached across, we've touched a spark
The story's just beginning...

# CHAPTER TWENTY-TWO

# THE FLIP SIDE

The music industry is driven by image, and I felt like a square peg in a round hole. I was determined to rise above it. I would have loved to be the perfect size, but I wasn't. And I was realistic about it. I was quick to make jokes at my own expense and often told the story of how a waitress had once asked me, "Dear, did you ever think you'd get so big?"

I wanted to keep on singing, but the media were interested in showing what an oddity I was. No one seemed to have any idea how hard I worked at shedding pounds. Sometimes weight dropped off after months of hard work, but like a bad dream it kept coming back. I never gave up trying and it was a constant battle for me. In the meantime, what was I to do? Should I hide my head in the sand? Or wait until I was a little more "camera friendly"?

I'd been the subject of an article in *Maclean's* magazine, interviewed on CBC's Midday by Valerie Pringle, and mentioned in a range of newspaper articles. An interview with Eric Malling from CBC didn't worry me. They did it in Sydney, bringing a crew of people who set up their lights and equipment in my house. I felt relaxed; I was getting used to interviews by this time.

The interview went along fine, with questions that I felt comfortable answering, until we got onto the question of my size. I showed him some photographs of my younger days.

"So, you were a dish then," he remarked.

I stared at him.

"I'm still a dish," I shot back, stung by the implication.

But how had I gained so much weight?

It wasn't something I wanted to discuss, so I countered by asking him about his bald head. That interview aired early in 1989, but I wasn't keen to see it.

◆　◆　◆

I try to turn aside criticism with a joke, but it doesn't always work. To one interviewer I said, "As big as I am, I could always be bigger."

In her article, she wrote, "That is hard to imagine. She fits snugly into a large armchair."

My appearance was usually an issue, no matter if I was interviewed for television, radio, or print. I was a "dumpy mother of two," a "heavyweight challenger for the title of pop queen," an "unlikely star." I had a cleft palate. I was over forty. Much as the interviewers might enthuse about my music, they usually wanted to discuss my appearance. Even those who tried to defend me made mention of the bad jokes, which only made things worse. These jokes appeared in leading Canadian magazines on several occasions: "Did you hear that Rita MacNeil has the flesh-eating disease? They've given her ten years to live." Or "Rita MacNeil is dead! She was wearing a Malcolm X T-shirt and a helicopter landed on her." Or "Rita MacNeil? Oh, you mean Eat-a-Big Meal."

Certainly not every interviewer I'd come across was willing to print the negative remarks about my size—many have been sensitive and supportive—

but in general there was an attitude born of the shallowness in the music industry: that a woman, if she's going to perform, had better look pretty good.

At least I was learning how to deflect that sort of thing, even if it continued to hurt. It wasn't something that was confined to the music industry either, it was something that came up from one day to the next. On a commercial flight on a small plane in western Canada I took the front seat near the bulkhead, as I was accustomed to doing, because it was more spacious. The band and crew members were with me and we filled most seats in the plane. A few, however, remained empty.

The attendant came along the aisle. "Sit in the seat behind, please."

"Why?" I asked. Surely she could see that it would be very uncomfortable for me?

"Because we don't put passengers in the front seats." She was irritated.

"Pardon me," I said. "This is where I usually sit."

What she really wanted to say was that I was too large and she thought she wouldn't be able to get into the cupboard.

"We keep this seat free," she insisted. "I'll get the pilot unless you move."

I stayed where I was. She didn't get the pilot.

This is something that I live with, just as I had to endure the comments about my cleft lip as a child. I am a tenacious soul, though, which works to my benefit.

◆ ◆ ◆

In 1993, I wanted to focus on things I was very proud of: Female Vocalist of the Year at the East Coast Music Awards, an honorary doctor of law degree from St. Francis Xavier University, and an honorary doctor of letters degree from Mount Saint Vincent University. We were able to establish scholarships for children of miners killed in the Westray mine disaster the year before, with funds raised from a benefit concert.

Instead of those things, all eyes were on me when I sang the anthem for game two of the World Series in October, even though it wasn't actually shown on television since a celebration before the game pre-empted the singing of the anthems. I was so excited to learn that I was to sing "O Canada" that I could hardly contain myself. At the SkyDome itself, I felt honored to be part of things and delighted to meet all the dignitaries. I was dressed in clothes that had been chosen with care: a red swing coat over black pants and top. My hair had been done, my make-up was on. I felt that I looked fine.

It was hard to go out and sing the anthem in front of all those people. I get jitters at the best of times, but a full SkyDome was enough to make me tremble. Still, I walked out on to the field to the roar of the crowd and sang the anthem with all my heart. My voice soared that evening. I am proud to be a Canadian, particularly at times like that. Then I stood back while Michael Bolton sang the American anthem. It was a fine moment for both of us, and together, amid the screams of the crowd, we went back together to the stands, where we had front row seats for the game. We kidded each other and bought peanuts that we shared. I cheered and yelled. It was a great evening, topped by the fact that the Blue Jays were doing so well.

The next day the phones were abuzz. Reporters were at my door as well.

"Have you seen the newspaper article, Miss MacNeil?"

"What newspaper article?"

"Well, the one that—well, the one in the *Philadelphia Daily News*."

"No."

It turned out that a sports columnist, eager to get in a jab at a Toronto journalist who had attacked the physical condition of the American baseball players, had turned his attention to me. He'd had a field day.

"Towns that need a forklift," he wrote, "to transport their 'O Canada' singer to home plate should think twice before describing the Philadelphia Phillies as 'unfit.'" "Caution, wide load model," he mentioned in the next breath, referring to me as Rita McCall. Apparently I made Roseanne Arnold look like Jane Fonda. Finally, he wondered if I'd been paid "by the pound, the note, or with Jenny Craig certificates."

It was some of the most mean-spirited "reporting" I'd ever seen in my life, if it can be called reporting. I pitied the man who wrote it. I was the target of his jokes, but he really did it as a retort to the earlier gibe in a Toronto paper that had "started it." Yet it also hurt, because I believed people to be above that. He didn't retract his statements, nor did the *Philadelphia Daily News* offer an apology. In fact, he pointed out that he'd done it in the spirit of "fun" and that Canadians were too "thin-skinned."

There was a flood of indignant mail on my behalf. Canadian journalists immediately leapt to my defence. Canadians as a whole were outraged by the insensitive account. Fans were up in arms and I was grateful for their support.

As for me, I had no comment.

Later, however, when asked if I would sing for another game in the World Series, I responded, "Yes, I'd do it, but only if they drive me out onto the field on a fork-lift."

◆ ◆ ◆

Once I had dinner with some executives from a major record company.

"I just want to tell you something, Rita," confided one of them. "When I first heard 'Flying on Your Own' I thought you were some young chick from England."

I waited.

"Imagine our surprise," he went on, "when we discovered that you were the singer—"

There was a silence.

"I mean, we just didn't think it would be you. You know, we thought that—well, we thought you'd be different."

He dug himself deeper. We were all embarrassed as he tried to smooth things over.

I met with the same kind of attitude when "Rita & Friends" went on the air. People didn't think it would work. I wouldn't look the part, I couldn't do the hosting. One writer for a major newspaper commented, after the program had gone into its second very successful year, that "only in Canada, the land of opportunity for the opportunity challenged, would this woman have her own television show." One would think the business of image would be confined to music videos or television appearances, but it is everywhere.

It was just as evident in radio. I once went to various radio stations to try to promote my music with the radio programmers, accompanied by a key person at the record company. Now that I was signed to a major label, it was important to try to get radio programmers to play the albums when they come out. It wasn't always easy, because not all my songs are "radio friendly." I follow my heart when I write them, though I try to be careful and keep myself open to advice. We weren't getting enough airplay, particularly with the major radio stations in Toronto. There were, of course, many other artists besides me who didn't get as much airplay as they would have liked. We set up meetings with people at the radio stations to find out why. At several of those meetings we were given the same sort of answers: my music didn't fit a certain format.

At one radio station, three programmers met with us.

"You know, Rita," said one, who seemed young and confident. He was hip, and it was clear he thought I wasn't. "We play music that caters to the thirty-five to fifty crowd."

"So?—that's me," I thought.

He went on, "We cater to the sort of woman who works—you know, she has a career—and comes home after a long day and puts on her radio. Well, she wants to listen to the kind of song that has the right message."

I wondered what he was getting at, but soon it was crystal clear.

"She's the kind of woman who's fit. She works out and eats right."

Ah, there it was. The slim career woman who wanted to listen to a slim singer.

"Well," I said, getting up. "I see exactly what you mean."

The man from the record company who was with me was speechless when we left. He couldn't believe what he'd just heard.

◆ ◆ ◆

It's very difficult for me to get clothes in my size, particularly in Canada. And it's often a trial going into clothing stores. Sometimes the salespeople stare at me as if to say, "What is she doing in here?"

"May I see your plus sizes?" I asked at a major department store.

"Well, this is what we have," the sales clerk explained.

She showed me a rack of clothes.

"No, I mean the higher sizes."

"Oh, well, we only go up to size 16," she sniffed.

Other times when I go into stores I am completely ignored as the sales-clerks chat by the register in an empty store.

I was delighted to find a shop in Nashville that was just heaven for me. Called "Catherine's," it was a place where I once spent hours. I found clothes that looked great and fit my body very well. Now, that was a shopping trip!

"Here's the blue one. The one in black. And a print," one clerk said, handing a few hangers of dresses into the change room.

"I'll be buying the place out," I told her.

Because it was difficult to get what I wanted in Canada, I started a clothing line with a Montreal clothes manufacturer. They were all set to get the "Rita line" going. I soon found out this was no easy road either. I had teamed up with Lee Kinoshita-Bevington, who did my clothes for the "Rita & Friends" shows. We talked about what I liked and he designed the clothes, often knowing exactly what worked for me. Together, we tried to get the "Rita line" off the ground, but it was destined for failure. When I went to the stores for the launch everyone seemed pleased at the styles and sizes, but retailers didn't want them, except perhaps Pennington's, and they weren't easy to convince. The retailers might carry up to size 24 or maybe size 26. I was hoping they'd go up to size 32, but that didn't happen. They didn't seem to be interested in that sort of customer. So it remains a battle. It's possible that I could do an independent line, but it requires a great deal of energy to get these things going. In the meantime, I remain a singer who wants to give people my music.

I think that people love to read about success stories, about everything working out well in the end. We all need happy endings. And it's true that I worked my way up from the bottom of the heap. Yet it's still not always easy. It remains a difficult road, with obstacles that one can't foresee. It would help if changes were made in the entertainment, fashion, and music industries, since they set impossible standards.

Maybe we should just let people be themselves by allowing them—and encouraging them—just to be the best at what they do.

# CHAPTER TWENTY-THREE

# RITA & FRIENDS

We had decided that an expansion to the Tea Room would have to happen. There were thousands of people coming through every summer and there just wasn't enough space for them all. Beginning in 1993 through to 1994, we did a major renovation. We kept the schoolhouse as the central space and built around it. New additions include the foyer, gift shop, kitchen, and another tea room adjoining the main one, making it very spacious.

Laura took on a major role in overseeing the expansion of the new Tea Room, and she mastered the business side very quickly. She has always been resourceful and a hard worker. Anyone who might think that Laura was lucky to be my daughter and get a job at the Tea Room should know it's the other way around: I'm lucky that she took her business savvy and came to work for me. Laura's sense of pride in the Tea Room makes me very proud.

In the midst of our planning for the renovation, representatives of the federal and provincial governments approached us to see if we needed further funding, so we matched the amount they gave us. The Tea Room is a key tourist attraction in Cape Breton, with a good track record as a local employer, and they wanted to ensure its success. I've always invited people to come and see for themselves how beautiful Cape Breton is. Even in the early days I urged them to visit, joking that they should bring their own tea bags. I wanted everyone to come and see the place I loved so much. However, there was an outcry locally when people learned that we might be given funding, and there was no way to point out our situation. As well, there were denunciations when word got out that we might not be using unionized workers, though it wasn't our intention to do that.

I received a doctor of letters degree at the University College of Cape Breton that spring, a real honor for me. Everything went smoothly, but at my fiftieth birthday celebration in May 1994 at a Sydney hotel, we worried that there might be demonstrations protesting the Tea Room. Yet that seemed to pass. We went on the June tour of Ontario, and in August 1994 we opened the new Tea Room. It was the realization of a dream I'd had over the years. The official opening, though, was not until 1995.

We had wanted to preserve the original charm of the school house, and it seemed to me we'd succeeded. Inside, on the mantel of the main room, was the eight-day grandmother clock, along with an antique radio, silk roses given to me by Leonard Rambeau, and the collection of teacups. There was a small room full of photographs of my parents, grandparents, Father Stanley, and even a photograph of me when I was a schoolgirl, as well as memorabilia from all the years since then. The kitchen was stocked with treats, like raspberry turnovers, apple pies, carrot cakes, and cookies. And the gift shop was full of teacups and tea cozies, as well as specially blended tea.

After all, it had started with a teapot and a tea bag.

◆  ◆  ◆

In 1993, my company, Big Pond Publishing and Production Limited, had been moved to Toronto to be closer to the Balmur office, which was in North York. We rented a space on the tenth floor of the building, since Balmur was on the twenty-fourth. The rent was actually cheaper than it had been in downtown Sydney, where we had our in-house operations as well as the Tea Room business. It was a major undertaking. Laura was now living in Toronto and Wade moved there in order to supervise Lupins. He was excited at the prospect of being close to the Balmur headquarters, because Leonard Rambeau was such a respected manager in the business. There was one catch: Leonard was not as much a part of things as we'd hoped, though we weren't quite sure why. We knew there were changes taking place within Balmur itself. However, when a top producer at CBC approached us with the idea of a televised variety show, Leonard was there to advise us that it was a good opportunity.

I had worked with Sandra Faire before, notably on the CBC Christmas special, "Once upon a Christmas," the year before, when we'd released the album of the same name with the many Christmas songs I'd written in Australia. The special had gone very well, and we'd all had fun, though we'd worked hard. They had done a great job of re-creating my grandmother's house in Toronto, and the woman who played Nana, Emily Butler, lent her Cape Breton charm to the show. Everyone loved her. And my daughter Laura played me as a girl. At the end of it we had a party, and I went as Charlie Chaplin.

A striking blonde woman who commanded attention everywhere she went, Sandra had impeccable credits to her name, having done the weekly musical show, "Ear to the Ground," as well as specials with many Canadian singers. I'd done the "Anne Murray in Nova Scotia" special with Sandra and I knew she would be a terrific person to work with. As with the Christmas special, she thought we'd be able to film some shows of "Rita & Friends" in Cape Breton, though that turned out not to be possible, because of budget cuts. Leonard and I were both very enthused about the idea, and we decided to go ahead. I was provided with a small office in the new CBC building, on the same floor as the production team, and when I first went to see it there was a plaque on the door with my name as well as Leonard's. Sadly, he was only there once, because by that time he was quite ill.

I was treated like a queen at CBC. From the first day at Studio 40 in 1994 I knew I was in the best of hands, because Sandra had the reputation of treating people very well and expecting the same high-quality work from them that she asked of herself. She was something to watch on the set, like a conductor with an orchestra. They paid great attention to detail. I have to say that I've never seen people work so hard: their days started early and went on well into the night. If Sandra was not around, then Trisa Dayot made sure that I was well taken care of. The other CBC executives— George Anthony, Ed Robinson, and Phyllis Platt—dropped in from time to time to offer encouragement.

Even though everyone assured us that all would go well when the first show was aired, there was no doubt that everyone was a little on edge.

"I never really thought about the risk until everybody started on about it," I said to one reporter. "Now you're all making me nervous."

What about my shyness?

"I'll just do my best," I told them. It was all anyone could do.

I wasn't the only one who was nervous. We were all too conscious of shows that had gone before us and failed miserably. It could easily happen to us. And so we were cautious when we spoke to the press. Sandra was hoping for an audience of 600,000 viewers. If there were 800,000 people tuning in she would be a happy woman. We had a line-up of interesting entertainment for that first show: Acadian Roch Voisine, Calgary's Jann Arden, RealWorld of Cape Breton, and Southeast Asian funk and rap group Punjabi by Nature. It was a live-to-tape show, which meant that we had a live audience, but the show was actually taped before it went on the air.

We got close to two million viewers for that first show. Sandra came right into the studio where we were taping the show and told us the news.

"1.7 million viewers," she said.

"Is that good?" I asked.

"Yes. It's wonderful."

Later she took Noreen and me into her office where she had spread out a little feast of cheese, crackers, and red wine.

After so much worry about the show not doing well, we could breathe a sigh of relief and settle into the rest of the season. The shows continued to do well throughout that first year, keeping a consistently high viewing audience. I began to have a little fun with it myself, learning how to write in my own lines when I felt the script didn't sound like me.

On the tenth floor of the CBC building, the stage was large and beautiful. There was a staircase down to it where choirs would sometimes appear and then come down to the stage to join me or one of the other performers for a song. Michael, the floor director, was superb, because he had to sit hour after hour keeping people calm as we rehearsed the show. Though there was friction after people had been working from early in the morning until late at night, he never lost his temper.

I would begin to work around nine in the morning and usually go through until evening. Sometimes it would be later because they would have to do retakes of certain sections. I might finish around ten o'clock at night and then be asked to do a retake. If I had to change my outfit for it, I'd go down to the dressing room, which was quite a distance away, change and come back. There were times we were all there until two o'clock in the morning.

Taping was never a one-shot operation. Halfway through a taping, it might be discovered that a light bulb had blown or that there were problems with the sound, so the whole thing would be done over, even though everything else had gone well. Each detail had to be perfect. I often had to stand for hours under the lights and there were times it got so hot that I'd be drenched with perspiration. Noreen would get me a damp towel to put around my shoulders. My greatest relief after tapings was to go to the dressing room and change into something comfortable.

I was provided with all kinds of support so that I could concentrate on the show. The halls were abuzz every Friday night, just before the shows. Young performers just getting started would be pacing nervously back and forth. The seasoned performers would be relaxed, old hands at this sort of thing. We always had good laughs with the hair and makeup artists. And I bantered back and forth with the wardrobe designer, Lee Kinoshita-Bevington.

"Lee, look at this plunging neckline—I can't wear that."

"You'll look great."

"Here, pin me up a bit."

"Well, maybe just a tiny little adjustment…"

"You just do that so you can get close to me," I told him, as he pinned me up.

"How did you know?"

He stepped back to look me over.

"I'm waiting for you to make the miniskirt, you know," I said.

"Oh, that's coming up. I've got the fishnet stockings ready."

I had a comfortable dressing room, filled with fresh flowers, and I always took my two little Yorkshire terriers with me. Noreen took care of all the little details that I might forget, and I was also provided with a driver, Mike Turner, who got us back and forth to each and every show and helped in a myriad of ways that went beyond the call of duty. Ever sincere, he did his very best to please. He was a gem.

I often told him to go into the dressing room to read his paper, and a few times I asked if he wouldn't mind watching the dogs for me while we were taping. Both are purebred dogs, with numbers tattooed on their stomachs. I came back to find him a little distraught because he had left the dogs for a couple of minutes and came back to find things not quite as he'd left them.

"It appears," he told me earnestly, "that someone has tampered with the dogs."

"What's happened?" I asked, thinking the worst.

"Well, someone came in and wrote something on their bellies in black marker." He paused, looking mournful, as this information sank in. "They got the both of them."

◆　◆　◆

The first year was a learning experience for me. I'd never hosted before and so I had to learn how to do it. We also wanted to showcase the talents of newer, obviously gifted musicians. There is enormous talent in this country and both Sandra and I were keen to emphasize it. We had some great performers on that show in the first part of that season, like Michelle

Wright, Crash Test Dummies, Prairie Oyster, Susan Aglukark, and a host of Nova Scotian musicians. In the winter shows of 1995 we had such performers as Bruce Cockburn, Jane Siberry, Murray McLauchlan, and Buffy Sainte-Marie.

I was a little unnerved by some of the big-name artists we'd invited to the show. Joni Mitchell was a guest in that first season, and it overwhelmed me to meet her. The audience was electrified before she came out on the stage. No doubt everyone there could think of at least one song of Joni's that evoked special memories. She came out and gave me a big hug, and then stood for a minute or two talking with me, holding my hand all the while. I was touched by that. She was a marvelous performer to watch, not only as a result of her strong presence, but because of the way she played the guitar, her fingers moving like lightning.

Tom Jackson, star of "North of 60," was another guest on one of the shows. He sang and then came over to chat with me.

"How are you?" I asked.

"I'm fine. How are you?"

I was about to compliment him on his performance, but the words got scrambled as I looked at him.

"I don't think you know—" I began. I blushed and put my hand up to my face, as the audience went into convulsions. Everyone could see how close I'd come to swooning. I walked away and then came back, the audience still laughing. "I'm a mess, that's all I know," I told him.

We danced on that show afterwards, which was sheer delight.

And I didn't swoon.

◆ ◆ ◆

I was entranced with so many of the performers. When Buffy Sainte-Marie made an appearance later, I literally had to be hauled out of my room before I could get up the courage to go and talk to her. I was struck by the power of her presence too, with her pride in her rich native heritage revealed simply in the way she carried herself. Bruce Cockburn was another consummate performer, whose fine musicianship was a joy to behold.

When I had to do a number with the Barenaked Ladies, I was a little nervous, but one of the musicians rehearsed and rehearsed with me, practically holding my hand to get me through it.

We were still touring during this period as well, though the load was slightly lighter because of "Rita & Friends." In November and December of 1994 we had a full tour through Ontario, with one date in the United States and eight in the Maritimes. We would have preferred more dates in the U. S. but at least one show would help in getting going. By then we had done a "documercial," to promote my music there. It was a thirty-minute televised package aired in the United States, and though it was an expensive initiative, it was popular in upstate New York, Pennsylvania, Washington, and Florida. So it gave us a good idea of markets to pursue. It was because of this that we had the date in the upstate New York just before Christmas in 1994. North Tonawanda was a sold-out show.

So it didn't help that I got sick on the Christmas tour. When one person in the band or crew gets sick, everyone else gets it. This time it was strep throat, and I had such a bad infection that I couldn't use my voice. I had to cancel three shows in Ontario, but I gradually improved. I could sing a little, but I couldn't talk much at all. When we went to North Tonawanda, I was able to put on a good show, but it took everything I had. I gradually improved, but we still had the O'Keefe Centre to do in Toronto, then Kingston, Montreal, Ottawa, and a swing through the Maritimes before getting back to Sydney on December 21st. Those Christmas tours—that one and another the year before—were the most successful we had ever done. It was a real joy to do them.

It was mandatory to decorate the tour bus with Christmas lights, a tree, and mistletoe. It was also the custom to watch "The Grinch That Stole Christmas," as well as "Spinal Tap." We did so much Christmas shopping that we'd have to send our suitcases home, fully packed, and buy hockey bags that we filled with presents. The band members were always playing jokes on each other, on us, and on the crew members. At one point on that Christmas tour, the crew strung up a toy lamb and dropped it down in front of one of the band members at intervals throughout the song, just out of sight of the audience. And once the crew was responsible for completely wrapping the band's van in what looked like green garbage bags: it was covered in green plastic and then wrapped with chicken wire so that wire cutters had to be used to get rid of it. In retaliation, the band filled the heater vents in the crew's van with confetti. They also managed to fill the van itself with bags and bags of popcorn.

We were working with the very able Tinti Moffatt at Balmur, who was really acting as manager since Leonard had become sick, and made plans to do another album, this time in Nashville. We made sure that some of the tours promoting it would be done south of the border. Our brief tour in the spring of 1995, beginning in Erie, Pennsylvania, and ending in Branson, Missouri, with stops in Indianapolis and Rochester, was really an effort to get a foothold there. But I learned that Leonard died that spring and I mourned him. He had been such a firm believer in my music and a true gentleman as well. I saw him only once when we were taping "Rita & Friends" and it upset me deeply to see him so ravaged by the cancer that eventually killed him.

We released the "Porch Songs" album that year, this time with a different producer. We did the entire album in Nashville at Don Potter's studio. Known for his work with the Judds, he himself was a very humble man, whose guitar playing was captivating. We went for a down-to-earth sound and were pleased with the results, though I thought my vocals might have been a little off in one or two places. Songs like "Field of Daisies" were written on the front porch of the old MacLellan farmhouse in Big Pond. I had been reminded of the times when I'd looked over the fields and had seen white daisies scattered through the green. I wanted to evoke the fleeting wonder of those summer days I'd known as a child:

I like to lie in a field of daisies
And feel the sun shine down on me
I have often walked Glengarry Road
In the warm summer heat
And I've seen the land

Pass from hand to hand
And the tourists they come and they go
When the sun goes down
On this patch of ground
It's where I leave my soul.

So much had happened to me over the last few years that when I was able to stop for a moment and realize where I'd come from, I was able to find tranquillity.

Everything might have changed in my life, but Big Pond remained the same.

# CHAPTER TWENTY-FOUR

# REALIZING THE DREAM

We had a tightly packed schedule in the fall of 1995, promoting the tour and taping for "Rita & Friends." In September, we had two weeks in Toronto doing the show and then a month of touring the West. Then it was back to tapings and more touring. In November, though, I went home to get ready for a very special occasion. My daughter was getting married. We had the house decorated from top to bottom and the parlor looked especially beautiful. In a quiet ceremony in my house, surrounded by only family and friends, she was married to Dana Lewis.

I was drawing closer to my family. It seemed time for Wade to take over my career, now that he had been involved for such a long time. Laura was back in Sydney, like her brother, and had been in charge of the Tea Room for some years. I thought we could make Lupins Productions a family affair. By early 1996 we decided not to renew our contract with Balmur in order to work independently, with Wade acting as manager.

During the tour in Florida early in 1996 I felt tired. I didn't think I was at my best, though the audiences were everything I could have asked for. And there was turmoil among the band members, so there was a lot going on behind the scenes. I felt the pressure of breaking new ground, as I always did, but I didn't feel the same support from the band. I was exhausted by the time we got home. And in the summer we were able to put out "Joyful Sounds," another Christmas album, as well as a Christmas songbook. It was good to be doing things on our own. And I felt, at last, a sense of relief about my career.

"If you make mistakes now," said a friend, "at least they'll be your own mistakes."

It was true.

"Rita & Friends" was moved to the Wednesday night slot in the fall of 1996, which meant that fewer viewers were watching it, though it remained successful. It also meant that the show might be cut altogether, so all through the fall we waited to see if the axe would fall. While we were taping, I lived in Granite Place, in a furnished condominium once owned by a doctor who had been the son of a well-known Canadian actor. Everything there had been left just as it had been, even papers on the desk. I was very careful not to disturb things.

For the two months I was there, I felt Christopher's presence near me. It was a very gentle presence and as a result I felt at peace the moment I went through the door after a long session of taping. I treasured those nights. I would sit and reflect, and it was as if I was with him. I felt him when I looked out over the balcony at the trees framing the cemetery nearby. At times I even talked to him. It was a very creative time for me, since I wrote quite a number of new songs.

One of the things I enjoyed most about that period of time doing "Rita

& Friends" were the occasions when Sandra would take Noreen and me out for lunch or dinner. She had excellent taste and we always went to the finest restaurants that Toronto had to offer. Noreen and I might arrive ahead of Sandra, who would come into the restaurant in a rush, apologetic about her lateness. Everyone in the restaurant was aware of her presence, from the busboys to the chef. We had excellent service, with the waiters hovering over us, anticipating our every need.

"So what do you think you'd like?" she asked me.

"Oh, maybe the chicken," I said, trying to figure out the Italian menu.

Then the chef would appear suddenly at our table, kissing Sandra in greeting. He would always recommend something for us, beginning, of course, with an appetizer. When the food arrived, piping hot, she made sure it was exactly what we wanted. She always made us feel like the most important people in the world.

Yet a door was closing on "Rita & Friends" and we all knew it. Sure enough, word of the show's demise came soon enough from CBC executives. It was a disappointing way to end such an excellent three-year run. The last night, a party had been planned. I didn't think it was unusual because each week we had a wrap-up party after everything was over. At ten or eleven o'clock on Friday night we'd all go into the Green Room for pizza and beer. This night would be special because my sisters, Mary and Ann, and some of my friends from home, Janice and Elaine, were there. And I knew it wouldn't be the usual party. This was really the end of it all.

Instead of going to the Green Room, though, I was taken to the studio where we had done all the tapings of "Rita & Friends." I was surprised by what I saw. On the stage small tables had been set up. Caterers had brought in food, and wine was flowing freely. It was the beginning of a show that the crew put on as a way of saying goodbye. Each of them did a skit, a dance, or a song. One of the highlights was when Mike Turner got up to do an impersonation of Elvis. Usually a shy man, Mike put his heart and soul into the role and it was wonderful. Apparently he'd been practicing for two weeks with Noreen whenever I wasn't around.

It was very difficult to leave behind such a fine group of people who had all worked so hard. I had the time of my life there, enjoying a challenge that I'd never expected would come my way. And after all my misgivings about hosting a show on television, I'd been awarded a Gemini for Best Performance in a Variety Program in 1996. Many people approached me after the cancellation of the show to say how sorry they were that it would not be continuing. That was good to hear. It told me that the show really had worked, when so many had been convinced that it wouldn't.

◆ ◆ ◆

Like Sandra, who had decided to leave CBC and start her own production company, we went on to other things as well. With Sandra at the helm, we did a special for CTV, this time a Celtic celebration, which was shot on location at the Tea Room, in Big Pond, at the Savoy Theatre in Glace Bay, and at Fortress Louisbourg. There was a rousing quality to the music when the members of Leahy played their fiddles, and a haunting nostalgia to Mary Jane Lamond's songs. Ashley MacIsaac fiddled wildly, and the Chieftains offered their special Irish music, and the Men of the Deeps sang from their hearts. I was so proud to have the special shot in Cape Breton, a place where such music has been kept alive by young and old.

We put out another album, "Music of a Thousand Nights," a reflective work. In writing some of the songs I was thinking back to earlier times. Songs like "Troubadours" harked back to the times of Dougie, Jerome, and especially Joella. "Married in the Sixties" was written for Mary and Johnny:

> It's a very Mary, married
> In the sixties room
> Just enough satin with a hint of lace
> A three-legged table with a photo or two
> And they're standing in the frame
> So young and strong
> And thirty years later she's as true to her picture
> As she was to his love.

And you can tell they've grown familiar
In some ways they've grown apart
But even in their distance
They're connected by the heart
And there's a gentle wind
That's blowing round the door
And married in the sixties
It seems so long ago...

Beyond my music, we were becoming involving with helping younger musicians. Douglas September is one of these very talented newcomers, a poet with a guitar in his hand. His manager, Tony Boone, who helped so much in getting him started, died in a tragic accident in Ithaca, New York, in the early summer of 1998, at the young age of twenty-eight. When we lost him, we were reminded once again to take the time to cherish family and friends. We can only celebrate his life by continuing to make music.

Go where the music is playing
And we'll sing like we've never before
And we'll open our hearts to a world that is ours
And we'll sing till we can't sing no more.

Steal me away like a call from the wind
There is so much here to remember...

Without music, we would never stop and listen to our hearts. It is a gift of the soul, a gift of healing, a gift of joyous spontaneity. I sang first because I was compelled to, as if it were a freeing of my spirit, but soon I realized I was giving a part of myself to others. To watch my mother as I sang in the kitchen or have my father ask me to sing "Danny Boy" was a privilege. And singing to all the audiences around the world who have cheered me on has been a privilege too.

When I look back over my life, I think I've been very fortunate. I never expected to come so far, especially at times when I was close to giving up. If it hadn't been for the dream of singing, I would never have travelled this road. It may seem at times that I've been on a treadmill, with the constant workload, the time away from family, the sacrifices made in a world that is not as glamorous as it seems. I often felt that I was two people: the private person and the public one. Sometimes it was hard to believe that I was that very public person: the singer to whom fans wrote long letters filled with love. I had only my dream of music when I began. I carried it around with me like a precious little seed. Yet it is remarkable that so long as a seed of a vision is planted, it can flower into something greater than anything ever imagined in the beginning.

With the passing of time, I'm now at a point where I can look back over the years of my career and appreciate how much joy they have given me. During my many tours it was the excitement of each new place, and returning to those places to find people still eager to hear my songs, that inspired me to continue. In the old pub days, it may have been fun, but it was also difficult to play above the noise level. With the respect that came with the concert stages, when audiences sat in complete silence to hear my every word, it was a chance to trust and to give my heart. I was never disappointed in the audiences. Night after night, even when my performances were not what I might have hoped for, they forgave me and continued to applaud. They accepted me as a human being who was not perfect.

While it may not have been easy in terms of the business side of making music, the audiences erased those problems. Once I was on stage, sharing songs that were both old and new, it was obvious why music was my life. I am very grateful to those audiences: the people who buy the albums, go to the shows, and send me countless good wishes for continued success. I can only thank them with a song.

It's for you
I give my heart and soul
It's for you
I wish the sun to shine

It's for you
This day and all my life
In all I do
The love comes through
It's for you

Take this heart
I'll wear it out for you
Take these eyes
They cry when you feel blue
Take these arms
That reach to comfort you

All my life
All my love
It's for you

All my life
All my love
It's for you

When the wind
Blows around your door
When you fall
And you're not sure
Most of all
When the day is through
Think of me
All my love
It's for you

All my life
All my love
It's for you

I've accepted awards and accolades on the run to something else, it seems, with no time to reflect on them. They were always thrilling to receive, especially when I walked down the aisle in a cap and gown, awed to be beside such learned people. Given that I never graduated from grade twelve, I was always so proud to hold the degree presented to me. Each time I thought of my parents and how proud they would have been. They wanted all of us to do well in school. As I looked out over the faces of those who had studied hard, I was reminded of what it takes to achieve goals.

I could never have done this without my parents, my siblings, and my children. My family is my anchor. Even though they are gone, my parents gave me the strength and desire to continue. And my brothers and sisters, all quiet, strong people, have always been there for me. All seven of them could write their own books. They have all lived amazing lives, approaching life in a positive way and making the best use of their talents. I never felt that it would be fair to bring them into the foreground in these pages, yet I am deeply grateful to them for inspiring me, always, to go forward.

My children are my greatest gifts. Laura is an exuberant spirit, whose humor always delights me, as does her sense of style. I'm fond of teasing her about it. I always knew she would become the wonderful woman she is, able to walk on after she's made mistakes and launch herself into the next project. It is because of her that the Tea Room functions so smoothly. Laura and Dana are happily married with a family, which makes me a grandmother.

Wade is a quiet soul, full of humor and humility, who has always done his very best for me. He has been around my music for a long time, and now it is his turn to take charge. Both my children have inspired me to be the best I can, for their sake as well as my own. When I look into their eyes and know they are doing well, it brightens my day. Yet of the many lessons I've learned, one is that I can't make things right for them when they are going through times of difficulty. Each of us has moments of sorrow and moments of joy. We have to take those moments that are joyful and cherish them.

David, who lives in Sydney, is still very close to us. He has never missed a Christmas with us in years, and he is just as proud of the children as I am. We are truly lucky to have such a good rapport.

Good friends are hard to come by, but Noreen is one of the best. She has always been there with a heart of gold. Not only is she gifted with great common sense, she also has a wonderful sense of humor. Few can tell stories like Noreen, who will often stand to tell a really good one, hands gesturing and feet tapping. Then she delivers the punch line, hands on her hips. Not only can she see things as they are, laced with a bit of comedy, she is kind and caring with people who want autographs after a show or those who just want to shake my hand. She is the one who videotapes when we are on the road, with over a thousand hours of videotape to her credit. Above all, she has been like a rock through all the changes of my career.

It is because of these people and so many more that this dream came to pass. It has been quite a journey so far. Yet even in the middle of it, there have to be moments when I have time alone to remember what life is really all about. Those are the times when I jump in the van and ride out to Big Pond to spend a day or a week by the Bras d'Or. I walk the shore as the waves roll in, sliding in lacy edges over my feet. I am grounded there. Because I can go to a place that is my haven, I can go back to the world with all its demands. It is there that I know that I have been richly blessed, not only to have lived my dream, but to have shared it with others.

Take heart and seize the day
Some things we may not change
We must never
Make a place where dreams will die
Lose our hope
Oh, we must try
To save the child within us.

Think of the sun on high
Cradled among the clouds
It comes shining
If the star is too far
Gather the stardust now
We must never
Make a place where dreams will die

267

Lose our hope
Oh, we must try
To save the child within us.

There is a part of life
We may not understand
We are shaken
Kind as a heart can be
It only goes so deep
We must never
Make a place where dreams will die
Or lose our hope, we must try
To save the child within us.

I have a dream, I have a journey
Whatever the cost, it won't be easy
But if you and I start together
I know that we can dream forever.

# DISCOGRAPHY

Please visit Rita's Web site at
www.ritamacneil.com

write her at
c/o Tea Times
RR #1, Big Pond
Cape Breton, Nova Scotia
B0A 1H0

or e-mail her at
mail@ritamacneil.com